Horrid Child

By

Luke Twigg

Copyright © 2025 Luke Twigg

ISBN: 9781918038705

All rights reserved, including the right to reproduce this book, or portions thereof in any form. No part of this text may be reproduced, transmitted, downloaded, decompiled, reverse engineered, or stored, in any form or introduced into any information storage and retrieval system, in any form or by any means, whether electronic or mechanical without the express written permission of the author.

PREFACE

Hello. I'm Luke Twigg, and I'm different. Different to most people. It's sometimes difficult being different. Different isn't accepted by everyone. Most people don't have the time or inclination to discover why someone is the way they are; they just take them at face value and judge accordingly. So be it. But there have been times in my life when I've contemplated carrying a little sign to show those who've not met me before. A sign rather like a deaf person might carry to explain that they're hard of hearing. I wasn't sure how I'd word my sign, though I wanted it to explain that I'm an unusual, nervous, insecure, complex character due to certain circumstances I've experienced, and I'd add something like "but please bear with me because I am also essentially a good person who means well". I contemplated that because all too often I felt people got a poor initial impression and that they might be more accepting if they understood me more. After all, a major part of us human beings is the culmination of our experiences and DNA. But it occurred to me that no card would be big enough to incorporate everything I'd want to say by way of explanation for myself. Anyway I didn't do it, because it would have made me seem odder still, and plenty of people go through far tougher things than me yet come across far better. Instead, I decided to put it all down in a book and, well, here it is...

1.

THE 'DON'T YOU WANT ME?' BABY

At some point in my early life, I heard a story about myself that made sense of much I'd felt until then. The story was of how my father, too squeamish to attend my birth, requested the midwife display a signal from the window by which he - from the safe distance of a different part of the property - could tell if he'd had a son or a daughter. The signal was to be white for a girl and black for a boy. As I have often thought, the day I was born was a black day for my Dad.

Maybe after two sons he longed for a daughter. If he was happy to have a third male, it soon became apparent he wasn't happy to have this one. And what my Dad did, said, or thought, not just influenced but dominated my family. I would gradually come to imagine that, when my mother brought me into the World, my father and brothers took one disgusted look and said "Oh no, do we have to have him?"

It wasn't long after my arrival that parents in Britain were first able to discover during pregnancy the gender of their child(ren), and I did sometimes wonder what Dad would have done had he known then a third boy was on the way.

I was christened Luke but Dad called me 'Horrid child', and so often that I didn't doubt that's what I was.

As a consequence, I felt a disappointment and different from the outset. Different even from my own intimate relatives.

By virtue of my father's job as a teacher in a boys' boarding-school in Devon called All Saints, as a family we then lived in what outwardly appeared rather grand staff accommodation nearby: the east wing of an elegant but isolated old mansion named Hartson House. It was haunted, but neither Dad, Arthur, nor Mum, Jean, nor my brothers, Matthew and Mark, appeared to notice. Only me.

My earliest memory is of a face. Just a face, no body. The face of a middle-aged woman staring so intensely that it shook with great severity. It stared and shook, stared and shook, stared and shook at me night after night from the same position, high to the left at the south end of my bedroom. And, being just a baby at the time, I screamed.

I believed that my mother and father could protect me from anything. So it was deeply unsettling for me to discover that, even when taken in to the security of their bedroom to escape the staring shaking head, I still saw it in there…and they didn't.

Although I would always remember it happening, I would never remember any family discussions about it. Maybe spirits, or whatever this was, were taboo. Maybe because no-one else saw what I saw, there was nothing for them to say on the subject. Or maybe they simply didn't give it a second thought. Whatever the reason, it added to my sense of solitude.

I would one day be asked to describe a moment which best illustrated my childhood, and I chose not the spooky lady but an occasion when I was left in a pram in a park all alone for what felt like forever, bawling my eyes out and yelling my heart out to no avail. No-one heard me and no-one helped me. Not for a distressing amount of time anyway. Somehow it was representative of that critical era for me. Despite my tender age when in that pram, I wondered if my parents would ever go back to fetch me. Or, more importantly, whether they wanted to.

'Wanted' was the key word for the child me. Somehow I knew I should be wanted but felt I wasn't. Nowhere near enough, anyhow. When as a teenager I first heard the theory that people 'choose their own parents', my immediate thought was 'If that's the case, why would I have chosen ones who didn't want me?'

I never doubted that was true of my father, in whom I only seemed capable of arousing emotions of annoyance, anger and frustration. Dad's rare moments at home were even more rarely spent with me. No hugs, no hand-holding, no genuine encouragement - just the occasional ruffle of hair and otherwise endless scalding from this tall, willowy, stern man with the down-turned mouth. Dad was born in 1930, but yours truly would most associate him with the humourless, harsh Victorians.

Mercifully, Mum was a contrast. A foot shorter and wider, with welcoming arms and a jollity that burst forth when Dad was absent, she gave affection. Yet I, reckoning that may not meet with paternal approval, was sometimes suspicious it was simply compensatory. Besides, Mum had plenty on her plate, being a district nurse, beauty counsellor, wife and mother of three.

A problem for me was: the less I felt wanted, the more I wanted to be wanted – and that made me even harder to be wanted.

Not me an admired, independent, bold boy, but an unappealing, clingy, whingeing wretch. What was it my father's French aunt kept telling me? "Luke, you are a silly bébé, you always want your Mummy!" Much as I would like to have disagreed with that, I couldn't.

I wasn't so self-absorbed that I thought my parents' lives should be devoted to me, but at times I didn't easily accept that they had other priorities including working lives to lead. "What was your problem? You were lucky to have parents…you were living in a mansion…and you had a nanny" were among the arguments thrown at my older self, mainly by my older self. But the disadvantages of not feeling love from those who mattered most obliterated any consideration of middle-class comforts to this needy kid.

The way I saw it was: even if my parents had been free to spend all day every day with me and still been able to live well, they wouldn't have wanted to.

The same went for my brothers. They were both older and closer and had formed an unofficial club which I was never going to be accepted into.

There were moments, such as when the three of us stood at the roadside in 'toy' police uniforms and saluted as Queen Elizabeth II passed through our village in a Rolls Royce, when we were temporarily a trio. But, for the majority of the time as far as I was concerned, Matthew and Mark were a duo and I was solo.

Surprisingly early on, I sensed that being solo was a personal failure. In fact, it would not be an exaggeration to state that from the time I was a toddler I thought that I myself was a personal failure.

Being the youngest, I had to remain at home for a couple of years after my brothers started school – making their 'club' appear to me all the more exclusive and myself all the more excluded.

When I alone attended a local nursery school, the first thing I remember seeing there was my reflection in a full-length mirror in the classroom, which made me melt into tears. I didn't like what I saw.

It was only later in my life that I would ask myself why I so wanted my parents and brothers when I was convinced they didn't want me. But for now they were, and this was, my world. It was all I knew and I couldn't see beyond it.

2.

MY START BELONGS TO DADDY

My existence was one of relative isolation anyhow. When I was five, as a family we moved to another boys' boarding school, at the other end of the country: Parkstone Prep in rural Northumberland. Dad was now Headmaster and Mum the Head Matron, so the school building with its 30 acres of grounds became our home…except it never would really be ours, we were just the latest tenants. In external appearance at least, it was a bit like living in a stately home. Aside from the fact that it was in the middle of nowhere and the sash windows rattled eerily in breezy conditions, you'd imagine this to be an idyllic place to live, but not to a youngster who had no friends and was unlikely to make any for many years to come. All the space and facilities any kid could dream of, and no-one except disinterested brothers to share them with during the holidays, which made my sense of failure all the more acute. I might as well have been an only child.

In term times we were joined by approximately a hundred boys, and all of us were referred to by our surnames, with Minor, Major and Max added to differentiate the seniority of siblings like us. The extent to which my mind was so focused on my own issues meant I didn't think what it was like for all these others being sent away to boarding-school so young, especially the one black and two Asian pupils whose different skin colours compared to the rest of us would alone presumably have presented a challenge. I only ever noticed a few homesick kids there and then not for long, as ironically my parents did a good job of creating a warm family atmosphere. But the school was also my home, and to my mind they were invading it for several long stretches of the year. It was tough enough sharing a mother and father with two brothers, let alone lots of unrelated kids who, because their parents were paying big fees, were as entitled to be there as much as I.

I struggled, Matthew faltered, but Mark shone. Even to my then undeveloped mind, the extent to which the three of us flourished was in direct relation to the amount of encouragement we received from our parents. Or rather, from our father – the true wielder of the watering-can of nurture to these buds.

From the outset, Mark was the one on whom Dad blatantly bestowed his attention and appreciation, his hopes and dreams. So Mark couldn't help but shine. He was Goldenboy. And his siblings wilted within his shadow.

For Matthew, this wasn't so much of a problem – they were buddies as well as brothers, and one thing Mark could never take from him was the two-year seniority. For me, two years younger than Mark and many more years younger emotionally, it was crushing. And I was all too easily crushed.

Mum tried to ensure her affection was fairly distributed, but again the extent to which we three boys each felt loved correlated to how loveable we were ourselves. And Mark was a lot more loveable than us other two put together.

Not knowing any better, I clung where I could - to Mark in particular, perhaps hopeful some of his magic would rub off on me and I might become more acceptable on the father front.

That was in the school holidays when parental – most importantly, paternal – attention was better attained. But, even when I did get a few minutes with my Dad, nine times out of 10 he'd turn negative or nasty. Although I never stopped trying to win him over, that was like repeatedly putting my head in the mouth of a cannon which then blew me to smithereens.

Dad moaned and complained about most things: the cost of living, the drop in standards, lack of organisation, machinery that failed, poor pronunciation, people in positions of responsibility, and…me. Among the words Dad used most frequently were 'appalling', 'awful', 'dreadful' (or, as he pronounced it, 'drettful'), 'ghastly', and of course where I was concerned 'horrid'. All of which he'd utter with venom in his voice, as if hoping the people or situations he was condemning would really feel his wrath. A stock phrase of his was: "I wouldn't do that if I were you." He was telling the truth too, as he was never one for taking risks. He was afraid of flying, heights, hospitals, dentists, most animals...you name it.

I'd already inherited Dad's dentophobia. It didn't help that the surname of our family dentist was Grindrod. I viewed him as elderly and evil. He certainly lacked compassion for me. The first time Grindrod attempted to inject my gum with one of those large late Sixties syringes, I screamed and knocked it out of his hand, and the needle stuck into the linoleum floor of the surgery as I ran for the door. Years later when I saw the movie Marathon Man, I instantly associated Grindrod with the sadistic ex-Nazi (played by Laurence Olivier) who performs dental torture on his student victim (Dustin Hoffman).

Due to Dad's fear of flying, none of us travelled by plane. Dad made us go everywhere in a car with him. He would hardly ever let Mum take the wheel when he was a passenger. It was almost acceptable in those days for men to have a chauvinistic negative attitude towards 'women drivers'. Ironically, Mum was perfectly proficient and Dad's driving was abysmal. He rarely changed gears above third and relied on the brakes alone for slowing - so heavily that the pads would wear within no time and the rest of us in the car often felt sick. The phrase 'Are we nearly there yet?' might have been invented with my brothers and me in mind. Late 1960s/early 70s estate cars (ours were Hillmans) were practical not comfortable, and the back seat especially seemed so narrow as the Twigg boys fought for space and with one another. "Will you three stop squabbling!" shouted Dad, as his left arm swung back in our general direction to smack knees, heads or whatever it took to restore some kind of order.

The slightest noise would irritate Dad, particularly any repetitive noise which he'd react to as if it were a slowly dripping tap of the kind used in Japanese water torture. Yet, as he drove, he himself would conduct the most bizarre repetitive habits. If, for example, he turned the radio on or off or changed its wavelength, he'd then touch the same button again and again and again until something inside him seemed satisfied. That applied to other knobs, switches and levers too. He was also forever shifting in his seat, especially waggling his head around from the neck as if the two didn't fit together and therefore caused constant irritation. From my shared seat behind Dad, I watched his strange routines with a combination of fascination, unease, and some sympathy at his evident discomfort. Yet I also found it hypocritical considering he would get angry if I so much as fidgeted slightly.

The tension in Dad radiated from him, never more so than when we went as a family in the car. His stressed presence alone would transform its confined space into a pressure cooker, and every time we boys tested his intolerance I half-expected the entire vehicle to explode into an inferno. Knowing the extent to which Dad's troubles troubled me, I was amazed at my brothers' ability to ignore all this in him. Mum tried ignoring it too, but Dad wouldn't let her – at least not for long. As far as he was concerned, she'd married him so she'd not only have to put up with him but take the brunt of everything too.

A classic example of what did Dad's head in was when any of us, Mum included, ever chewed gum. He tried to ban it in our household, and if he ever caught us with it or at it he'd 'hit the roof'. He may have regarded the appearance of a person chewing as scruffy, rebellious and low-class, but I reckon it was the repetitive sound which really got to him. On one typically tense car journey, Dad made Mum spit out her gum, which he grabbed from her hand and hurled from his window as he drove us along...only for the wind to blow the gum straight back and get stuck on his jacket. Our initial reaction was to laugh, albeit nervously, and predictably the over-active volcano that was Dad swiftly erupted.

Dad also loathed any bickering between us boys. Yet we'd always been under the impression that he didn't get on with his own brother, our uncle James. In fact, Dad didn't seem to get on with many people, certainly very few who Mum cared about, including her parents. That actually provided some relief as it meant that holidays were largely divided between respective sides of the family. And, while Mum would dutifully join in visits to Dad's folks, he rarely did the same for hers.

It was striking how much those two families were reflective of this contrasting couple. Mum's parents and brother were easy-going and enjoyed a laugh. Dad's parents, brother and sister were altogether more serious, reserved and formal. Visits to his folks were about being on best behaviour all the time. It was as if Dad never wanted the family he'd come from see flaws in the family he'd formed. With a nod to a Thomas The Tank Engine character, this was The Thin Controller. And woe betide us boys if we didn't act within his control.

The plus side of visiting Dad's side was that, as well as being based in Devon, they had a flat in the Riviera resort of Antibes. It was right by the beach, its surrounding area tres charmant, and the weather and food usually divine. Dad insisted his wife and sons speak French (with perfect pronunciation) to the natives and never say a word against them. On one of our endless drives through France, I once commented on the murky state of a river we crossed, and Dad bellowed at me with feral fury: "How DARE you say that about this beautiful country, you horrid, horrid, HORRID child!" Dad lived 99% of his life in England, yet if France played any other nation – especially England - at sport, he supported France and to an absurdly blind degree.

Mum's parents also lived in a South Coast seaside resort, but in England. Of course the temperatures tended to be a lot cooler in Sussex than on the Cote d'Azur, yet the family atmosphere was always a lot warmer...mainly because Dad rarely came too. I never asked why that was. No need to; that situation suited me just fine.

For me, the best thing about Grandma and Grandpa was that they ran what was officially termed a Confectioner & Tobacconist. So I really was like a kid in a sweetshop more often than I would otherwise have been...and I'd happily have lived in one if my extremely sweet tooth had its way. I also enjoyed going with Grandpa early every morning to get his paper from the newsagent opposite, mainly because he'd hold my hand which suggested he at least cared about my safety.

Breaks spent at their place in Worthing traditionally included going to see a film or stage show. I enjoyed them all, but the one I'd remember most fondly was just for one joke. The Welsh comedian Wyn Calvin began his act by telling the audience at The Pavilion Theatre (as he presumably did everywhere he performed): "How kind of this lovely venue to put my initials on my dressing-room door…" Once the proverbial penny dropped, that prompted an all too rare moment when our entire family group laughed out loud. Such was the joy of good-old fashioned humour then.

My other favourite tradition of those stays was an evening meal including my favourite dessert of rice pudding and tinned peaches or mandarins, washed down with Coca Cola or lemonade.

With or without all that sugar inside me, I was an active kid, always wanting to play…mainly football. Easily bored, I needed to be creative. My mind worked overtime. I'd look at cloud formations and arty patterns on tree-bark, curtains, wallpaper or whatever and see unintentional figures and faces. I liked walking past other people's properties when I could glimpse inside them, made cosier by lights at night, and always assumed they were happier homes than my own family's one. At night at my maternal grandparents' place, I liked hearing traffic outside my bedroom window where the roads unusually comprised enormous concrete blocks. Sometimes I'd peek at the people in the cars and wonder who they were and where they were heading. I found it reassuring seeing folk awake when those upon whom I depended slept.

I felt allowed and able to use my imagination while with Mum's side of the family. When Dad was around, projecting his darkness and discipline over me, I was stifled...and constantly on edge because he was. So I welcomed times away from him.

Had it not been for Dad's difficult domineering nature, I would have enjoyed being with my paternal grandparents more. Certainly I'd only ever remember experiencing kindnesses from Dad's father, known as Grandman, who walked me to the local bookshop to buy me a Tintin annual and to the jeweller for my first ever watch. To a child overwhelmed by a sense of rejection these were unforgettably thoughtful and generous gestures. Also charmingly, whenever Grandman saw us off after a visit, he'd stand at his front door waving a white handkerchief.

The only occasions I was shown a semblance of the parental pride I saw other kids get was when we three were introduced to, or paraded in front of, friends and family. Yet it was visits to elderly relatives that I disliked most. Sure, they were usually kind to me, but if it hadn't been for that I would never have wanted to visit them at all. Unsavoury smells, bent bodies, gnarled old hands and wrinkly cheeks had me shuddering to my core, especially at having to kiss them on arriving and departing – kisses which were wiped off with sleeves the moment I stepped out of sight. Objections to such visits were swiftly overruled. "You will damn well go, you horrid child!" Dad would roar, over-heating like a malfunctioning boiler. "You know how much they enjoy seeing you..." was the calmer Mum approach. But what really persuaded me was the money these old folks would present us boys with when we left. Coins, and especially notes, were some consolation. And, to my uncharitable mind, compensation.

One visit to a very elderly great-aunt in France will remain with me for the rest of my life. With dwindling eyesight, she took a tin of biscuits off a shelf, lifted its lid and, perhaps told I had an extremely sweet tooth, offered them to me first. To my horror, there were spiders crawling all over the biscuits. I swiftly withdrew my hand and declined the offer, only to receive a fierce stare from Dad across the room, and through his clenched teeth a hissed "Horrid child, TAKE ONE AND EAT ONE!"

As a family, we were unlikely to ever go hungry. But Dad wouldn't tolerate us wasting food. I say 'us' in that I assume it happened to my brothers as well, but I can only actually recall this happening to me. If I failed to eat everything on my plate at meal times, he'd sternly threaten "You will jolly well sit here until you do. There are lots of starving people in the World who'd kill for this!" Similarly, if I objected to having to wear clothes previously worn by Matthew and Mark, Dad demanded I consider my good fortune compared to the poverty-stricken. I knew nothing of the starving and/or poor people he referred to. I hadn't met them, and they weren't shown in the publications I read or programmes I watched on television then - that's how narrow my life was – but I wouldn't have dared doubt Dad was telling the truth. Neither did I mind most food we were served, but liver with its sinews and sour milk with bits floating in it turned my stomach. I vowed to myself that if and when I'd one day be able to make my own decisions, I'd only consume what I wanted.

A popular phrase among people of a certain age then aimed at the disappointing youth of that era was 'You don't know you're born!' Indeed, none of us could imagine the incredible hardships of living through wartime, but a) it wasn't our fault that we weren't around then, and b) in my Dad's case, he was 15 when WW2 ended, and he spent all six years of it in the safety and calm of the English countryside, so it was unlikely to have harmed him much. I might have understood his virtually permanent state of displeasure had he been battle-scarred, suffering from post-traumatic stress disorder, or something to that effect. Yet I knew that wasn't the case. What I didn't know and couldn't work out was what his problem was with me.

My early sugar addiction was sealed by the then common practice of serving desserts with lunch and supper, biscuits at coffee breaks and cake at tea time, not to mention a weekly allowance of sweeties. The fact that my Grandma and Grandpa ran a confectioners could also have been to blame, as could their daughter, my mother. I suspect she felt bad about the way Dad treated their youngest son, which mainly involved ignoring and berating this boy, and Mum knew how comforting sweets, cakes and puddings could be. She was partial to them herself. It showed in her physique.

No-one needed comfort from Dad's tyrannous reign more than she and me. Consumed as I was much of the time with trying to fathom and cope with apparently being detested by my own father, I became increasingly aware of his hostility towards Mum too. He dismissed her opinions and needs as if they didn't matter at all against his. He'd put her down – often to the point of humiliation – in front of others. And he'd frequently reduce her to tears through the brutal insults he'd shout at her. Their arguments may have mostly taken place behind the closed door of their bedroom, but the volume of his shouting and her whimpering could all too easily be heard from some distance away. Painful as it was to listen to, it was also strangely compelling. I suppose I wanted to be on-hand in case Dad was ever violent towards Mum...even though my feeble frame would have had stood no chance against him at 6'4" and 15 stone. So it was small wonder Mum comfort ate. She smoked and drank too but, considering the circumstances, surprisingly not to excess.

To Dad's credit, he'd gone from being an extremely heavy smoker to giving up completely. As a result, he and the house smelt better but the channelling of his nerves and tension from then on would often have his family wishing he was still on the cigarettes.

Dad and his moods ruled. Once his mind was set, that was it. No-one could question him – not Mum, not Matthew, certainly not me. Just occasionally Mark. It was as if Dad's entire aura comprised black clouds which frequently turned into storms so ferocious I'd be prepared to do whatever it took to avoid or defuse them.

Aptly, Dad's chocolate of choice was dark (mine then was white). One day when the school pupils were to return for another academic year – which meant that for most of the following few months my parents would be even less available to me than normal – I hatched a plan. It involved popping to the local shop and buying a bar of Bourneville. I then knocked on the door of Dad's office where he was up to his neck in paperwork, phone calls, and all sorts of comings and goings. His secretary beckoned me in and, the instant I made eye contact with my father, I stretched out my right hand to give him his gift...and burst into tears. The treat – though maybe more my crying – worked a treat. Dad asked his secretary to give us a little time alone, he pulled me towards him, thanked me for the chocolate and asked me what the matter was. I could hardly speak for sobbing, but managed to splutter out an "I love you, Dad!"

I can't remember his reply. If he said he loved me too, whether then or at any other time, I either didn't hear it or didn't feel it. The phone rang, someone walked in on us or whatever, and our bonding session was over. Sadly that was to typify my relationship with my father. The precious few treasured times never lasted and always seemed to mean everything to me and nothing to him.

At night, but only during holidays, Dad would bend over our respective beds and kiss us, his three sons, on the forehead one by one. A fleeting moment from which lingered the unique smell of Euthymol toothpaste battling to keep his halitosis at bay (I did say dentists were among his fears). And that was about it on the fatherly affection front for me. Most of the rest of the time, he was terrifying and I was terrified. Scared shitless of my own father. Literally too. For one excruciatingly embarrassing phase I messed my pants repeatedly. But there was no gentle parental discussion about it. Instead, the sternest of matrons was despatched to march me up to the top floor bathroom and forced me to sit on the toilet as she blocked the door shouting "You will not leave this room until you have done a poo in the loo", or something to that effect. Just what I needed, of course: to be terrorised into sorting myself out.

When that didn't work, I was taken to the local hospital...to see a psychiatrist. At least my parents took me there themselves. But I remember they gained pleasure in telling me the shrink's finding: that I was 'performing' in this way to gain attention. What I don't remember was any change in Dad towards me as a result. I got the impression his verdict was that I was the only person responsible for my problem.

At least Mum made some effort towards giving me one-on-one time, albeit in an unusual way. She took me with her shopping. But that frequently meant wandering round women's clothing stores as she pondered over what to buy, and waiting an eternity while she tried things on in changing rooms. Occasionally she sought my opinion which was pointless as there was probably no-one else alive on the planet then who knew less about women's fashion than me.

When visiting supermarkets with Mum, I'd beg her to buy me sweets, and she got me to fetch sanitary towels and tampons from the relevant shelves. I'd no idea what they were and, even if I had, the thought of being useful to my mother would have exceeded any cringe factor.

Maybe Mum, as I suspected of Dad, wanted me to be a girl, because she also had me accompany her to the hairdressers. The other women in the salon seemed to relish having a boy in their midst, and I'd take full advantage by acting up in whatever way I could to make them smile or talk to me. 'Showing off', as Dad would have described it had he been there to spoil my rare moments of fun. My highlight was being seated next to Mum while her barnet was setting under a hood drier. All this at least meant I was out of Dad's hair, in Mum's care, and receiving some required company and consideration.

On a visit to the weekly market in the local town, I saw something I wanted – probably sugary. So I went over to Mum having seen her a couple of stalls away in her houndstooth-patterned coat, tugged on that and asked if she'd let me have the small amount of cash I needed. No response. I tugged a little harder, then heard an 'Oi!' in a voice I didn't recognise. It was another woman of similar appearance and almost identical coat. She was annoyed, even suspicious, and I was mortified at my mistake, apologised profusely and went in search of my real mother.

There were often rewards and quick fixes for me in the shape of sweeties, like throwing fish to seals or drugs to addicts. I consumed a scary amount. Candy and cans of fizzy drinks in particular made my behaviour hyper. That, combined with the extent to which my Dad made me constantly perturbed, resulted in a tendency to blurt things out, sometimes inappropriate things too. I just couldn't help myself.

I remained a deeply unhappy child. In fact, although over a thousand children would attend Dad's school during his 11 years in charge, I never met one as miserable and anxious as me.

A photo still exists of my father's side of the family all together in his sister Lizzie's back garden in Barnstaple. I'm sitting on a little stool in the front row, upset to the point of tears after yet another angry tirade from Dad. It's a sad memento, but typical of how I felt then.

3.

LOSING AND MY RELIGION

I was sad when Dad's Dad, Grandman, died in 1969. Of old age, I believe.

I was only eight at the time. No-one I'd ever known had died before, as far as I was aware.

When my mother broke the news to me, I asked her what she meant by it. I recall being told it meant I'd never see Grandman again, but I don't think it was explained why that was, though Heaven was probably given as his new whereabouts.

Knowing that Heaven was the reward for good humans, I reckoned my grandfather – having bought me my first watch and Tintin annual – richly deserved his place there.

Perhaps sensing this was a rare opportunity to bond with Dad, I set about searching for him, overflowing with sympathy. I found the familiar lanky figure in an upstairs corridor, and what he'd just learned dawned on me: I could see my father, but my father would no longer be able to see his. Not that that appeared to be affecting him as much as it did me.

"Why are you crying?" he asked, apparently startled to have this sobbing boy suddenly clutch him round the waist. "Because Grandman's dead!" I exclaimed, secretly thinking "Why aren't you crying?"

I wouldn't learn the answer to that until a long time later. But I would never see Dad sad over losing his Dad.

The following year there was another death in the family. My mother's brother Paul, her only sibling, suffered heart failure at 40. In contrast to Dad's lack of reaction to his Dad's death, Mum was absolutely beside herself at this shocking news. She shut herself in the bathroom, in distress. And that distress didn't let up – not for ages. Not ever, in fact.

I will never forget how Mark and I responded on being told the above news by our father. We looked at each other and briefly giggled. We definitely didn't consider it funny nor mean to be disrespectful, and I don't think either of us ever forgave ourselves, but we couldn't help ourselves. This was a family who lived on nerves, with Dad being the 'nerve centre'. He seemed incapable of relaxing and was permanently uptight, and therefore so were his offspring whose nerves manifested themselves in smiling or laughing. The more serious the situations we found ourselves in, the more we couldn't help but react that way. It was mortifying.

Not long after these deaths, Mark and I were sharing a bath and while in it discussed which of us three brothers would die first, when he said "I will". Whether he actually believed it or had a premonition, I've no idea. But that memorable chat proved we were both now aware lives were limited. And I knew that, no matter how much confidence and strength Mark radiated which made me want to be close to him if not actually be him, he like all of us was going to depart this planet one day and therefore could never be totally relied upon to 'be there' for me. Besides, as with Dad, there were increasing instances where Mark didn't allow me near him and pushed me away.

Some months after losing our Uncle Paul, Mum took us boys back to Hartson House, the mansion we used to live in, to visit a lady in another of its apartments. Over afternoon tea, Mrs.Chaucer unwittingly asked Mum how her brother was. This harmless enquiry caused Mum deep upset. Tea was abandoned and we left.

I was amazed at the extent to which Mum mourned her brother. It was serious grief. Maybe I just couldn't imagine feeling much at all had my brothers lost their lives. They didn't appear to care for me, so I didn't care for them either.

Perhaps it was part of her grieving process but I remember Mum regretting gifting Paul so many chocolates to satisfy his sweet tooth, but as a nurse she'd have known there must have been far more major contributing factors to his early demise. And I didn't notice that stopping her trying to cheer me with sugary treats, but that was fine by me then.

For years, Mum looked for signs. Signs like white feathers, which some believe come from angels – more specifically, people we've known who've passed on and become angels, as if the feathers have fallen from their wings. On a country walk with Mum once we came across a bright white feather on the ground. She was quite excited. I said nothing so as not to detract from the tiny hopes she clung to, but I was thinking 'Do you really think that's there for you? What of others who walked that way...was it not meant for them too? Is this really a sign or simply a case of a bird having recently shed a feather in that particular place?'

Soon Mum was taking an interest in spiritual matters. She was fascinated by The Bloxham Tapes – recordings famously made by a hypnotherapist of what sounded convincingly like past life regressions. She would have liked to make some kind of contact with her brother if she could but, although she consulted a psychic or two, it wasn't achieved.

For all her fascination in that direction, and the fact that her extended family had a fairly distinguished history within the Baptist church in Britain, Mum was not a religious sort. Even if she had been, there was no chance of us three boys being brought up as Baptists. As far as this family was concerned, what Dad wanted Dad got – nothing else even got considered. Thus, as Dad was a devout Catholic, his sons would automatically be too. He said prayers by his bed at night, and he made us do the same. He went to church on Sundays and holy days, so we had to too. He'd attended Catholic schools, and now we did as well.

Much as I then usually tended to behave in ways that I thought might appease Dad, I didn't try to share his dedication to his religion. To me church buildings were often sinister and spooky, the hour-long services bored me rigid and seemed to drone on for days, and I was far too self-conscious to let anyone hear me singing. Above all, I just didn't 'get it'. I saw no point in all these people reciting like automatons age-old lines in worship of a 'being' whose existence there was no proof of. And I understood even less why the monks and priests we sometimes met would voluntarily take on restricted, dull existences in devotion of this one unproven 'person'. I considered every second given over to 'God' was a waste, and I'd far rather be playing than praying.

At Parkstone Prep, religion – albeit the Catholic version of it - was part of the curriculum. The school had its own chapel – an endearing room of panelled walls, wooden pews, patterned white ceiling, and to the left of the altar a side section with a curved wall of windows looking out over the garden. Much nicer than old austere church buildings, yet still I never wanted to be in there on my own. The association of religion with things beyond my sight or knowledge, including 'the Holy Spirit', unnerved me.

At the back of the chapel was a Confessional – a dark enclosure so small that only one person could sit either side of a grille: the priest and a member of his congregation. After certain services, pupils would sit in the chapel's rear pews in a queue to visit the priest in the Confessional. While waiting we were expected to contemplate what bad things we'd done, or even thought, in order to confess those 'sins' to the priest and wait for him to punish us accordingly. They weren't punishments in the usual sense – we'd only be ordered to go back into the chapel and recite a few Our Fathers, Hail Marys and maybe other prayers, as a means of seeking forgiveness from 'Our Lord', ie God. I found the entire experience awful. As an innocent child being raised in a basically civilised environment, I never did anything really wrong, and with a Dad like mine I wouldn't have dared anyway. Even I knew eating too many sweet things wasn't a crime. Okay, so I had negative thoughts about a few people I encountered, but hey wasn't that just normal? And were such things considered sinful, I'd have been tempted to point out 'Well, if God really made us and all we are, then why am I apologising to him? Isn't he to blame for my faults and weaknesses?'

Though I knew I hadn't been bad in this life, the fact that I wasn't feeling loved within it did make me wonder if there was something to talk of paying for the sins of a previous life.

Being an exceptionally withdrawn child, I didn't want anyone else knowing my intimate thoughts and secrets. So when it came to confession, I thought 'I'm not telling you that!' We had to address priests as 'Father' – not a great association for me – followed by their monastic first name. Here was Father Phillip. He was the school chaplain, and a close friend of my parents, especially my Dad. After being grim-faced serious in Confession, he'd attend lunch or supper in the school refectory, cheerily chatting away to staff and pupils alike. I didn't trust anyone, even a priest, to not pass my private information on, so I only went to Confession once or twice. In fact I remember my Dad questioning me on later occasions why I hadn't gone again, so the priest must have at least told him that much.

Confession, Catholicism as a whole, and my Dad the doom-laden disciplinarian...they all drilled into us kids: do bad things, even think bad things, and there will be negative consequences, ultimately Hell to pay. I could never have imagined that concept would infiltrate so much of my life.

In school holidays I had to be dragged kicking and screaming to church. When I was successfully dragged there, I'd make a nuisance of myself. I'd try to get Mark to giggle, I'd doodle on the distributed leaflets, or tap my fingers or feet which I knew would annoy Dad.

Dad and Mark – when I would allow them - took their religion extremely seriously. They recited the prayers and sung the hymns with great gusto. Last thing at night, they'd kneel at their respective beds with clasped hands and closed eyes, sincerely muttering prayers to the Almighty...whilst Matthew and I just did the bare minimum when we knew Dad was watching.

I couldn't help but think that, if this God they worshipped was as good as they seemed to believe, why were these two not among the most happy and pleasant people I knew? Dad especially was miserable and moody much of the time. So, if I had doubts as to whether I was right about not sharing their faith, they didn't linger long.

If there was anything earthly that Dad regarded as seriously as religion it was sport, particularly cricket. He'd been an exceptional young cricketer himself, and still played whenever he could. Cricket was the compulsory Summer sport at school, and we brothers all tried hard to be good at it. Winning Dad's appreciation was everything then. And as usual it was Mark who did the winning, Matthew did reasonably well, whereas I was just okay. Those were the likely podium placements whatever sport we played.

Already feeling a loser in life, I loathed losing at sports and loathed even more the fact that Mark was always winning. Yet he loved the fact that I was always losing to him and hating it. "That's 10 wins to me and none to you!" he'd taunt, repeatedly as his tally increased. Now I could see why goldenboy Joseph in the Bible was sold as a slave by his brothers but, as my only other brother's loyalty was with Mark and not me, there was no chance of any such plot developing between us. Though I wouldn't have imagined them hesitating over swapping me for a few shillings. Or even just giving me away.

Then one day an opportunity arose for me to not only stop Mark's winning and taunting, but to stop Mark full-stop. We were in the school gym...rifle-shooting. This was holiday-time so the required supervision of this activity was ignored. We both fired the little metal pellets through our respective .22 barrels aimed at marked paper targets 10 metres away. After the allotted amount of attempts, Mark swaggered confidently towards the targets. Even before he reached them, we both knew I'd barely scored if at all, and he'd bagged a number of bullseyes. Predictably the taunting started. "25 wins to me, and none to you!" or whatever it was. Mark was bent over staring with glee at the targets. I bent open the barrel of my rifle, inserted a pellet and aimed. I may have been a poor shot but, fuelled by my freshly ignited jealousy, I doubt I'd have missed what I considered then to be his very big head. Nor did I think I would ever miss him in any other way had I succeeded in killing him. I didn't go through with it, of course, though I suspect that was more to do with how that would have affected my existence more than his.

There were subsequent occasions in our childhood when I wished Mark was dead, but not as many as those on which I wished our Dad dead. Such strong thoughts for such a young person, perhaps, but I could not stand the fact that my own father was so disinterested in and unpleasant toward me. I figured that Mark was, to a degree, following that example. And I was puzzled as to why the fair-minded God of theirs not only allowed this to happen, but also granted Mark the ability to outclass me at everything, thereby really rubbing my nose in it.

If there was any sport at which I thought I might at least one day compete favourably with Mark, it was soccer. Somehow, despite never having had a word of encouragement in any department of my life, I was beginning to gain something resembling hope in my footballing skills. I actually believed I was quite good at it. During a Summer stay with Aunt Lizzie and family, I practised dribbling a ball around assorted objects in their garden – over and over again until I was ready to take Mark on. My subsequent challenge went well for me, nudging that one tiny niche of aspiration up a notch above zero, and instilling a sporting passion which was self-generated rather than paternally-appeasing.

I supported Leeds United FC. They had no connection with my surroundings or acquaintances. I chose them because their acclaimed successes in the late 1960s and early 1970s made them winners when I felt like an all-round loser.

Around that time, I wrote to the Leeds manager Don Revie requesting a trial for the club. I got a polite letter back explaining this wasn't the normal procedure. He could no doubt sense I was not to be taken seriously anyhow. Playing well for the Under-11 team of your prep school may have felt impressive to this child of no expectations, but it hadn't really occurred to me that there were only about 100 pupils in the entire school and none of our sides stood a chance against most others in the vicinity, let alone the country. That was a measure of how the closeted existence I led in such a restricted environment prevented me from having the faintest idea of what the real World was like.

When I attended my first professional football match, I instantly realised the vast gulf between my basic abilities and those of these top players. It was Middlesborough versus Portsmouth and even the smartness of the pitch surface impressed me massively, let alone the skill and speed of what was performed upon it for 90-plus minutes. The biggest surprise came about 30 minutes in when the ball was booted into my section of the crowd…and I picked it up and hurled it back to the winger waiting to do the throw-in. Not just a personal thrill for pathetic, insignificant me, but a moment in which my real world literally came into contact with my dream world. Fleeting but fantastic, proving it was actually possible to some degree.

4.

DEFINITELY DADDY'S HOME

You might have thought that being the Headmaster's sons would have put my brothers and I in a position of resentment from the other boys in the school. For those seven years, very little happened to indicate as much...not to Matthew and Mark anyway. And I don't think what I experienced was due to my Dad's status – though a lot to do with the effect he was having on me. Nearly all the other pupils seemed accepting of the situation. Maybe if any did have a problem with it, they'd have felt reluctant to cross the boss's family.

To be fair, literally, Matthew, Mark and I led identical lives to everyone else, and slept in the dormitories like they did. When a bunch of boys including me caused a commotion after lights out one night, Dad bent each one of us in turn across his left leg, pulled our pyjama trousers down and smacked our buttocks with his bare hands. Same for all but strange to me, partly because he never did it during holidays when he was at his harshest. Otherwise about the only difference was the fact that our family had its own accommodation in the school to retreat to, and none of us retreated there more than me.

When terms ended, we three Twigg boys remained at the school as the rest set off for their respective homes around the country, some around the globe. That to me suggested unrestricted adventure for them but also – with my Dad's dire warning 'I wouldn't do that if I were you' ever ringing in my ears - potential danger. So, while I was comparatively stuck, I felt safer that way. But I did assume that they were all returning to more affectionate and cheerful families than mine.

I spent too much holiday time on my own, often wandering the mansion and its expansive grounds alone and lonely. At the eastern boundary of the school gardens was an ornamental wrought iron gate which I'd stand behind staring through it at the main road in the far distance. I wasn't interested where the road literally led to in a local sense, but the fact that it represented escape – ultimately to places where I believed I'd be happy one day. It was all about 'one day', because I somehow knew that in the meantime I had a lot of dissatisfaction and disharmony to endure. Not unlike a prisoner contemplating the day he'll eventually get released following a long sentence, although I had committed no crime.

After a few years, our family accommodation moved from rooms within the school to a cottage on the edge of the grounds. It was a very old cottage with thick stone walls and low ceilings. One night, Mark saw the ghost of a sailor beside my bed. I didn't find that out til years after we'd left there because our parents swore him to secrecy in case I was freaked out. So maybe they did remember the effect the Hartson House spook had on me. Anyway, they were right: I probably wouldn't have wanted to stay in the cottage a moment longer.

I was disturbed enough as it was by its oppressive atmosphere - not due to the spirit of this cottage's past but to that of its current chief occupant. Dad's darkness filled every room he entered, especially the living room we spent most of our family time in. Northumberland was frequently freezing and so was the cottage. During holidays I took to wearing several sweaters at once, to cope with the cold and to make my puny body look bulkier than it was. A bar heater was the most effective way of warming up, yet Dad couldn't bear it being used, certainly not with both bars on. "Turn that ruddy thing off!" he'd seethe. "You're wasting electricity and money!" Similarly he insisted we only had the cheapest toilet paper which was so sharp it nipped your bottom.

Dad pretty much always decided when we watched television and what we watched. And he inadvertently used it as an object of his endless gripes. For example, if a man with then fashionably long hair appeared on-screen, he'd say something like "Look at the state of him! Scruffy so-and-so. What kind of example is he setting to the boys of this nation?" And although Dad could happily watch cricket for days on end, he was forever criticising batsmen who didn't play the way he'd been taught. "Foot nowhere near the ball!" was his most common complaint.

Some of what and who I saw on the magic box in the corner of our front room was awesome and aspirational, and felt unattainable like a dream world full of fantasy figures. Mum was enamoured of movie stars and Dad admired some from the small screen. Those Dad liked I looked closely at in the hope of emulating whatever qualities I could detect in them that he found admirable.

Of the people on TV who impressed Dad, most were women he fancied - which he'd happily make clear to all of us regardless of how that might have made Mum feel - and entertainers who made him laugh. The latter included Joyce Grenfell and The Goons (who were really from before my time but still shown a lot), Morecambe & Wise, Victor Borge, and Mike Yarwood. Those were truly exceptional performers so the rest of us Twiggs generally liked them too, but there was an element of showing appreciation to appease Dad. I enjoyed hearing him laugh at these stars and their shows, partly as it meant he might for a while at least be less likely to pick on me for something. His loudest laughs were reserved for quick-witted responses given by bright guests on panel shows. It didn't occur to either of us that those 'spontaneous' ad-libbed comments were probably prepared in advance. All I knew was that if I tried smartarse quipping, I wouldn't raise a single smile – only frowns for 'showing off' - so I shouldn't even think about it. Which made my blurts all the more mortifying.

Pretty much any telly his sons liked Dad dismissed as "utter codswallop" or "unintelligent nonsense". He also had no time for the slushy movies Mum enjoyed. Maybe he didn't want to see her cry – not because that saddened him but because it went against the stiff upper lip upbringing he'd had.

Mum was English but had been raised in India, where her father worked on the railways during the Second World War. She talked about that time as if it was the happiest of her life - those halcyon years with her beloved brother whom she now missed so sorely, and her parents whom she continued to adore. A favourite tale of Mum's was how she'd met stars of the silver screen when they toured India with ENSA (which officially stood for Entertainments National Service Association, and jokingly stood for Every Night Something Awful). She still treasured the autographs of greats like Noel Coward and Jock Perkins. Mum told me Perkins had thought she in her early teens had at least the look of a potential movie actress and requested the permission of her parents to take her to Hollywood. Very sensibly they refused. Occasionally, when Mum would be sat beside me watching what Dad angrily labelled "sentimental twaddle", I wondered if it was the schmaltzy plot which got tears streaming down her cheeks, or the knowledge of what might have been. The high-life in Tinseltown or struggling along in bleakest Northumberland with a turbulent marriage to an impossible husband...? No contest, surely.

Dad also seemed in awe of famous folk. On occasions when certain people popped up in the press or on TV, Dad would say "I was at school with him" or "I used to teach him" or "I know someone who knows him/her" as if it gave him a kind of kudos. I just hoped that one day he'd proudly say of me "that's my son!", but I very much doubted that would ever happen – more likely "that's not my son!".

My youth was largely unhappy – that was the part involving my disapproving father and brothers. I sensed there was a better life to be had, like those evidently enjoyed by many of my fellow pupils, and by many people I saw on television. Of course there was plenty of unpleasantness on telly, but I didn't watch that. Although admittedly I did like playing with toy soldiers and plastic guns which pumped ping pong balls, for me there was more than enough darkness to deal with in real life, so why would I seek out more on television when I was supposed to be relaxing?

When Dad wasn't sat reading The Times or doing its crossword, there was one thing he always insisted on watching on TV or listening to on the radio: the news. Whenever or wherever he could, he devoured it, and got absorbed by it. Whoever was with him at the time was shushed into silence. No-one was allowed to move a muscle while the news was being broadcast. It was as if each bulletin was revealing the death of a monarch or a declaration of war. If I hadn't let Dad listen, he'd have declared war on me. I evidently annoyed him enough as it was, and that would have tipped him over the edge.

Part of the difficulty with Dad was the fact that he'd rarely show his true colours to anyone outside his intimate family. He could be in the midst of an almighty temper tantrum with us at home, yet if visitors ever arrived he'd immediately transform into charm personified, and very convincingly too. The visitors would be none the wiser and, had I told them what had really gone on shortly before, they wouldn't have believed me.

All I ever seemed capable of doing with my brothers, as with our father, was irritating them. I was, in their eyes, the archetypal annoying youngest sibling.

Mark shared a bedroom with me but little else. On the other side of our far wall, Matthew had his own room. He was the eldest, so that was his right. And he took good advantage of it, entertaining friends, playing music and probably doing a lot more besides. His taste in music then was much more mature than my own. Jimi Hendrix, Deep Purple, Yes, and King Crimson, for example. I wasn't keen on hearing any of that stuff, especially when I wanted to sleep. But there were other artists he played whose music I did enjoy, such as The Beatles, The Doors, and early Elton John. Now I'd discovered something capable of lifting my spirits almost as effectively as sweet foods.

My personal preference was for the pop of that period: the so-called 'glam rock' in the bizarre guises of Gary Glitter, T-Rex, Sweet, Slade, Mud, David Bowie and so forth. Wholesome music appealed to me too, particularly The New Seekers whose beautiful lead singer Eve Graham became my joint first crush along with cute little Dana of All Kinds Of Everything fame. Several hit singles I'd play repeatedly on my record-player, including Gonna Make You A Star by David Essex which I loved everything about, including the title's pledge – 'How fantastic it must be to be told that', I pondered. One afternoon I replayed that song so often that my visiting Grandpa urged me to stop. I could only bear a couple of spins of its B-side Window because the boy screaming on that resonated in the darkest recesses of my soul.

The Sunday evening rundown of the UK singles charts on BBC Radio 1 meant more to me than anything I learnt at school, and I'd record each one on a tinny tape machine for posterity.

What enthralled me most were the international teen idols of the time: David Cassidy, Donny Osmond, and to a lesser extent Michael Jackson. They were only a few years older than me, yet in a different stratosphere in terms of togetherness and sophistication. Incredibly talented, good-looking, cool, charismatic, confident, globally desired and in-demand – especially by young girls – they were absolutely everything I wasn't. All three even appeared to get on famously with their brothers. I enjoyed their music, and lapped up any media coverage they received.

One day I was walking along the stretch of main road I could see through the ornamental gate, when I noticed a 7-inch vinyl record lying in pieces on a fence-post. It turned out to be Donny Osmond's chart-topper Puppy Love, with its blue circular centre bearing the logo of the American record label MGM. To me and my then limited horizon, it seemed astounding that something created thousands of miles away around one American boy in the entertainment industry should even find its way to this desolate spot in the back of beyond. That alone was success on a scale beyond my imagination.

Donny and co were conquering the World, performing live to enormous audiences who hung on their every word. And there was hopeless little me with no discernible ability, even less self-belief, and definitely no fans. Never mind making pop records, when it came to just buying my first one, Crocodile Rock by Elton John, I couldn't do it. Beset by shyness, and scared of standing at the head of a shop queue to put my request to an assistant, I bottled out and nagged Matthew to do it for me. He did it too, albeit begrudgingly.

There was much more distance between Matthew and myself than just our four-year age gap. Not too long after I joined Parkstone Prep, he left there for public school. And, during holidays, he hung out with Mark and not with me.

Of our utterly unfashionable family, Matthew came the closest to being even vaguely trendy. He embraced early 70s clothing and hair styles, as well as the hippest music of that era. I truly considered him cool when a brown paper bag arrived in the post for him one morning, containing a copy of the banned record Je t'aime…moi non plus by Serge Gainsbourg and a breathy Jane Birkin.

The bottom line was: Matthew was acting his age and making an effort to fit in with the times and his friends whom he attracted in quality if not quantity. In stark contrast, even as I gained in years and height, I remained a child inside. A timid, frightened, awkward child. Matthew's determination to be 'one of the lads' meant associating with someone as undesirable as me was never going to happen. I reacted by being a pest, embarrassing him in front of his mates, which only succeeded in increasing the barrier between us. As my own family wanted little to do with me, it was hardly surprising I struggled to make friends myself.

Then, in what seemed to me at the time like a giant step forward at a young age, Matthew was swiftly moving on from just having male friends to having girlfriends.

5.

IT'S DIFFERENT WITH GIRLS

Girls were almost alien to my early life. I was, after all, one of three brothers being raised and educated in an isolated boys' boarding-school. A Catholic school at that, where there was virtually nothing to provide the first awareness of sexuality to this most naive of nerds.

There was certainly no sex education in my Dad's school, nor in his home. If there was anything to enlighten me on any of the three TV channels Britain had in those days, I was not allowed up late enough to watch. My mind just slowly, though unintentionally, began gathering images and information. But it made little sense and I didn't try to make sense of it, probably because I sensed it was taboo.

An elderly lady joined Mum and I for afternoon tea one Sunday. This woman was so pious and set in her old-fashioned prudish ways that she might as well have been a nun. On the TV – switched on to keep my boredom at bay – appeared classic paintings of bare-breasted women. Our visitor was appalled. Ignoring the fact that the featured pictures had been created a century or two before, she exclaimed "That sort of thing should never be shown on television at this time of the day!" But even I, who hadn't so much as clapped eyes on a real naked breast since presumably sucking on my mother's as a baby, failed to see how these ancient innocuous images could be a corrupting influence.

On another Sunday afternoon, I was playing soccer with a superball against Mark in our living-room, with Mum and another visitor just metres away. Mark got a goal and, in my annoyance, I blurted the C-word. He instantly scolded me, in such a way you'd have thought I'd said the most disgraceful thing of all time. "You must never EVER use that word" he warned. And I didn't – at least not for another decade or so. I'd no idea where I'd picked up that expletive, nor what it meant. I just assumed, if Mark's reaction was anything to go by, it was a heinous crime to utter it.

I reckon it was that Summer when I got my first glimpse of what a female looked like 'down below'. A very young cousin wandered naked in the French flat on a shared family holiday and, although I knew I shouldn't be staring at her most intimate part, I was transfixed. Maybe my sixth sense told me to make the most of it as it'd be far too many years before I'd see a girl 'in the flesh' again. Funnily enough, around then I recall hearing that children born to cousins would turn out 'dotty', a polite word for nuts.

A few days later, that girl's mother pitched up on the beach in a bikini and suddenly I got a stirring in my own undercarriage. Never mind the embarrassing consideration that this was my aunt – my Dad's sister, for Gawd's sake - my concern was that something was threatening to show in my all-too-tiny swimming trunks, and I ought to hide it. So I rolled on to my front where, to my horror, the soft movement of the sand beneath my body only made matters worse. I must have remained face down on that beach that day for quite some time until things calmed down, which meant my back was red raw from the sun. Not a dream introduction to desire.

Far too often from then on, one part of my body demanded attention, and dealing with whenever possible. I'd never have dared share this awkward situation with a soul. I just decided that this was to be my problem, my secret. There was nothing or no-one to advise me on the best – or most satisfactory - way of resolving such scenarios...except Mother Nature. But then 'came' the next problem of what to do with the end product. One night, in a state of desperation, I used a handkerchief and subsequently scrunched the damp result into a ball which I hid in my bedside drawer as quietly as I could so Mark wouldn't wake and cause a scene he'd doubtless never let me live down. But worse was to happen. The next day, Mum beckoned me into the bedroom, showed me the manky hanky and demanded "What is this?" I lied and said it was glue (the only vaguely similar substance I could think of). She knew perfectly well what it was, and warned me never to do it again. I was shocked to the core, not just by Mum's discovery but the fact that she was prepared to embarrass me with it. I just hoped that when she said 'never again' she was only referring to my use of a handkerchief. She would have known more than anyone what a super-sensitive boy I'd become, and that nothing could be more deeply intimate than my first brushes with sex. If that episode had any effect it was to send me further inside my already very withdrawn self, and determine to not let anyone else ever be privy to my physical feelings.

To my immense surprise, one of the pupils at Parkstone Prep, Vincent Lakehurst, invited me to stay with him and his family at their house near Middlesborough. This was extraordinary for me because a) it suggested I was liked by someone, which I'd never imagined possible before, and b) it entailed spending nights at the home of people I wasn't related to. Once there, I remember being struck by the warmth of this boy's parents towards him – although I dare say they might have been keen to give a good impression to a son of the Headmaster of his school. However, if they were, it all threatened to fall apart on my first night. Vincent's sister Karen, who must have been about 12, somehow let it be known that she not only fancied me but wanted to kiss me. Rather than be flattered, I was horrified. Not because she was in any way unpleasant; rather, she was cute and polite. I can only assume I regarded her openness as shocking, especially as I considered anything to do with attraction/sexuality (call it what you will) should be kept private and not shared with anyone. Whatever my reaction was it resulted in this poor girl being reprimanded by her parents. She must have thought me very weird...and she wouldn't have been far off the mark.

Then Dad's school started taking girls. Only a handful at first, but two took my fancy and one of them – named Georgia - all but took my breath away. The problem was I didn't have a clue what to do about this unprecedented ardour. And, even if I had, the knowledge would have been pointless given my total lack of self-confidence.

Maybe the incident involving Karen Lakehurst had an influence because I disclosed my fondness for Georgia to another boy at school, called Mike Trailer. This ended up with the pair of us approaching Georgia in a passageway and persuading her to say which one of us she'd rather kiss. Very childish but, hey, we were children. Anyway, she chose Trailer. I was crestfallen at that, and jealous of him, but at the same time I wasn't in the least surprised. To me that girl was gorgeous, that boy was cool and handsome, and I was unappealing in the extreme.

Naturally, the girls had their own separate accommodation in the school. And, as there never were more than six of them in my day, they remained in the same place throughout. We boys, on the other hand, moved dormitories as we gained seniority. In the dormitory I moved into at about the age of 11, a couple of the other boys would have after-lights-out discussions about the female sex... and, in the most basic sense, sex with females. I had nothing to contribute, but listened intently even if a lot of it made little sense to me.

Somehow a pornographic magazine made its way into the dormitory, and when I glimpsed pictures under torchlight I was mesmerised. I even managed to secrete myself a small photo of a nude woman sitting on a garden swing. I was either given it or stole it, but I certainly treasured it. And kept it well hidden, aware it was forbidden.

Once, in the cottage, I caught my parents in bed together. This was unusual because they had two separate single beds with quite a gap in between. It was also shocking because I didn't think Mum and Dad liked each other, let alone loved each other...which I assumed was a requirement for intimacy.

Around that time – perhaps as a direct result – they revealed that Mum was pregnant. I was thrilled. Finally, I'd have someone to play with, maybe boss around, and hopefully deflect Dad's hostility away from me.

Not long before, on a trip to a local farm, I got to bottle-feed a newborn goat and felt remarkably privileged that this vulnerable little animal trusted me, so the thought that I might soon be doing that with a baby sibling was thrilling.

Catholic acquaintances joked that there'd finally be a John to follow Matthew, Mark and Luke. But, if my Dad had wanted a girl when I'd come along, he'd have been even keener now to have a Jane rather than a John.

However, within too short a time, came another revelation: Mum had lost the baby. From a personal point of view, it felt like a candle of hope had been snuffed out. I was devastated. So much so that I was allowed to miss lessons that day.

I wonder how upset Mum was about her miscarriage. She had an awful lot to cope with as it was, with three sons and countless schoolchildren in her charge. And had she produced a fourth boy, Dad might have been even less accepting of him and maybe taken his disappointment out on Mum.

In an attempt to cheer my Calcutta-born mother, I made her a card on which I sketched the face of an Indian lady with a red dot on her forehead. Knowing from past chats with Mum that the red dot indicated the Indian lady was married, I drew an arrow from this dot and wrote above that 'Divorce Spot' in an early shot at irony. My joke wasn't just lost on her, she assumed I was suggesting she would or should split from Dad, and the pair of them enlisted Father Phillip to assess and reassure me. Somehow at about that stage in life I learned what adoption was and, as I felt neither wanted nor understood in this family, I wondered if I myself had been adopted.

Once a week at this prep school there was a letter-writing class, presumably to ensure all the boarders satisfied their parents by hopefully telling them what a good education they were getting and how happy they were. As I was living there with my Mum and Dad, I wrote my letters to grandparents, uncles and aunts, which was a blessing in the respect that I wouldn't have wanted to begin my letters with the traditional word 'Dear' when addressing my father.

6.

LOVE ME LIKE MY DOG

Christmases and birthdays were a source of some warmth and excitement in our household, at least as much as Dad would allow them to be. Those occasions in my childhood all mildly resembled the legendary 1914 festive truce in the trenches of World War One when soldiers from opposing sides briefly halted hostilities to shake hands, mingle, play football, and even exchange cigarettes and souvenirs. In our case, Dad would be nicer than usual…for a while at least…but sadly it never lasted long before he was back to his difficult old self.

I usually made the most effort to get gifts for the rest of the family that I knew they'd want, because I wanted to be noticed let alone appreciated, even just for a matter of moments. Christianity decreed that it should be about the giving rather than the receiving, but I loved the receiving more. In fact, I literally couldn't wait to open presents. For a brief period as kids, Mark and I got into the habit of 'snooping'. This entailed finding where our parents hid our gifts and making small slits in the wrapping-paper to discover in advance what we'd be getting. Either I made a bad job of this before one birthday or Mark betrayed my confidence, because when I entered the parental bedroom that morning there were no gifts laid out and Mum simply said "Why don't you fetch them because you already know where they are?" I pretended I didn't know what she was talking about but she and Dad clearly knew I knew. It spoilt that birthday for me. I was embarrassed and hurt to the extent that this would become an enduring sad memory of my life.

My birthday was the only day on which I was guaranteed a degree of attention. Or so I thought. On my 11th, I think it was, that day started like any other in the school holidays. Everyone in my family got up, washed, dressed, and breakfasted as normal. There were no wishes for me, no indication that this was in any sense a special occasion. That was until eventually my parents asked me to get in the car because they were going to drive me somewhere. They took me the few miles to the nearest town where we stopped outside a house in a street I'd never been to before, and they led me to the door of that house refusing my pleas to explain what was going on. It's an illustration of how I felt at that point in my life that I went from believing my family had forgotten my birthday to suspecting that my parents were about to give me away. That is what I really thought as I was introduced to a nice but unfamiliar couple and shown to the back of their home.

Then their kitchen door was opened to reveal, lying in an endearing mess on terracotta tiles, a litter of puppies. It was a heavenly sight for me, whether or not compared to the scenario I'd just been envisaging.

My parents must have remembered the joy I'd got from an aunt's Dachshund and how, due to its body shape, that made turns like an articulated lorry. No sausage dogs here but I got down on my knees to hold and cuddle these funny, furry, wriggly, adorable little creatures and heard a rare positive instruction from my Dad: "Choose one of them." I turned and looked up disbelieving at him stood in the doorway. "Can I really have one?" I asked, and he and Mum nodded, confirming the best gift of my youth.

I would happily have taken them all. But I noticed one was lying on its own, separate from and largely ignored by the rest of its family. I knew how that little pup must have felt, and I knew it was the one for me.

'It' was a she, by the way, though because of other meanings I still cannot bring myself to attribute the correct term 'bitch' to that bundle of innocent goodness.

If getting me a puppy was my parents' attempt to provide a substitute younger sibling for me in the wake of Mum's miscarriage, it worked. And, if it was intended to provide me with the attention and love I craved, then it was aptly a masterstroke.

Dad named her Lulu, claiming he simply liked the name – though one day he'd admit to me that that was the name of a woman he then had his beady eye on. He seemed happy for me to have a dog, but he didn't seem happy to have her around him. Rather, he hardly let her near him, shooing her off chairs and beds and from his general vicinity as if he considered her diseased. And when she slept a lot, as puppies are prone to, Dad said "What a great life Lulu has lying around all day. If I'm ever reincarnated, I'm coming back as a dog!" I realised he wasn't being entirely serious, but I felt compelled to speak up for Lulu and her fellow canines. "But dogs don't live very long, they can't talk, they can't eat what they want when they want, they're dependent on humans to do most things like opening doors or windows…to name but a few things. You really want your life to be like that? I hardly think a dog's existence is an improvement on your average human one. If it's lying down a lot you begrudge them, you could do that too. Personally I think, because dogs bring so much joy, they deserve lots of rest and sleep, and much more besides, and we should respect and appreciate them in the short time they're with us."

Not someone who took kindly to being challenged, particularly by me, Dad's response was simply "What do you know, horrid child?"

Tenderness from Dad to this dog was similar to how he was with me; just the occasional quick pat if Lulu was lucky. At least I now knew of one other living being who went through what I did. Except in Lulu's case Dad's behaviour was even less understandable. Like all pups, she hadn't a bad bone in her body (except when she sometimes ate those she found outside) and was impossible to dislike. To my mind, she was already a finer creature than any person I knew, certainly including my family and me. Mum made the excuse that Dad had had a fear of dogs since being trapped in a classroom by one at a previous school. But not only was that many years before, it was a great big Alsatian, and Lulu was just a little Pomeranian.

I swiftly learnt that actually Lulu was way more than 'just a little' anything. Her impact on me was immeasurable. Having felt utterly unwanted and disliked up til that point in my life, it felt amazing to have this adorable animal resting her head on me, licking my face, excited whenever she saw me, and never wanting to leave my side. Unlike almost all humans I'd encountered by then, she didn't judge or criticise me and was always consistent. She didn't care what I did, said, even wore. She'd just be with me whenever she could, and when she looked at me it was always with love and devotion.

Lulu particularly enjoyed me rubbing her chest and tummy as she lay on her back, with her tail thumping the floor in delight. Each time she'd raise her paws in a futile effort to defend herself, which was endearing but made me realise how powerless little creatures like this would be were they to ever encounter hostility.

Lulu was the first true friend I had, the only true friend in my childhood, one of the truest friends of my whole life. That's what dogs are if you treat them right. I adored Lulu, the love she gave me, all the times we spent together – even playing with balls which she was remarkably clever at.

Okay, conversations with a dog were always going to be one-sided for the most part, but at least I could say what I liked to Lulu without fear of negative responses. She unquestionably brought light and love to my life – most importantly, unconditional love. Yet I can't say she changed my situation, nor the attitude of others towards me. Being worshipped by a dog wasn't suddenly going to make me more appealing to other humans. I soon realised dogs latched on to anybody who loved, fed, watered and walked them, but I lapped up Lulu's canine affection in the absence of it from anyone else.

I also noticed that Lulu endeared herself to everyone despite never speaking a single word and with only the one serious facial expression, as well as spending a lot of time lying around doing nothing. I could not fathom how to make myself endearing, though as a human I had infinitely more capabilities. Lulu needed the capabilities I had – to feed, water, walk her, and so on – just as she would have depended on them from whoever owned her. So it was understandable she looked up to me. After all, I looked up to my brother Mark because of the capabilities he had that I lacked.

I considered Lulu an intelligent creature, yet when I talked to her, it was usually either the classic canine instructions like 'sit', 'down' and 'here', or the classic canine compliment 'good girl'. Like the vast majority of dogs, mine remained as pure of intention as the day she was born, so she couldn't really be anything but a good girl. I imagined her thinking 'I'm not stupid, so you don't have to keep telling me I'm a good girl because I know am!'

Nothing is ever really a dog's fault. But, on one unforgiveable occasion when I was frustrated and angry, I punished Lulu for a minor misdemeanour by shouting, smacking her bottom and tossing her into a bathroom. As I slammed the door shut behind her, I caught the little finger of my left hand in the hinges and was writhing in agony for hours afterwards. It was as if something or someone had spoken for the little creature without a voice, and dealt me the karma I deserved. I remember saying to myself "You have the wherewithal to harm animals like Lulu in this life, but if you do and there's a next life your roles might be reversed and revenge will be theirs." I was infinitely more respectful of her from then on. Few moments would ever make me feel as guilty as I did over that isolated incident. There was never any excuse for unkindness towards living creatures. Maybe I was now the 'horrid child' Dad referred to me as.

I felt neither liked nor likeable. I couldn't bear myself. If I'd been asked why that was, however, I suspect the explanation I'd have given would have been "Well, my Dad can't stand me, my brothers don't want anything to do with me, I've not got any proper friends as such, and I haven't a clue why that is."

Whenever I watched a film that had an admirable leading man, I would afterwards adopt aspects of that character in my mind - his voice, swagger or whatever, …probably an inner desire to be likeable, admirable, everything I wasn't. And, of course, within a short period of time any trait I'd adopted to convince myself I was remotely heroic wore off, and I was back to being my sad self again.

Plenty of boys aspire to be like their fathers. I didn't. In fact, I vowed to never be like mine. I must have made the mistake of telling Matthew, because for the rest of our shared time on Earth he'd use as a hurtful weapon the phrase "You're just like Dad", which he knew was the last thing I wanted to hear.

Of course I couldn't help but share some our father's physical characteristics. I was rapidly getting tall like him. Six foot at the age of 12, in fact. Plenty of people said they envied me that, but I hated it. I didn't want to stand out, literally or otherwise. Dad's constant picking on me, particularly in front of others, left me wanting to just blend in with the crowd, stay under the radar, not be noticed in any way - at least not unless I could do something to make myself impressive.

If there was one person on the planet I wished I was more than any other it was my brother Mark. He had what I most coveted at that point: paternal admiration and adoration. The confidence that gave him in turn led him to be admired and adored not just among our family, but by everyone who encountered him. It enabled him to tell jokes and stories, even do impressions, and always achieve the desired response: laughter, appreciation, respect, reverence, almost deification… In my desire to be like him, I'd occasionally try his jokes, stories and impressions out, yet they all went down like lead balloons. I had more tumbleweed moments than the entire genre of spaghetti westerns.

Ironically, there were times my disappointed Dad would turn to me and ask "Horrid child, why can't you be more like Mark?" If only he knew how hard I was trying to be.

I was now discovering there was a lot for me to learn from animals too. There was I often wanting gifts, clothes, records, sports equipment etc, when really I already had enough, and there was Lulu who was perfectly content with just a toy or two as her only possessions.

I found it especially appealing when animals behaved like humans. I noticed with Lulu that they needed to be given confidence too - mainly confidence in their keeper/provider, and to know the parameters required of them to abide by. Viewing their lives with my human perspective, I thought about how frustrating it must be for dogs having to rely on humans to do crucial things for them. And though none would give it a thought obviously, each would live while major events would be happening in the World yet be totally oblivious of them.

Being super-sensitive and having to entertain myself much of the time, I'd think unusual thoughts. I remember becoming convinced that my dog had been Queen Victoria in a previous life. There was nothing in Lulu's appearance or behaviour to indicate that, so I had no idea why....at least not until I noticed a painting on a wall at a historic house showing that very monarch with Pomeranians at her feet. Strange, but true. But no, I didn't treat Lulu any differently after that.

Dad had remarked upon canine reincarnation, but as a young human I didn't recall having had any past existences myself, though I had some moments of déjà vu. I was however baffled that I was part of a family that I didn't feel wanted me to be, and maybe my overactive imagination was a means of escaping the pain of the rejection I felt. But, as Dad had put it, 'What did I know?'

7.

WHEN I DISSED THE TEACHER

When pupils at Parkstone Prep reached their final two years there – at the ages of 12 and 13 – they became eligible for casting in school productions. Here was my chance, you might have thought, to get attention. And, as I was cast as a major biblical figure, a chance also to be notable. Unfortunately for me, it was the Virgin Mary I'd be portraying in a nativity-themed play, and I was devastated when I realised that would entail wearing women's clothing. If my parents really had wanted me to be a daughter, maybe this was a step towards fulfilling that wish. But I'll never forget the feeling of utter humiliation standing in just my underpants as Mum put a bra on me as the starting-point of my costume. Had I been more worldly-wise, I might have questioned how she could be sure Mary wasn't flat-chested, but even if that were the case I suppose this was a way of showing the character was female among the all-male cast. My squirming must have meant Mum and Dad then had good indication that their youngest son was unlikely to become a crossdresser one day. The bra-fitting alone was enough to make me want to run away and hide. But I knew there was no escape, nowhere for me to run to, so instead I just willed and willed the production to not take place. And then, suddenly to my complete amazement, it was indeed called off. We were told that an oil and/or petrol strike was going to severely reduce attendance, so that was it: no show!

Rarely in my life would I feel such relief. Were my wishes, if not prayers, answered? It was a nice thought, but if so what about the desires of the other participants and planned audience members who presumably can't all have wanted it cancelled? I kept any thoughts I had of it maybe being a miracle to myself. Had I shared them with my family, I fully expected my father and brothers to say 'You getting personal help from God...why would he help you? In your dreams!'

Had that play gone ahead, I'm sure I would have backed out of it in some way or other – probably by feigning illness, my usual chosen excuse. I'd never have had the courage to perform in front of an audience in the substantial role I'd been allotted, especially as it was female and I'd effectively be in drag. I was so incredibly self-conscious that, despite craving attention in a personal way, I couldn't bear the thought of being the centre of attention in a public way.

In morning assemblies at Parkstone Prep, Dad would raise the issues of the day. These occasionally included crimes committed within the school (though never anything really serious) that he'd ask the guilty boys to own up to...usually with threats that all pupils would suffer if the culprit(s) didn't come forward. I was way too fearful, ironically of Dad, to have ever done anything bad. Yet I was also way too anxious, because of Dad, to bear the awful atmosphere in that large room as everyone stood silently waiting in vain for guilty parties to make themselves known. For a while, irrespective of my total innocence, I was so tormented by these tense scenarios that I'd blush to such a degree that my scarlet face would glow in the crowd. Following one such occasion, Dad took me to one side and asked if I was the person who'd stolen the missing geometry set or whatever it was. Fortunately he believed my pleas, which was an indication that he did at least know this son of his well enough in that regard.

Looking back, it does seem strange that Dad was far better at dealing with the 100 or so other boys in his school than his own three at home, and that he was so much more relaxed in term-time than during holidays. To me, he was like a chef whose skill was in catering for the masses but wouldn't have the first idea how to host his own dinner party.

Once when addressing his pupils, Dad relayed the notion that bullies tended to be cowards, yet ironically I knew him to be both. Only very rarely did I consider him even close to heroic. One was a moment when, taking us his family out to an evening meal in a pub, we spotted a man lying face down on a grass verge looking distinctly dead. Knowing his fear of so many things, I expected Dad to keep driving. But, to my surprise, he stopped the car and rather than let Mum – who was after all a trained nurse – attend to the apparent casualty before we knew the score, Dad made the approach himself, only to find the man fast asleep after drinking too much.

Otherwise I'd quite proudly observe Dad making smart, witty speeches in front of appreciative audiences from assemblies to annual events like Speech Day, and being charming to the point of reverential when dealing with parents, staff, pupils, shopkeepers, whoever. Just not with his youngest son. But there it was. And there was I always struggling because of his inconsistencies, and truly terrified of holiday-time Dad.

I was aware that, for most families, meals at home were bonding sessions, with everyone joining in and pooling conversation, concerns, celebrations, etcetera. Our family meals were not like that. During term times we all ate in the school refectory, but scattered in different areas of it. During half-terms or a week or so before or after each term, our meals were served in the staff dining-room with whichever teachers or matrons were around. During the rest of the holidays we'd eat together either in the cottage or wherever else we happened to be. I dreaded meals attended by my Dad, especially in the staff dining-room when we had company. Dad didn't take pride in presenting me or giving me a platform of any kind. Any conversational contributions I made he usually ridiculed and criticised. I remember once sheepishly requesting pocket-money to buy a record (a 45" vinyl single) which was in the charts at the time. I felt like Oliver Twist asking for more gruel and getting a similar reaction. In front of fellow staff, Dad demanded to know what record it was and, when I told him, he replied: "Never heard of it...ghastly pop...bloody noise...horrid child...why don't you listen to some decent music?"

Most of the music I played Dad would dismiss as 'noise'. It was as if his taste was all that mattered.

He delighted in making me his laughing stock, the butt of his jokes and mockery. Not the nourishment and encouragement children more than anyone need. With Dad setting that example in his dictatorial fashion, my brothers believed it was right for them to do the same. Thus I took on the role of family fool. I didn't like it, and I had no idea how to change it, though in a perverse way it was a means of gaining attention. Ultimately it sent me deeper inside my shell. I didn't even dare answer a telephone until I was 12 and a half.

Another thing Dad would do when we as a family were in company, particularly at mealtimes, was flirt with other women whether they be waitresses, matrons, guests, whoever. Mum would silently put up with it and sometimes attempt to laugh along with it, as if she felt obliged. She must have felt so belittled, and it happened countless times. But Dad's flirting was pathetic and, as far as I could see, got him nowhere. Perhaps the women concerned were embarrassed it was happening in his wife's presence.

My parents were reasonably sociable. But if ever they held parties, or played host to the Over-60s Club Christmas dinner at the school, I remained upstairs and refused to attend. I felt so bad about myself that I didn't think anyone would want to meet me, let alone talk to me. I was sure if I were to get into conversation with someone, I'd only say something dumb. And if it wasn't me making an ass of myself, my Dad was sure to make me look an ass in front of other people. So why put myself through it?

To add to my laughing and blushing at tense moments, I was busy blurting too. Saying things, however inappropriate, to break that tension...yet in doing so often making it worse. My flaw was never as bad as what I've come to know as Tourette's Syndrome, but I couldn't keep a lid on it. And due to my hatred of being focussed on, I'd never forgive myself these blurts.

When it came to academic performance, I was a pupil of extremes. In English and Art, I usually did very well. But then the teachers of those subjects, who just happened to be a married couple, were exceptional. Their respective enthusiasm rubbed off on me, and they gave me what I lacked within my family: encouragement and, where appropriate, praise. In English, my essays and stories were marked sufficiently high for me to have them read out loud. Similarly in Art, my paintings and drawings qualified for being displayed in the school corridor, and a few even got declared the week's best. To think I was actually considered good at something was a relief me. A glimmer of confidence – something I'd previously known little of – began to emerge.

Art classes were especially inspired. The teacher, Wendy Jones, would tell us about interviews her sister – a journalist on the New Musical Express – was doing with the hot pop stars of the day. I couldn't begin to imagine the thrill of meeting, let alone talking to, idols of that stature. So fascinated was I that I took to drawing pictures of famous people, copying from press photos mainly. These were not so much my personal celebrity heroes but more my father's favourites. I probably thought that, as he admired them, he'd appreciate images of them, and possibly appreciate me more for creating them. Any tactic I could come up with, I guess.

Interestingly for someone who, typical of his generation of male Brits, sometimes spoke out against foreigners (the fact that he was himself half-French evidently didn't count) and people of different skin colours, Dad was most in admiration of two black sportsmen: the West Indian cricketer Garry Sobers and the American boxer Muhammad Ali. Dad spoke of Ali in particular with the kind of reverence he usually only reserved for God. So I drew and painted numerous pictures of Ali, and watched and read everything I could on him. And when in due course Dad directed his veneration towards others in the public eye, I'd do their portraits too.

One History class, the teacher Corporal Hank Parker – a former member of the American military - immediately got everyone's attention by revealing he'd played golf the day before behind four members of the then dominant Leeds United team. He held up a handful of tees he said these golfing footballers had left, offering to trade them for sweets. It was a measure of how much it meant to me to have something once owned by a sports stars that I was prepared to give up a packet of Love Hearts.

My interest in celebrities grew. I was given a book in which to note down the birthdays of family and friends, and instead I inserted those of famous people. Strange perhaps seeing as I didn't know any of them nor looked to have any prospect of ever doing so.

As a family, we saw the occasional star on stage in shows we attended. Three times Mum took me and Mark on coach trips to London, and on each one she saw a different actor we recognised. The most memorable was when she discreetly pointed out comedian Kenneth Williams about 50 metres from where we then were on the Tottenham Court Road, as if spotting a rare prized species on safari. He looked like he would not have appreciated being approached by autograph-hunting well-wishers, so reluctantly we left him well alone. In later life I'd realise seeing a well-known person on each visit to the capital was quite some hit rate, but at the time it made me think London was full of them, which was an exciting thought.

On a school trip to hear Cy Grant sing locally, and at a garden fete during a Summer break in Kent opened by the BBCTV newsreader Robert Dougall, I got their signatures. I was dazzled at seeing these people 'off the telly' for real and to have their signatures. Had I met any of the pop stars whose music I loved and who Mrs.Jones' sister interviewed, I'd probably have hyperventilated with excitement.

The Jones' were among a group of inspiring teachers Dad recruited for Parkstone Prep – which may have been luck on his part, but I prefer to consider it good judgment. Another was Tarquin Lyon, a unique English eccentric with a penchant for waistcoats, old sports cars, model railways, and occasionally even a monocle which made him resemble the popular puppet of the day, Lord Charles. Lyon taught Latin, though I for one found him more riveting than his subject. If he couldn't get me interested in Latin no-one could...and he couldn't. As some of us were fond of reciting:

> *Latin is a language*
> *As dead as dead can be*
> *It killed the ancient Romans*
> *And now it's killing me*

Latin was like God – it needed to exist for me to believe in it. As for Mathematics...tests asked for measurements of the angle of a shadow off a lamp-post or calculations of the number of sweets left in a jar if X number of kids had taken two each, for example. I didn't see any point and lost interest.

In Maths and the Sciences, I was a non-starter. Oddly enough, I'd won a prize for Arithmetic as a five-year old at nursery school, but didn't pass a Maths exam from then on. I never liked the Maths and Science teachers I had. That might have been because I didn't like their subjects, but maybe I didn't like the subjects because I didn't like the teachers. Or perhaps they just weren't good teachers.

One such teacher was an odd little man called Spencer Trout. After he supervised or refereed sporting activities, he'd join the boys in the shower...wearing just a beige jockstrap, at which many of us stared in disbelief. It didn't seem right having one of the staff virtually naked and showering beside boys who were totally naked. He was married with children and I'm not saying he had ill intentions – that wouldn't have crossed my innocent mind then – but it looked and felt strange. I was even more unsure of him when, in a Biology lesson, he asked us pupils to put our hands up if we'd yet experienced an erection. There was no way I was going to put mine up (hand, you understand) and make this intensely personal admission in front of the entire class, and I was stunned at how many others were prepared to. I got the impression that the 'yes' lads were keen to suggest they were 'grown-up' in at least that respect. That didn't interest me; weirdly the more childish I felt, the more secure I felt. Had I been truthful about my own experience of erections then…they were an uncomfortably frequent occurrence. But, hey, I had nobody else to play with! Thank goodness there were locks on the toilet doors.

Masturbation for me – and I presumed others, though I'd never have asked them - would ideally involve visualising or viewing images of somebody I found attractive. I rarely encountered real females, and never intimately thus far in my life, so these were nearly all famous ones I'd see on television or in newspapers and magazines. Although it didn't occur to me then, these actresses, presenters, reporters, experts and pop stars had often got where they were because they had good looks as well as, and in some cases irrespective of, talent. I remember wondering if whoever I fantasised about during masturbation could somehow sense what I was up to, possibly feel a little tingle. Had that been the case, certain celebrity ladies would have felt tingly all day and night thanks to boarding schoolboys alone. I wouldn't envisage them performing any form of sexual act as I'd no idea what the real thing was like. In fact, even if I wanted to undress them in my head, I wasn't entirely sure what I'd see if I did. Their pretty faces and/or feminine figures were sufficient for me. If I'd known it'd be another decade before I would get intimate with an actual woman, that would have been a deeply depressing thought.

This silly little rhyme did the rounds at the time:

> *It's a man's occupation*
> *To stick his cockulation*
> *Up a woman's ventilation*
> *To increase the population*
> *Of the World*

I committed that to memory convinced its naughtiness made it cool, but I didn't properly understand it. Similarly sexy lyrics in pop hits I heard tended to go right over my head, and there was always a risk I would sing them aloud at school.

My confusion was epitomised when in 1972 I asked my mother if the Cat Stevens' hit I Can't Keep It In was "a rude song". She wanted to know what made me ask that, and I said "because it's a man saying he can't keep it in…" She sensibly said "No" and changed the subject.

By the time I reached puberty, the school changing-room became a very awkward place indeed. Some of my contemporaries started cupping their private parts in one or both hands as they dashed in and out of the showers or communal bath, so I did the same. It was as if we felt like freaks and were ashamed of the hair suddenly sprouting above our willies, as we called them. This bizarre behaviour naturally attracted the attention of the other boys, and the resulting banter caused me such embarrassment that I dreaded bathing and changing after games. One unfortunate lad called Reynolds, who was a little challenged in the mental department, was also massively endowed in the groin department, so predictably he was subjected to quite brutal teasing. That would have taken him some getting over.

The second Maths and Sciences teacher I had difficulties with was one Jim Blackfoot. A sturdy build with a tough character to match, he was the sort I could imagine having been a bully himself as a schoolboy. In my penultimate year at Parkstone Prep, he took it upon himself to give us senior boys secret sex classes. I'd like to think his only motivation was the fact that it wasn't part of the school curriculum but he believed it should be. I was amazed at some of the clever questions posed by my classmates. But I listened and observed in silence, not knowing what to say or think. What I did think though was that these illicit lessons were a betrayal of my Dad and that I was playing a part – albeit a silent one – in that. I'd been taught that if someone was up to no good, especially an adult, you report it. And, as I was ever in pursuit of Brownie Points from my father, I betrayed Blackfoot to him. Some there then would have called that 'peaching' – their term for telling tales – and labelled me a 'peach'. An afternoon or two later, by the sports fields during Games, Blackfoot grabbed me by the elbow, wagged an index finger in my face and said exactly what he thought of what I'd done. It was a disturbing encounter and I was suitably disturbed, partly at the realisation that Dad might have named me as the source.

Blackfoot also taught Carpentry, and I was afraid to attend his next lesson. If he told my classmates what had gone on, he didn't do so in my presence, but I was so on edge throughout that I had a blurty moment. Another boy wound me up about something, and in retaliation I picked up a piece of wood and poked a finger back and forth through the round hole I'd drilled in it. Blackfoot, doubtless seizing his chance for revenge, wasted no time in reporting me. I was duly summoned to the Headmaster's office where Dad asked me to explain what I'd meant in making that gesture. I didn't answer because I didn't want to try to put it into words, and I was scared Dad would punish me as he always aimed to treat his sons the same as any other boys in the school. Yet he and I both knew what I'd done referred to a sexual act I could only have learnt about in Blackfoot's secret classes. I escaped with a caution, but I suspect Blackfoot paid a higher price because I don't recall him returning the following term.

Blackfoot's departure was a relief for me. But that dark episode, and the likelihood that he let on about my betrayal to others in my class to explain what became of the sex lessons, made me want to quit Parkstone Prep. Odd that here was I hoping to leave a boarding-school which was my home – partly to avoid its headmaster, my father - in order to be sent away to another.

My parents seriously considered my request, taking me to look around St.Justin's, official prep school to my next educational destination Stourback Abbey. But I knew from past sporting fixtures against them that they had no doors (never mind locks) on the toilet cubicles, which alone crossed them off my list. To me at the time that was barbaric and unacceptable, and to a wiser me years later it was downright dodgy. That was only exceeded by another alternative, Longford Priory, where all the boys were forced to run and/or swim naked every morning. The 1970s was a period of naivety and advantage-taking, and this was able to happen. Two decades on, allegations of historic abuse were brought against staff at both schools by former pupils and I wasn't in the least surprised.

It was hard to know then how I'd have fared elsewhere as a boarder, without the safety net of my parents to fall back on. I'd find out soon enough when moving on to public school. In the meantime, I did stay at Parkstone Prep where everything and everybody was familiar. It has to be said that, without Messrs Trout and Blackfoot – and thankfully now we were without them – the teaching staff were of great quality and character. Dad was given credit for that. He also earned praise for allowing his office to double as a living-room in which all the pupils could play.

Dad enjoyed a warm respectful relationship with his pupils, showing great interest in how they were getting on, giving them exactly the right amount of encouragement, and discussing most with fondness and admiration during the school holidays. I doubt anyone was more aware of that than me, to whom he was the opposite at home.

More baffling still was the way in which Dad insisted I was an eternally obedient boy, with demands like 'be good', 'don't get into trouble', etcetera, yet openly praised the kids who were a handful, who played up. One Parkstone Prep pupil ran away, causing a major manhunt involving the local police. Had that been me, I can only imagine being yelled at or smacked senseless for a long time after. Yet within weeks at the annual prize-giving, Dad awarded that wayward lad his personal trophy, The Headmaster's Character Cup, and later made him Head Boy. It left me as confused a kid as there could ever be. So a big challenge was trying to understand my father's thinking, let alone why he was so disinterested in me and what I could do to change that.

A chance cropped up at the end of my last Summer term at Parkstone Prep to make an impression on Dad at the one sport that always had his attention: cricket. It appeared a fateful opportunity too because it was an away match against our biggest rivals Longford Priory.

I'd had a fruitless afternoon as an opening bowler, but now as the No.11 batsman going in with just six balls to survive and four runs required for victory, I had a shot at glory let alone redemption. Just before I entered the fray, Dad instructed me to play as safe as possible for the first couple of balls, and ideally get our more recognised batsman Piers Finch down the striker's end. But I gave no thought at all to the concept of getting my eye in and patiently waiting for loose balls to lash out at. I decided I'd be a hero from the outset and smash the debut delivery way beyond the boundary for a massive winning six. The bowler had barely released his leather missile when my head was already tilted skyward in anticipation of the ball's flight...and my stumps were duly splattered. I was dismissed - for a Golden Duck - Parkstone Prep were defeated, and Dad was devastated. Rather than allow me to join my teammates in the minibus back to school, Dad made me get in his car where I got a stinging clip round the ear and an apoplectic "I told you what to do. Why didn't you darn well listen? What use are you to anybody? Worthless child! Horrid child!"

That hot-headed recklessness on the cricket pitch said a lot about me as a person. What I'd done was like a sporting form of the blurting I did through sheer nerves. Of course the result meant my school and I were losers. And henceforward this was the reference for a fools-rush-in side to me that I'd duly call Front Foot Luke.

Privately I didn't think I was the only one to blame. I felt I was overdue a generous helping of good fortune from God, the allegedly fair figurehead I was having to devote so much of my life to. Only a fortnight before I'd been favourite to win the Throwing The Cricket Ball contest, yet hadn't even made the Top 3 due to some uncharacteristically wayward efforts. I was becoming convinced that even the Almighty didn't consider me deserving of success. So maybe Dad and Mark were rewarded for their devotion to him.

If it wasn't for the fact that I did well in Art and English, received positive responses from the teachers of those subjects, and had the unconditional love of a dog, I would have felt a complete personal disaster area. I was constantly frustrated by a lack of affection, attention and interest, and almost everything about Dad made me an anxious wreck. On two separate occasions, my blurting so annoyed other boys that I was given a black eye. Because of the way Dad always talked positively of the other boys and negatively about me, I'd gotten to thinking that I was inferior to them, and always the one in the wrong in any disagreement. Besides, the fact that these two lads didn't think twice about hitting the Head's youngest son showed the extent to which I must have caused annoyance.

In my last year at Parkstone Prep, Ron Dutton, a fellow leaver of burly build and cold character, put me in a headlock for no apparent reason. I barely knew him and had done nothing to provoke him, and he had no axe to grind with my parents either. It was as if he just flipped. We were in an empty classroom situated in an outbuilding where there was no-one around to rescue me. Not only was I alarmed at the absence of motivation, the venom with which he held me in his powerful grip was shocking. I was sure that, if I tried to wrestle my way out from under his strong arm, he'd break my neck. And the more I expressed my frustration, the more he seemed determined to make me suffer. I decided my only chance of resolving the situation was to say and do nothing, in the hope that would eventually bore him into submission. It did work, but only after what seemed an eternity.

Rather than toughen me up, these demonstrations of physical aggression just made me all the more insecure. I hoped I'd leave them behind on moving to my next school, where I assumed older boys would mean more mature boys. Nobody was warning otherwise. Dad did summon us leavers into his study during our last days and warned us about, of all things, the possibility we might experience wet dreams and develop crushes on older boys. That was supposed to be part of a broader talk about the birds and the bees, but he bottled the rest – maybe because I was among his audience and we both knew he was never one to discuss such matters.

From what I could tell, most pupils emerging from Parkstone Prep under Dad's leadership would rightly claim to be content, confident, balanced individuals. But there I was at 13 years old and over 6 feet high, still totally a child who felt so small, unloved and lousy. When I'd reach middle age I'd increasingly come across stories of people who claimed to have been abused as children. But that usually meant sexually, which was never the case with me. No, I would have considered my young self way too repellent to have earned even that sort of attraction from anyone, especially my father to whom I was a horrid child.

8.

BIGGER BOYS DON'T CRY

From the time of our move north in 1966, Arthur Claude Twigg had identical plans for his three sons all set out. We'd each attend Parkstone Prep til the age of 13, take the Common Entrance exam and, providing we passed, go on to five years at Stourback Abbey for our public school education.

Stourback was only about 10 miles from Parkstone Prep, but my differing experiences at the two schools were to be a million miles from one another. I had no idea what to expect though.

Matthew had left Stourback a year early, the term before I arrived, but he'd made a few quality friends there who I'd liked. I gathered that Mark was faring very well, as he always did, and he was not only in the same school, he was in my House (one of 10), St.Anselm's, two Years above me.

Dad had been to Stourback (and St.Anselm's) too, so his sons were continuing a tradition he was proud of. After all, it was not just 'a top public school', it was 'THE top Catholic school in the World'. Or so Dad told us.

The complicated, tense, anxious person I knew Dad to be, it wouldn't have surprised me to discover his days at Stourback were disastrous. In fact, he'd been something of a hero there. Academically, he was clever, gaining a scholarship to Oxford University. But, more importantly in the minds of testosterone teenagers for whom sporting prowess was the ultimate, Dad was a star at cricket. So much so that he opened the bowling for the 1st XI in all his five years at the school, eventually becoming captain, and he would go on to play for Oxford at a time when future England legends were also in the team.

Dad's own legend lived on, on the walls of Stourback's main assembly hall – known as The Grand Passage - and the St.Anselm's refectory where the names of the House's achievers were expertly painted onto elegant wood boards for posterity. But that wasn't going to help me now, anymore than the man himself was.

Judging by the extent to which Dad complained about the amount of belongings Mark and I took to the school, and to which he stressed over loading and unloading them from the car – his eyes screwed tight, his tongue sticking out to one side of his mouth, and his face purple with the strain – thoughts that this was my first day of a potentially difficult five-year journey were clearly nowhere near his mind.

We had left the polite, peaceful, ordered scenario Dad had helped create at Parkstone Prep, travelled a mere 20 minutes in the family Hillman, yet arrived at a completely contrasting scenario which resembled a madhouse of near Hogarth proportions. St.Anselm's House, to be precise – an unspiring red brick building with overexcited youths leaning and hollering out of its multiple rows of windows from where there were varying genres of music blaring at alarming volume levels. No sign of neat prep school uniforms; the only dress code here was a jacket and tie, of which few were worn with pride.

It was as if there was no-one in charge. Yet down the front steps to greet us bounded a chubby cleric, complete with black habit and white dog collar, introducing himself as the Housemaster. In an attempt to ingratiate, Father Anthony explained to me that this was also his first term with St.Anselm's. I got an immediate sense that he didn't have what it would take to handle what was practically a riotous situation. As he led us inside, the chaos was even more intense. Teenage boys of all shapes, sizes, attitudes and demeanours were shouting, strutting, shoving...

Once we'd made our way up to the junior dormitory, the true atmosphere of intimidation kicked in. Like one of those scenes from a western where the instant a stranger enters a busy bar it falls silent, everyone stops what they're doing and just stares at the anxious newcomer.

It was a large long room, all in dark wood, and on either side eight identical iron beds with accompanying cubicles. Mark found mine for me, and was in the process bombarded with catcalls and questions about the arrival of his kid brother. My instant reaction was to smile nervously at the interested parties in the hope that would disarm them. But there was nothing warm about the looks I got back. Only mocking and brutal. A kind of 'Who do you think you are, daring to even be in the same room as us?'

Among that reception committee on the opposite side of the dormitory, I spotted a silent staring Ron Dutton. Several years together at my father's school would, I assumed, have earned me some support and loyalty from him. Yet, when I caught his eye, he swiftly looked away as if he didn't know me. Or, more significantly, as if he didn't want to know me.

It had taken me a matter of minutes at Stourback to realise I wasn't going to settle or succeed there, to realise I was in the wrong place. It was certainly no place for a Mummy's boy. For most of my spell at Parkstone Prep, being the Headmaster's son had given me some sense of security. Yet if that school at times felt like an open prison, moving to this enormous establishment already felt like being transferred to a severe jail of lawlessness. Little did I know it but this was akin to being sent into war without any weapons or armour.

Nobody told me Matthew had left early because he wasn't happy there. And you might have thought, the type of character I was then – or rather the lack of character I had then – should have made my family doubt my ability to tackle the challenge that clearly lay ahead of me living away from home for the first time in an unforgiving all-boys public school. If it occurred to my father and brothers, they said nothing. Maybe they thought this was the toughening up I needed.

If Mum had concerns, she was probably reassured by the fact that the school was run by seemingly kind priests and monks...and have assumed I'd still have protection with Mark being in the same House. Indeed, if I myself had any doubts as to whether I would sink or swim at Stourback, I'd have been sure that Mark's support and popularity would keep my head above water. Yet as I turned round to him for moral support in that dormitory that first afternoon, he'd gone. And, reflecting now, it's as if he never did really return. In their silence, looking away and walking away, he and Dutton were effectively refusing to be my safety nets. I suspect they both foresaw me as a threat to their credibility, so they instantly disassociated.

Stourback was a massive place compared to Parkstone Prep. The central building comprised long corridors with wooden floors smelling of polish, off of which there were classrooms, laboratories, lecture theatres, toilets, store cupboards, etc. A wide stone passageway led through to the Abbey church and its adjoining monastery. Pupils weren't permitted in the monastery – it was like the forbidden kingdom you could only catch a glimpse of where the clergy would be floating around in their black habits with hoods, resembling a dark Klu Klux Klan.

The 10 Houses were in separate buildings, all with their own corridors, dormitories, refectory, chapel, and so on. St Anselm's was on the north-west side of the scenic plain on which Stourback nestled. As with the central building, its flooring comprised patterned pine tiles, and halfway up many walls was an oak panelled facade.

The cubicles at the wall end of each bed in the dormitories had clothes-hanging space, a small chest of drawers and a sort of bunker that when closed could be sat on. Pupils would sleep in dormitories for their first three years, and in that time these cubicles were the only real personal space available. Yet, with 15 other pupils making their presence felt in the same room, they weren't sufficiently enclosed to provide privacy, so hardly anyone sat in them for reading or suchlike. They were basically just places to store your stuff.

Twice a day the House common room switched from being a games and TV area to become the chapel for Mass and prayers. Next door to that was the Housemaster's study where, when Fr Anthony was present, he requested relative silence so newspapers and books could be read and he could play his beloved classical music.

There was no family accommodation for me to escape to here. In that respect, I was just like all the other boys. However, there were about 750 others – so many that most you'd never meet despite attending the same school for five years. The ones who mattered to you, like it or not, were the 75 or so in your own House because that's where you spent most of your time when not in classes or playing sport. And most important of all were the 15 (approx) in your Year in your House because it was them with whom you shared dormitories and were seated with at desks and meals.

It didn't help that I'd turned up a term later than the rest of my Year. They already all knew one another and, while I yearned for a welcome, I sensed the opposite of that – disgust that I should have the nerve to wander onto their territory. Being an outsider was not a safe status in St.Anselm's House with the Year I was in.

It was a little easier outside St.Anselms, in the main school where I was one anonymous fish in an enormous pond. Mercifully lessons were for pupils from every House. But save for a lad in my English group (Timmy Thompson) who sobbed with homesickness throughout our first few classes, I reckoned very few at Stourback could match my immaturity. I was a needy gangly kid with no base, no backbone, no balls.

Not literally no balls, I hasten to add. Good thing too because the New Boys' Medical partly entailed Stourback's doctor holding each pupil's scrotum and requesting a cough. I never found out what this was meant to ascertain; I just knew it was something we all had to endure. Thankfully these medicals were one-on-one private encounters rather than tackling a long line of awkward schoolboys simultaneously. But it still felt a ghastly invasion of my privacy and I dreaded there being a pretty young female nurse present who might excite me as underpants were lowered for this inspection. It didn't take much to arouse the 13-year old me, which was a worry because in this unnerving new environment I didn't want to stand out in any sense.

Mum had kindly spent a long time making a dressing-gown for me to wear in my 'new school'. But as the robe was bright red, long and a little ladylike, I already knew it was not something I should be seen in at Stourback, so I hid it away and reverted to my old dull threadbare blue one.

As someone who always felt the cold, I needed a dressing-gown as a kind of extra blanket at night. Northumbrian weather was unreliable most of the year, but reliably bitter in Winter. With 16 people per dormitory, inevitably some wanted windows open all year round while the likes of myself wanted them shut on at least the cold days. But I was never one whose opinions counted; I was just constantly at the mercy of others' decisions.

A Dormitory Captain in my first year was Dexter Troupe, an aspiring actor with a flamboyant camp personality, who would swan around in his silk dressing-gown, an empty cigarette holder between his lips, like a wannabe Noel Coward. Two years younger and with none of his nerve, I could only admire his audacity and, because he inevitably took a lot of flak, the fact that he already had a comedian's ability to handle hecklers. The only quick retorts I'd ever come up with would be blurts – misjudged, misfiring, ill-advised blurts.

Dormitory Captains were supposed to keep discipline, but there was precious little of that. All Stourbackers were teenage males, and most were preoccupied with appearing cool in front of one another. School Captains, House Captains and Dormitory Captains were all conscious that, if they became officious, the boys in their charge would laugh at them.

As someone who needed his sleep, and needed silence to sleep, I was dismayed at all the unchecked disruption in the dorm at night. Walking (mainly to the toilets and back), talking, larking, farting, burping, wanking....it was all going on, and it did my head in. No serious efforts were made to stop it, and no way was I going to try.

I took to sticking a transistor radio or audio cassette tape player under my pillow - the former to tune in among the crackles to Luxembourg on 208 Medium Wave, and the latter to play tapes of The Carpenters, Rod Stewart, and the then new hit musical Joseph & The Amazing Technicolor Dreamcoat. I'd listen to them through an earpiece on a wire – my lifeline to a more cheerful world - until the worst of the dormitory disturbances had subsided, or until I fell asleep through sheer exhaustion. Even then I'd often be woken in the night by weak bladders, attention-seekers, sleeptalkers or sleepwalkers. One boy, shortly after nodding off, would suddenly sit up, shout something incoherent, run to the other end of the room, touch the Fire Door, return to his bed, shout again, then nod off. There was no point in the rest of us closing our eyes before this bizarre ritual occurred, or he'd have only woken us. As if it wasn't already like living in an asylum... After a while he was given his own room, lucky fellah. I'd have tried it myself for that outcome were it not for the fact that two loony sleepwalkers in one dorm would have seemed suspicious at best.

Rather like the distant road I'd gaze at through the ornamental gate back home at Parkstone Prep, I now just had stars and sometimes the Moon to peruse from the small row of windows high in the junior dormitory on those long, lonely nights. I imagined pleasant places the same galaxy was visible in, and wished I was there rather than here. My public school prison sentence was underway.

9.

HOW DEEP IS YOUR HATE?

Late one Saturday afternoon I wandered into the junior dormitory to be hit by the hideous stench of sick. Not on the floor, not on any beds, but in the bin. The big black rubber receptacle by the door was inches deep in vomit. Several boys, obviously the worse for wear, were in a kind of drunken huddle at the other end of the room. Turned out they'd got tanked up at the local pub. They were 13 and 14-year olds, yet someone had served them. This happened most weekends. If they couldn't find a friendly barman, they'd buy or steal from the off licence, consume far more than they could manage, then chuck it all up. Far from tempted to join in – not that they'd have wanted me to - I was pretty much put off alcohol for life and would never understand the likes of them who boasted about getting drunk or being off their heads, or why they'd think those were things worth crowing about.

I got the impression they thought it made them seem more mature. Maybe they were keen to become adults as soon as possible, which would have been ironic considering the amount of actual adults I'd met who said they themselves wished they were still young. But then there was I feeling my unhappy youth was dragging on, yet I'd heard one or two elderly people saying life for them was going by far too fast for their liking.

It soon became clear to me that having no haven, no sanctuary, was going to prove a problem. I pined for privacy, but the dormitories were constantly busy and noisy. Sixth Formers from neighbouring rooms would frequently invade the dormitories, sometimes smoking and/or drunk or high, as if to show their seniority or sense of rebelliousness.

An intimidatingly large senior who occasionally came into the junior dormitory during the daytime, ignoring the fact that one or two of us were present, entered also the cubicles and then laundry bags of a couple of then absent boys, took small items of clothing out, and 10 or so minutes later returned to put them back in. I learnt that his young targets were known as a 'pretty boys', apparently because they had quite feminine faces. But sexuality was still something of a confusing blur to me, and a big taboo. I never told a soul about the laundry looter, partly out of Britishness, but more because I felt it wasn't wise or my place to question those older than me. So his strange activity went on unquestioned.

The row of nine basic 'bathrooms' on the ground floor of the House were divided by slim walls that fell two feet short of the ceiling. Lying in a bath one evening in my first year, I looked up to find the laundry looter leaning over and gazing down at my naked torso. In sudden shock, I sat bolt upright to obscure his perverted view. "Ooops, wrong cubicle!" he exclaimed, disappearing rapidly. I'd almost jumped out of the skin he'd been staring it, and then did jump out of the tub to belatedly cover my midriff with a towel. But again I said nothing of it to anyone, and kept out of his way whenever our paths crossed again.

I imagined confident teenage boys in a co-educational state school, who slept at home, would by now be boasting about having some form of intimate contact with girls. Here at this isolated Catholic boys' boarding-school, the sex boasts were mainly of masturbation – a preoccupation of young males, never more so than where it was the only satisfaction...to hand. I daren't even discuss that then; I kept such matters to myself. When I learnt of the age-old myth that guys who masturbate too much lose their eyesight, I did wonder if Stourback would one day become a school for the blind.

One night an aptly cocky character informed the junior dormitory there'd be 'a wanking competition' adding "When you do it you can think of whoever you like, they'll never know! The first to come, wins" – perhaps not an ideal precedent for the future. Half a dozen participants created tent shapes with their knees under the regulation sheet and two blankets which shook as they frantically set to it. Then after about three minutes the victor raised dripping slimy proof in his fingers for all to see.

No sooner had this gross contest completed than a few senior boys, including the laundry looter, charged in and started stripping the beds. Despite not being among the competitors, I dreaded being exposed in that way. Silently, rather like praying, I willed and willed them to leave me alone, and surprisingly, mercifully, they did. After the cancelled play at Parkstone Prep, I considered this the second example I'd had of a miraculous response to a secret plea. But it may well be that only the pretty boys were targeted by the bed-strippers, and pretty was not an adjective I'd ever have used to describe myself.

In search of solitude one afternoon, I wandered up into the wood at the back of St Anselm's and found a bunch from my Year smoking roll-up cigarettes, some of which gave off a sickly stench. "Have a fag!" I was urged by Pat Butler, a greasy-haired urchin whose olive skin was pockmarked by acne. "No thanks" I replied politely. Holding his burning cigarette out towards me he pressed more vehemently: "Just a few puffs!" I looked straight at him to see he was likely to get aggressive if I continued to decline his offer. His eyes were glazed and he began laughing. "I tell you what" he said. "I'll give you one pound if you have a drag from this fag, and I mean inhale properly." Our exchange had by now garnered the full attention of the small crowd, baying for me to obey. "One pound per drag?" I checked, thinking of the decent amount of sweets I could buy with that. "One pound, I promise" he said. I took the thin glowing item in my fingers, held it to my lips and sucked in. An unpalatable taste, smell and smoke filled my mouth and nostrils and I coughed and spluttered to the great amusement of the assembled. On recovering, I extended my open palm to Butler and gasped "Pound please." Butler bent down to the ground, picked up a pile of dirt, and poured it into my hand. "There's your pound...a pound in weight!" he chuckled, as did his cohorts.

The majority of my contemporaries already appeared to me men of the World. I was discovering that, of the 15 in my Year at St.Anselm's in the mid to late 1970s was a core group of about five arrogant entitled individuals, including the rebellious smokers, drinkers and druggies. That handful of members of the influential in-crowd at St.Anselm's were for me precisely that: a handful. Compared to them, I was leading a nun-like life, Dad having always drilled into my psyche that I'd pay a heavy price if I didn't tow the line at all times. But the taste of most alcohol did not appeal to me, and when as a teen I'd been permitted a few sips of wine it upset my all too frequently nervous stomach. Cocaine I believed to be dangerous, and cigarettes bad for your health and breath. The extent to which I was already addicted to sugar suggested it was a blessing fags, drugs and drink were not my thing.

There were another eight not quite so self-assured and trendy lads but who were accepted by the cream so would clearly survive. And then there were two others who totally lacked esteem and were utterly uncool, and I was one of them.

My fellow walking catastrophe, one Stephen Banks, had dark, greasy curly locks, dandruff on the shoulders of his dated jacket, and terrible halitosis. His whole lean, pale, spotty self always looked like he could do with hosing down. He was shy, secretive and an awkward conversationalist. It was galling to be lumped with such a loser, but it appeared – or at least our peers had decided – that that's what I was too. Looking to avoid further condemnation by being seen as a kind of sad duo, I distanced myself from Banks, but it made no difference.

I wanted to be popular, and definitely not picked on or persecuted. I'd have settled for being ignored or made to merge into the background. Previously at Parkstone Prep, even when I felt uncomfortable in the company of other boys my own age, I'd find one or two amongst them with a sympathetic nature - boys who, whatever they thought of me, would to some degree still treat me as just another kid. Without that, my unfortunate natural tendency was to look to others to protect me. In my public school

House, however, there was no ally. Not even my own brother, the apple of my father's eye who already had a sturdy self-belief about him. I wanted Mark's strength and popularity, but he didn't want my weakness and unpopularity.

As for Ron Dutton, I should have taken heed of the aggressive way he'd suddenly turned on me in our final year at Parkstone Prep. For since I joined him at Stourback, I found not an iota of compassion within him. His coldness was disturbing. Perhaps that was his way of ingratiating himself with the in-crowd who were similarly devoid of warmth towards me. He gave the sinister impression of a bully who looks you straight in the eye and warns: "I know how to break you and I will".

Rather than feel empathetic through our shared history, Dutton used the knowledge it had given him to seek advantage over me. He knew how proud Dad was of having his three sons at Stourback, which usually cost a fortune to attend. As the Head of one of its main feed prep schools, Dad was getting a sizeable discount on our fees. Dutton knew and reckoned it was kudos falsely gained, so he soon spread the word, and I was condemned as 'cheap'. Just me, incidentally, and not Mark – no such weapons were ever used to attack him, I assume because of the confident, positive persona he displayed.

This word 'cheap' would be included in jibes about me and my family living 'Oop North', which were usually delivered with stereotypical northern English accents…even though none of us Twiggs had one then. Most Stourback pupils hailed from the Home Counties, and these particular ones considered themselves superior to 'northerners'. Apparently attending a northern school wasn't an issue, but living there was…even if only for a decade like us. It made sense of something our Surrey-based cousin Sam had said to Matthew, Mark and I when we first moved up: "If I ever come to visit you, I'll have to put my dark glasses on." He made out he was joking but I believed in the old adage 'Many a true word is said in jest', and he never did visit. Dutton and the in-crowd might have claimed they were joking too, but it was another 'stick' they found to verbally beat me with.

It all made me nervous, naturally. And, as ever, my nerves manifested themselves in smiling. No-one had made much of an issue of that before. Now those smiles were mocked and mimicked, made to look and feel like inane grinning. Among many uncomplimentary things, I was called 'goon' for the grinning, 'lollop' because of my uncoordinated skinny frame, and 'Twiggshit', 'Puke Pig' and a lot worse just for their entertainment.

I was now not even liking my own name, reckoning Luke and Twigg both sounded weak when I so wanted to give off at least a hint of strength in whatever way I could. But I was hardly going to get away with switching to something akin to Butch Champion at this point.

Not only did I get privately frustrated at lacking confidence, I took a secret dislike to overtly self-assured – 'cocksure' I secretly called them - boys, especially those I didn't think deserved to be. I was not just jealous but astonished at their extra confidence. They had what I wanted.

First Year pupils at Stourback were obliged to form part of the school's Combined Cadet Force. Second Year pupils could choose from the Air Force, Army or Navy, – but we still all spent Monday afternoons marching on the quadrangle carrying rifles. I had no interest in becoming an airman, soldier or sailor, partly because the itchy uniforms made me want to scratch which we were forbidden to do while on parade, and that restriction alone was enough to put me off for life.

But in Stourback's Cadet Navy, I did enjoy a trip to a minesweeper when a member of the Royal Family was brought on-board. We all received a photo of ourselves with the then Prince Charles, and I proudly pinned mine to my desk in The Study Hall. Within 24 hours, I found it burnt to a cinder by a cigarette or lighter.

Needing comfort more than ever, I stashed what I hoped were private supplies of sweets and fizzy drinks in my dormitory cubicle. But they were duly stolen in raids where the perpetrator(s) left clear evidence of break-ins, as if to emphasise their utter contempt for me. One night as everyone was supposed to be preparing for bed, I returned from my bath to find over half the dormitory standing in front of their cubicles holding my cans of Coke and giving me a chorus of 'cheers' as they tore off the ringpulls and necked the contents. I knew if I looked annoyed, that would be what they wanted. Instead, a nervous smile burst across my face which infuriated me as it encouraged their cheers to turn to jeers. I couldn't win.

I had no choice but to live with these aggressors and their relentless invasions of my personal space and pressing of my buttons. Dig, dig, dig, jab, jab, jab, poke, poke, poke, on a daily basis, year in, year out. It was mainly words rather than deeds, psychological not physical, but still ruthless.

The usual suspects mocked the increasing gap between the bottom of my trousers and the top of my shoes, as I was then growing at Triffid-like speed. So, the following school holiday, I begged Mum to buy me a new pair that reached right over the top of my Size 10s. Anything to avoid further criticism.

The day we were returning to Stourback for my second year and Mark's fourth, I requested a record be played for my Dad on BBC Radio 2....and it was, just as he was driving us to school. Dad seemed pleased, and so was I til later unpacking in the junior dormitory Dutton mentioned he'd heard it too. Pretending to stick two fingers down his throat, he said deliberately loudly "Made me want to puke Puke, you sad little Daddy's boy!" He knew how to hurt, but little I was not though I felt and wished it, and he couldn't have been more wrong about me being a Daddy's boy...much as I aspired to be.

In the refectory one lunchtime I was getting goaded by Kev Cooper, an especially irritating twerp who proceeded to pour masses of pepper and salt over my food. Admittedly meals at St Anselm's were abysmal anyway – which was inexcusable considering the cost of attending this school. But, egged on by his pal Pat Butler, he succeeded in his quest to wind me up and, pacifist though I was, for the first time in my life I came close to retaliating with violence. What kept me sitting there letting this happen with blood boiling in my veins were several thoughts. I was much bigger than Cooper and, such was my fury now, I could have caused him serious damage, but I'd recently seen in the news a man receiving a life sentence for murdering another with just one punch to the head. Besides, Cooper was part of the in-crowd and, were I to launch a physical attack on him, the others would doubtless pile in on top of me and, fuelled by their evident hatred of me, I'd have then been the one seriously injured. So while I was actually aware I might forever regret doing nothing, I was sure I'd have regretted more doing something should it turn out disastrous for both of us.

After that lunch, I was standing at one of the urinals in the House toilets (or 'bogs' as they got called) when suddenly I was pushed mid-pee into it and, partly due to a consequent spraying, slipped into a heap on the wet floor. An unexpected bonus for Butler and Cooper who, maybe because they were both determined to get me to flip, must have followed me in. They now headed towards the sinks in hysterics, clearly expecting a reaction. I was of course appalled and enraged, unable to imagine anything worse that didn't involve serious violence. But I still did nothing, doubting it would have made a difference even if I had as these two particularly appeared hellbent in their campaign against me. Their laughter continued. "Oh dear, Twigg, have you wet yourself?", "Twiggshit, you smell worse than normal!", and so forth. I just stared at them thinking, but not saying, "What did I ever do to you two to deserve that?" But they were already making their exit.

Pathetic perhaps, but that actually was the question I most wanted answering…even though they and I knew the answer was 'nothing'. I wasn't a threat to them in any way. Their bullying was unprovoked. I assumed they then went off congratulating each other, pleased with what they'd done, and maybe discussing what else they might do to me in future – probably to poo in my bed were it not for the stink that literally would have caused. The need in them to repeatedly torment someone was beyond my comprehension, especially when it was without motive.

It was scary realising I was not just never going to be part of the in-crowd, but I would instead be forever rejected by them. They didn't just dislike me, they loathed me. Oh boy, did they loathe me. Some demonstrated pure malice. Had I been the arrogant sort, I'd have half expected a comeuppance. But I was anything but. I had no confidence with which to put others' noses out of joint. Non-confrontational and a 'goodie-goodie' who always played by the rules because I daren't be anything but, I never did or said anything provocative to them or anybody, I just quietly tried to get on with my life, yet they goaded me endlessly. As my own father regarded me as a 'horrid child', which I really wasn't, what were the likes of Butler and Cooper?

I knew I was not just harmless, but soft-hearted and kind. In fact, I was such a sensitive soul that, if I ever so much as accidentally upset someone – by my blurting, for example – I'd not only be deeply apologetic, it would bother me for some time after, and disturb my sleep. Yet I could see these tormentors slumbering soundly in the dormitory.

They were different animals altogether, with anger and anarchy already part of their make-up. It was fitting that impacting on Britain at that time was punk rock and its rebellious disciples. I, in contrast, was like an example of why well-meaning people are told never to touch wounded/vulnerable creatures and then return them to the wild (which my going from my parents' prep school to this place seemed like), because those creatures will be rejected and even killed. I was discovering to my dismay that, once bullies sense your fear, and your inability to respond effectively, they will keep exploiting it – you become a bear to be baited.

I assumed that if I was despised within my own House, I had little hope of being appreciated outside it. After all I felt disliked, sometimes hated, by my own family and by now knew I had that effect on many others. Paternal, familial and now wider rejection weakened me critically. My school persecutors were predators and I was easy prey – evidently a target to be disrespected, defiled, and possibly even destroyed. I was a lamb to the slaughter - a long, slow, painful slaughter lasting half a decade.

All I could do was keep out of their way as much as possible. I never even used a urinal again. For the rest of my days that would be done behind closed doors.

10.

STUCK IN THE MIDDLE (OF NOWHERE) WITH THEM?

I remember confiding about my clean-living to another Stourback boy from a different House, and his response was "You're so bloody boring!" I was taken aback, embarrassed and deflated…for ages afterwards too. But it wasn't in my nature to then turn rebel to reverse the opinion of the likes of him or the St Anselm's in-crowd, and I'm sure they'd have seen through any such attempt.

Ever in search of a solution, at one stage I attempted to adopt a policy of politeness towards the in-crowd whenever I was unable to avoid them. I suppose that was to show them respect, though that was the last thing they merited. But my politeness was never going to change their minds about me. Rebellion was more their thing and I was not a natural in that department.

Here fearing my persecutors would never let up, perhaps unless I did eventually fight back, I just heard in my head Dad's words 'I wouldn't do that if I were you', and (apparently) Jesus' words 'Turn the other cheek'. There was no "Stand up and defend yourself…give as good as you get!" type of urging. In fact, no-one gave, or even offered, any guidance for getting on, for simply surviving. It was all left to me to discover for myself, usually by my own mistakes, and unfortunately I was a slow learner. The traditional advice given to the persecuted is to not react, not make the perpetrators aware of the affect they're having on you. But that's not easy when you live together in the same dormitory in the same school House. Besides, I was no actor and the bag of nerves I'd become ensured every modicum of hurt and fear was there for all to see.

It did strike me as ironic that my Headteacher father didn't properly prepare all his sons for the public school life he himself had been through. Of course every individual's make-up, circumstances and experiences are different, and Dad's own Stourback experience hadn't been so bad largely because of his sporting success there. But surely any smart-thinking, caring parent prepares their child for every eventuality...especially a child displaying such obvious vulnerabilities. I couldn't help but wonder whether, consciously or sub-consciously, Dad didn't want to arm me for the battles, and did want me to struggle, even sink.

Had someone sat me down and explained it was my lack of self-esteem that got me treated as worthless by my peers, there wouldn't have been much I could have done about it. As it was my own father who was the chief source of my self-loathing, and he showed no sign of letting up, I had little hope of salvation. This was a war I was never going to win. But I did view my dilemma as a puzzle that needed to be solved, and I'd have to do that unaided.

At Stourback, blind eyes were turned and insufficient done concerning serious issues such as indiscipline and persecution. Seeing as over half the staff were monks and priests lacking normal life experience and teacher training, it was small wonder they were mostly ineffectual. Some swaggered around the school displaying what appeared to me deeply inappropriate vanity. Others could barely disguise lusty interest in their young charges. A few were just plain weak and clueless, like my Housemaster who gave the impression he assumed discipline would just fall into place as he listened to the works of classical composers in his study. Maybe he thought he could rely on God to take care of everything. Or that the boys would sort things out among themselves to a large extent, perhaps as preparation for facing the outside World, but that surely would have been seen as a poor excuse for a lack of supervision and made the massive fees harder to justify.

The official line would have claimed struggles faced by pupils such as myself to be 'character-building', though it was anything but for me. I didn't have a recognisable character. If one was to emerge it would require careful coaxing and nurturing, and clearly Stourback was not the place for that. I was under the distinct impression I had to fend for myself no matter what was to be thrown at me, despite my having none of the required weapons or defences.

In books and films and stories I heard – ones with satisfying outcomes anyway – victims found ways to overcome bullying, often by overcoming their bullies. Having seen an excellent TV adaptation of Tom Brown's School Days, I read that novel hoping to learn more about how its eponymous hero successfully tackled the bully Flashman. But in reality I was so outnumbered for any physical response to have stood any chance. I had tried following the common 'Just ignore them and eventually they'll get bored and leave you alone' advice, but there was no sign of them letting up. It seemed I just had to accept that the way I was caused many others to detest me. And barring a personality transplant I couldn't see how they would ever let me be.

It didn't occur to me that factors in the lives of my detractors might have caused them to act the way they did towards me. It was perfectly possible that their own home circumstances were difficult and/or their parents didn't want to raise them most of the year. If, as an excuse for their behaviour, I'd been told then "Maybe they're angry at being sent away to boarding-school…", I'd have replied "Well that's not my fault. I'm not happy to be sent here either, but nothing I'm experiencing ever makes me want to take it out on others."

A big deal for me was the fact that, of my own brothers, Mark was very popular at Stourback and Matthew had made several good-quality friends during his time there…yet I had none. So I made it my mission to make friends. Certain weekends, Stourback pupils were allowed to be taken out by family or mates. It was obvious none were ever going to ask me to join them. I asked Jimmy Hales, a St Anselm's boy who wasn't part of the in-crowd but not rejected by them either, to join me and my parents for a pub meal. I reckoned Mum and Dad would be relieved to think I had a buddy, and I hoped I might gain an ally where I needed one most. He duly joined us, but never subsequently invited me to join any of his family outings nor showed me the loyalty I'd hoped for in return. Maybe he'd just fancied a free meal, but his friendship clearly could not be bought.

In some classes I found myself sitting next to a boy named Justin, who happened to be the best sportsman of my Year in the entire school. I was slightly in awe of him, especially knowing my Dad's admiration for sporting idols, and knowing how beneficial it would be to acquire my own cool pal. I was surprised to find he had time for me. But, being far more mature than myself, he reacted with mock horror when I asked if he'd like to join me for a coffee one evening - as if it was some kind of gay approach. However, we did go with a few other boys on trips to see Newcastle United play home matches – taken in the car of a slightly effeminate, scented, well-groomed man called Alan Paxton who worked in Stourback's admin department. I can't recall anything untoward happening, but decades later Paxton was jailed for sexual offences against a young boy and downloading indecent images of children. As for Justin...brilliant young sportsman though he was, he'd barely reach the age of 20 before succumbing to Leukaemia. A tragic waste of a decent and naturally talented person. And further proof that none of us knew what was in store for us.

Stourback was a seriously sporty school, where rugby union and cricket dominated. Mark excelled at most sports like our Dad. Despite my height and the assumption I might share my father and middle brother's abilities, I was only regarded as 'useful' at them. My deep unpopularity within St Anselm's meant I was last to be selected for the House sides, but fortunately that didn't apply to the main school ones.

Being literally left out in the cold was no fun in the often brutal Northumbrian Winters. I was skinny as a rake with only the regulation rugby shirt, shorts, socks and boots as defence against snow, sleet, driving rain and bitter temperatures, and often knee-deep in mud befitting a battlefield. At Full Back, I'd stand behind the rest of the team shivering and wishing I was almost anywhere else. Stretching sleeves over my frozen hands and raising the collar around my arctic neck was futile, but I did it anyway. I had no choice but to run around to keep from turning blue, and I did so in all directions with or without the ball.

To everyone's amazement, including my own, at the annual Stourback athletics competition in my third year, I fared remarkably well in the 400 metres. I overtook a couple of recognised runners and kept pace with the school's fastest, Matt Sly, who happened to be in the Year below me in St Anselm's. He won, and I came a close second. Afterwards an astonished Fr Anthony told me: "That was a shock. Congratulations on doing as well as you did." A kind of backhanded compliment, though any kind of compliment from him was rare, and praise from any source was precious as gold-dust to me then.

Sly, however, was worried I might steal his thunder...and maybe a title or two. He was, after all, already the school speed-merchant. One afternoon he suggested we race each other from St Anselm's to the Stourback sports centre. This time I passed him. Hours later, in The Study Hall, in apparent jest, he pulled me to the floor, jumped up in the air and landed with both feet on my chest. It hurt like heck and I struggled to speak, never mind stand, for quite a while.

There was no storybook outcome. I didn't suddenly become a sports star. I just did okay. I captained the school's 3rd XI cricket team and the 4th XV rugby team, but no-one cared about such lower ranks and barely a soul watched. Dad came to one of my matches, and consequently I played my striped socks off that afternoon, fiercely tackling opponents and making darting runs when I had the ball. I even scored an impressive diving try but, following my moment of triumph, I looked up from the turf to find Dad some distance away wandering over to another pitch to see Mark's 1st XV clash. He attended all of Mark's rugby and cricket fixtures, home and away. Mark captained the first teams at both sports – and I couldn't help wondering how much Dad's support helped him achieved that.

After the Romanian gymnast Nadia Comaneci bagged her three Gold Medals at the 1976 Olympic Games, Dad talked incessantly about her robotic impeccable discipline and the fact that she'd scored the first ever 'Perfect 10' mark. With his constant sniping at me – "do this...do that...don't do this...don't do that..." – I got the impression he expected perfection from me too. I was the same age as Ms Comaneci, but that's all we had in common; I was far from a champion at anything.

I was frustrated, sometimes furious, at not being gifted the ability to play better and beat more people than I did, particularly Mark whose old taunts still stung. Angry, above all, at not being able to impress our Dad like he did. Although I generally considered myself a mild-mannered person, when it came to playing sports like tennis or table-tennis as an individual, such was my hatred of losing that I'd hurl my racquet or bat around when things didn't go my way. And there were many times as a spectator of sport – let alone a player – that I'd hate the opposition to such an extent that I'd happily have seen them badly injured, even killed. At this time on the World stage of cricket, lightning-fast bowlers from the West Indies and Australia were knocking opposition batsmen over like the stumps behind them. I watched wincing but fascinated, and determined to inflict similar damage on school playing-fields. Dad had been a fine fast bowler himself, which I hoped would make me a natural. It didn't. I bought a book called The Art Of Fast Bowling by Dennis Lillee, the Aussie superstar who was the best at the time. With his thick black hair blown behind him as he embarked on lengthy run-ups and devastating deliveries, Lillee was like a human superhero. Sadly I was simply human. My attempts to emulate him failed dismally. Fortunately too, because if my desire to decapitate batsmen had been matched by his brilliance there could well have been casualties in those days when the only physical protection accorded school cricketers was a 'box' to cover their privates.

My preference was to field out near the boundary. If the ball was hit in my direction I had a little time to prepare for it. Otherwise, if there was sunshine – a rare commodity in Northumberland – I could enjoy that in relative isolation, and daydream, and think. I was forever thinking, usually of ways to improve my lot.

When playing a supposed friendly match for St Anselm's against another House, I temporarily stood in as Square Leg Umpire. One of our guys missed a shot and got himself stumped by the wicket-keeper. He was clearly standing several inches outside his crease, and the fielding side rightly appealed. But my team-mate was among the in-crowd and I declined the appeals. The opposition inevitably all turned on me – souring my poor reputation further within the school – but at the time I considered potential reprisals in the House later to be of greater concern.

Although it often felt like it, I was far from the only Stourbacker on the receiving end of unpleasantness. One of the History teachers, then close to retiring, had bent fingers from fighting in World War 2. Even an old and injured soldier couldn't escape scoffing from this rabble. When he tried pointing at the classroom door to expel a pupil from his lesson, his gnarled digit pointed instead at a wall which the miscreant walked into reckoning himself hilarious...and sadly most of the rest of those present thought he was too. Zero respect for this man's sacrifice for this country, to help preserve a future for all of us, and its apparent cost to him personally. I was mortified for him. I imagined that, if I'd tried to talk privately to him about it, he'd have just said something forgiving like 'Oh, boys will be boys', but I'd have expected to still sense his disappointment and pain.

Strange to think I was surrounded by the offspring of politicians, lawyers, captains of industry, celebrities, even royalty, and many would themselves one day take on those roles. Wealth and privilege, but no indication of positive values and decency as far as I could see. Certainly no consideration of others' feelings and failings; but instead a warped determination to dominate those they regarded as inferior or vulnerable.

If I was a parent paying serious money for my son's education at this apparently elite establishment, and I discovered he'd basically become canon-fodder, I'd have had him withdrawn immediately and demanded a refund. But at the time I considered it unwise to go running to Daddy, and doubted he'd listen anyhow.

I'd have thought that any person feeling so unhappily stuck in any institution, without any sign that their situation will ever improve, would at least contemplate escaping. Had I faced as an adult any of the disrespect I experienced at Stourback, I'd have left that environment entirely...simply walked out and away, never to return. But, although there were no actual gates to prevent that happening, as an obedient youth with an outlook restricted by elders and their rules, I didn't even contemplate such a thing. I just trusted and accepted that it was in my best interests to stay within the parameters set by my parents and teachers who somehow gave the illusion you were locked in when you weren't, and that there was no better place to be if you did dare leave. Indeed, I had nowhere else to go, certainly with only a few pennies' pocket-money. Home for me was not generally a preferable alternative to school. I was disrespected by males in both places. If I was from a happy family home, I'd have run off there...though maybe boys from happy homes weren't the kind of kids who got bullied. And, vast though the World was, I didn't actually have options beyond school or home, and I wasn't adventurous enough to even consider that there might be other possibilities. Or was it just me growing up with Dad's catchphrase 'I wouldn't do that if I were you'? Besides, a pupil disappearing from a famous public school would soon come to the attention of the police and probably the media.

Not only was my personal view of the World very limited then, rarely seeing beyond boarding-school boundaries, the majority of my thoughts were on my predicament at Stourback. Like I was used to doing at home, I spent much of my stint at the school contemplating the reason(s) for, and how to stop if possible, my persecution.

11.

OHHH COME, ALL YE UNFAITHFUL

The extent to which my focus was on feeling persecuted and trying to understand why and what I could do to stop or avoid it, meant my concentration in classes was well below what it should have been. My O'Level results showed that.

I either naturally had or developed good gut feelings about things, and that included never worrying about how I'd fare in exams. It wasn't that I was complacent or thought myself especially intelligent; I just somehow knew I'd do well enough in them without having to stress or do much revision…and that's what happened.

But when it came to my O'Levels, I only passed five, and those only just. On an afternoon home at Parkstone Prep at that time, Dad's deputy, Kirk Jacobs, asked me in front of a group of his pupils: "How come you fared so badly in your O'Levels? What on earth have you been doing? Results like that won't get you very far". With his pupils around him now also waiting for an explanation, I felt humiliated. 'What is it about me that makes people feel entitled to talk to me this way?' I wondered, but only in my head. 'Why don't they consider there might be a rational reason I might not want to have made public…and that I might actually be struggling personally?' This man was a senior teacher who should surely have considered such matters before speaking. And as he was not a teacher at my current school, was he really right to comment? I didn't think so.

Jacobs had a son of his own, Jerry, who'd been to Parkstone Prep and gone to a rival Catholic public school to Stourback, and by all accounts he wasn't faring at all well academically, yet the way Jacobs talked to me you'd have thought his boy was Brain Of Britain and a sports superstar in the making. Mostly what I observed were parents proud of their offspring. If only my Dad thought like that about me. But I didn't know what to make of Jerry Jacobs. He had a beautiful pet parrot he kept in a cage, which to me seemed like imprisoning a creature which should forever be free to fly wherever it wanted to go. And worse, he sometimes roamed the grounds of Parkstone Prep with an air rifle shooting defenceless wild birds. I wasn't convinced someone who did things like that merited admiration, but what did I know?

Committed Catholics like my brother Mark were surprisingly rare considering Stourback's global status within the church. We pupils had our religion and school chosen for us by our parents. Although a major point of attending Stourback was supposed to be its Catholicism, imposing religion on an audience of teenage boys in an increasingly rebellious era was an uphill battle. The imposition involved saying grace before all three meals of the day, attending prayers in your House and then in the main school every morning, House prayers again of an evening, and High Mass in the Abbey church on Sundays. There were plenty of optional services too, including House Mass every evening, and Vespers in the Abbey. Those optionals were poorly attended, as the compulsories would have been were we given a choice. Religious Instruction, aka RI, classes were similarly undersubscribed once they became voluntary from the third year.

At High Mass, rousing hymns such as Dear Lord And Father Of Mankind, To Be A Pilgrim, and the English public school standard Jerusalem could get the majority going. But for the non-sung worship, most attention spans were short. One senior Stourback priest used to give a nervous cough before he said anything out loud, so whenever he served Mass inevitably that got mimicked by clowns in the congregation causing widespread guffaws. At one Sunday service an altar boy stood so close to a candle that his cassock caught alight, and fire extinguishers had to be hurriedly fetched to prevent the lad going up in holy smoke. The fact that those were my strongest memories of churchgoing during five years at Stourback spoke volumes for my interest in it.

As with the broader Catholic church around Britain, if not the World, from the mid-1970s, senior figures put their heads together to try and think up ways of making their brand of religion more appealing. The traditionally inflexible Stourback clergy tried introducing a few Peanuts comic strip cartoons – those which contained Christian themes – in an attempt to gain the attention of the masses at Masses. But that lasted as long as it took most of us to read each of them: about one minute.

The Stourback clergy were enough to put me off. All of them every day bedecked in those slightly sinister identical black dresses of sorts. I didn't know how often they changed them, but judging by the smell of some not often enough. And, whenever I observed them praying, many appeared to be sniffing their own fingertips when hands were joined beneath their noses. Although never a devotee of religion myself, I was curious about those who were, like the fact that when saying prayers they tended to either have their eyes lowered in reverence or gazing upwards as if that's where they thought God and/or Heaven was.

Stourback had two shops inside the school – one selling sweets, the other uniforms and sports kit. There was also a Post Office, run by an elderly local couple. Next to that was a traditional red telephone box. This was the only phone available to the school's 750 boys, and it had to be shared with the general public – limited though they were due to the remoteness of the location. The degree of privacy the box permitted was limited too because bored pupils and passing yobs sometimes smashed its windows, and it wasn't completely soundproof even with a full quota of glass. Invariably there were substantial queues to use it in this era way before the arrival of mobile phones. So for any conversations I had in there I'd endeavour to keep my voice volume as low as I could, in the hope nothing I said would filter back to my Housemates and give them cause for further ridicule. I winced whenever whoever I was talking to asked me to speak up because they couldn't hear me. Fortunately, I only spoke to my mother at length, as she was my only real friend in the World aside from my dog.

They were my only motivation to go home for holidays and weekends. At least it wasn't far from Stourback, so I popped over occasionally - sometimes for a few hours, sometimes for a night or two on exeat weekends.

Once I walked into the staff dining-room at Parkstone Prep and was stunned to find my Dad in a passionate clinch with Denise Jacobs, wife of his Deputy Head. They were holding each other as close as humans can – a position from which they rapidly extricated themselves, mightily embarrassed. Whatever was going on, it didn't look good. The stupid thing was it could have been anyone barging in on them, including their respective spouses. They were lucky that I was so shy and Dad-fearing because, firstly, I walked straight out again, and secondly, I didn't mention it to anyone including them. Not for about a decade anyway.

Another time I returned home to the cottage unexpectedly. If I was hoping to surprise my Mum, I achieved it...though not in the way I would have intended. It was me who got surprised first, to find my housemaster Fr.Anthony exiting the front door as I was about to go in. On seeing me, he was positively startled. And he quickly leant back through the open doorway and shouted "Jean, Luke is here!" Not a man who'd ever had much time for me, suddenly he was charm personified, telling me how well he thought I was faring at school, etc. As I couldn't believe he would think that, it only made me realise quite how out of touch he was with what really went on under his rather sizeable nose. He never gave me the chance to ask what he was doing in my home so, when he said goodbye, that was the first thing on my mind on finally getting inside. Mum was hurriedly tidying herself and the marital bedroom upstairs, shooing me out of it when I went in there to find her. She seemed flustered but tried to appear relaxed, casually explaining that Fr.Anthony had himself dropped by unexpectedly, and she'd been very pleased to see him. She didn't seem quite so pleased to see me, but I was well used to that reaction from my family members by then.

There was a noticeable increase in cheeriness from Fr.Anthony whenever he saw me for a while after that. And, whenever I rang or visited home, Mum would quiz me about him and proffer her 'love' to him through me.

Then it was gifts. If I was going back to Stourback after being home for any amount of time, Mum would invariably hand me something to give to Fr Anthony. These started as small, often jokey, things. But on one occasion she handed me a parcel for him. I asked what it contained and, rather than avoid answering, she proudly unwrapped it to reveal a smart black jumper she'd spent ages knitting. Black was the only colour these priests could wear, at least while 'on duty' as it were.

I now realised that this was more than a simple acquaintance. And I concluded from the fact that Fr Anthony never gave me more than his best wishes to pass on to Mum that it was probably one-sided on her part. However, it did dawn on me that he had more to lose than Mum if any intimacy between them was ever exposed. Sure, Mum was married and the mother of two boys in his House, but he was a Catholic priest for whom sexual relationships were strictly forbidden.

Curiously though, Mum made very little effort to hide her fondness for him – almost as if she wanted them to be found out...perhaps in the hope he'd have to abandon Holy Orders to settle down with her. I wouldn't have known then but it could just have been that urge people in love have of wanting to tell the World about their situation and feelings. I've since heard it said that cheaters sometimes subconsciously want to be caught, maybe as they're behaving that way partly to make a point. Even in front of Dad, Mum would occasionally say things that I considered dangerous. I once pointed that out to her and she replied referring to an affair she said Dad had with a woman whose brother ran Longford Priory. So there was probably an element of revenge involved. If Mum was wounded, I didn't want to rub salt by telling her I found Dad in a clinch with Denise Jacobs. At least not then.

My greatest concern was that Mum's dalliance, affair, whatever it was, would become known within my House. I was enough of a victim without this. At least in that respect I should have been grateful that Fr Anthony didn't give out any tell-tale signs that something was going on between them. They only ever pecked each other's cheeks in front of anyone else including me, except for once when they hadn't realised I was watching from a distance as their lips locked for several seconds. I didn't need to see them having sex as Mum eventually told me about that in boastful detail. Considering their respective roles in my life, it was usually easy for them to meet without my knowledge as he knew where I was during term-time and she during holidays.

So besotted with him was Mum, and so desperate to share her excitement with about the only person she could trust, that I became her confidante as well as go-between. On the one hand I was fine about that as, for the first time in my existence, it made me feel quite useful and meant I got one-on-one attention from her. Also it entailed me being party to a betrayal of Dad, especially involving Mum who I'd long felt had suffered too much at his hands. Above all, whatever this situation was, it made her more happy and excited than I'd probably seen before. An added bonus was a little relief from my boredom, and distraction from my persecution.

On the other hand, I was disappointed that the target of her affections was Fr Anthony. He was a hopeless Housemaster, held in low regard by those in his charge, and evidently also a hopeless priest whose part in the affair seemed to me more sinful than Mum's.

I actually said to her: "Of all the men, you choose a priest…"
"They have their needs as well, you know" she argued.
"Yes, but their chosen path in life forbids it. He signed up for a life of abstinence."
"Well, he's only human."

And so it went on. Once again I was left thinking 'You adults set rules that you say must be abided by, yet you go breaking them and make excuses for others who do too.'

I already felt let down by Fr.Anthony in that he failed to recognise let alone tackle the problems I was facing in St Anselm's. I must have said as much to Mum because – maybe desperate not to lose her crucial ally – she soon attempted to rectify the situation.

One Sunday evening, when I returned to Stourback after an excursion of some kind, Mark took me to one side saying he needed to talk to me. Any expectation of having rare time with him swiftly soured as he explained that our elder brother had been seriously injured in a head-on car crash. Matthew was in a very bad way with multiple injuries, and plans were being made for us to visit him in hospital in Sunderland. However, we wouldn't be going at the same time. It had been arranged for Fr Anthony to drive me to and fro, and Mum advised me to use the journey to explain to my Housemaster why I was so miserable at Stourback.

On our first trip, after about 20 minutes of polite conversation, Fr Anthony introduced this topic and I duly poured my heart out while he made reassuring noises. But all this was overshadowed by the hideous sight of Matthew in hospital, his head swollen like a giant battered football and one of his legs broken in four places. Worse, his friend who'd been driving lay in a neighbouring bed blind in one eye...and I was informed that the driver of the vehicle they'd smashed into was dead.

Matthew stayed in hospital 16 long weeks, during which time Fr Anthony drove me on several visits, encouraging me to divulge what I could along the way. To this out-of-touch Housemaster, it must have been a handy insight as to what was actually happening in his House. But it turned out not to be the beneficial exercise for me that I'd been led to believe. At the end of that academic year, his official report stated that I 'lacked integrity'. More confusion for my head. Did this mean that, when he'd asked me to spill the beans, I wasn't actually supposed to? And this from a Catholic priest under a vow of chastity who was at the time f***ing my own mother....

'Like my father, even my Mum's unofficial man disrespects me' I thought. But then I thought further 'Not one person actually respects me!'

Ironically, one secret I never contemplated letting anyone in on was Mum and Fr Anthony's. For several reasons. 1) If I had, that would have meant the end of my involvement, my usefulness. 2) Mum was probably the only person in the World I trusted and cared about. 3) Mum had lost her beloved brother and Dad was a bastard to her, so I had precious little sympathy for him. 4) Not only did I think Dad wouldn't actually care very much if he did find out; I suspected he'd use it to justify his own behaviour and betrayal. So I had no problem with Mum cheating on Dad. We knew Dad to be difficult and unloving, to list just two of his faults, so Mum's misbehaviour needed no defending in my eyes. I just wanted her to be happy, and frankly I didn't mind if that meant Dad would be unhappy as my own happiness never appeared to occur to him.

12.

LOVE LETTERS STRAIGHT TO APART

In 1977, the Summer before I entered Sixth Form, my parents shocked me by revealing they were moving from Northumberland to Oxfordshire. Dad had landed a job as Head of another Catholic boys' prep school, called Cardinal's. It meant that, while I was at Stourback, they'd no longer be close by. In fact, this was easily the furthest they'd ever been from me. Contrary to what they and I might have expected, I wasn't bothered. All the time they'd been just 10 miles away or when I'd lived at home, I'd never felt their true support. Rather, it was around this time that I began realising the sad truth that would always remain with me: I had no firm foundation in life. What little I felt beneath my feet resembled sloppy blancmange not a solid basis.

I was surprised that Mum agreed to go when her relationship with Fr Anthony was serious…to her at any rate. Maybe the move south was an attempt to save my parents' marriage. I personally would have been happy to see them split, particularly if that meant I'd see lots of my mother and little of my father.

Just as I did in the early years at Parkstone Prep, at Cardinal's School I'd hang out inside our accommodation (again a flat on the same floor as the dormitories) as if I wasn't prepared to face the world outside. I felt free from harm in that flat – even Dad tended to be in better humour there than anywhere else – and the fearful side of me would like to have hidden there til I felt safe or strong enough to emerge, like a deserted soldier from Japan who made headlines circa 1970 when he was found on a Pacific island unaware that World War II which he'd fled had ended 25 years previous.

At the flat alone one day, I was nosing around in Mum's desk when I discovered a letter she was writing to someone. I spotted my first name and began reading. If I ever did know who it was addressed to, I no longer remember. But in it Mum was expressing serious concerns at the way Dad was towards me and how it was likely to affect, indeed damage, me in the future. I was dumbfounded that Mum had noticed for a start, because not even she had ever discussed that matter with me, and to see it there written down in black and white: THE problem of my life.

I never let on to Mum or anyone that I'd seen what she'd written. I've no idea if she ever sent it. If she did it made no difference, in as much as Dad didn't change towards me, though I did feel a little better knowing Mum was at least aware.

That letter could be credited with getting Mum and I talking a lot. She was confiding in me, and now I felt better about confiding in her. Maybe it prompted me to ask about Dad, because it was around that time that Mum told me he never got on with her mother and father and they hadn't wanted her to marry him. Most importantly, she explained "why Dad is the way he is"...

Which was that Dad's Dad - whom I'd only known as the kind elderly gent called Grandman, until his death in 1969 – had himself been a difficult, stern, domineering character. Dad had apparently been terrified of him and suffered severe depression as a consequence. That was at its worst when he was a student at Oxford University, despite him being a scholar and playing First Class cricket. He was given electric shock treatment, which was borderline barbaric and had such a serious effect on him that he had to take a year out before completing his studies there. The black clouds of depression stayed with Dad evermore – as did a deep dislike of his father whose grave he never visited.

Maybe from the moment I learnt all that – assuming it was all true - I should have hated Grandman after what he did to Dad, and sympathised more with Dad after knowing how his father treated him. But neither occurred.

At the time of Mum's revelation about Dad, I was a withdrawn, disturbed teenager, attributing most of my troubles to him. Despite what Mum said, I still hated Dad. After all he'd said and done to me and her, I couldn't bring myself to think 'Oh, that explains it. In that case, all is forgiven.' I wasn't convinced that what he went through was totally responsible for his behaviour. Above all, I thought, if he was damaged by his Dad being too severe with him, why did he allow himself to become an overly harsh father himself? Sure, Dad had played a part in bringing me into this World, and I was grateful to be here, but he undoubtedly damaged me…possibly because I was not what he hoped for. As this was my life to live and defend, I did not appreciate the harm he inflicted on me. And, I now knew, he never forgave his father either.

Dad was now only in his 40s, yet at home he was already about as intolerant as a person could be. And nothing wound him up more than me. I knew he couldn't stand my company, although he'd never have admitted that. I couldn't stand his either, and I would have admitted it. I stopped going on family outings, whether for a few hours, whole days, or even vacations. I preferred to stay at home alone with my dog, to avoid Dad and my equally uncaring brothers. I knew I was never going to win any of them over. Even the fact that they were prepared to holiday abroad without me suggested my lack of importance to them.

So for a fortnight of our first Summer at Cardinal's, I was left alone in that big old preparatory school and its extensive grounds. Mum filled the deep freeze with what she thought was enough to sustain me in their absence. My incessant comfort-eating ensured I devoured the desserts and cakes very swiftly. I'd never been taught how to cook and relied heavily on the then must-have new item: a microwave oven. I recall setting it to heat a chocolate éclair for about 10 minutes, and within less than two the cream pastry treat had literally exploded. Days later I noticed chicken sitting in a pan on the hob and decided to heat it to eat it. It wasn't long before a foul smell filled not just the kitchen but the entire flat - a smell that became unbearable. I took a close look at the source of the stink and discovered the pan was overrun with wriggling maggots. One of the most disgusting sights I'd seen, my eyes were as appalled as my nostrils. As quick as I could, I opened the kitchen window and hurled the pan out. The flat was on the first floor, so there was quite a crash as it hit the concrete below and its ghastly contents spattered some distance.

Despite that tiny trauma, I relished the time away from my family. No sooner had they returned than something happened which made me wish they were still away. I met a girl. Her name was Susan Taylor, she was the daughter of the school housekeeper, and she must have been about 16 like me. I was walking across the Cardinal's school playing-fields when I encountered her in search of stones she liked to collect and decorate. She wasn't an obvious beauty, but she was petite and pretty and most importantly she was female!

Susan struck up conversation and it wasn't long before I was privately thinking 'She'll soon come to the same conclusion as everyone else and won't want anything to do with a fool like me.' But, although I struggled to think of suitable things to say, she was kindly understanding and receptive.

From the moment we parted after an awkward exchange, my mind became overwhelmed with this situation. I'd actually met a girl, she was sweet and attractive, and I wanted to see more of her. But I was a ridiculously shy and self-conscious persecuted public schoolboy and I hadn't a clue how to win her over, even if she was interested in me...which I seriously doubted.

My desire to see more of Susan, coupled perhaps with a sub-conscious need to commit a courageous act, spurred me on to do something I couldn't possibly have imagined of myself. I decided I would go to her home (a bungalow halfway up the drive) and ask if she'd like to join me for a walk. It's impossible to exaggerate how huge and out-of-character such a move was for me then, and protests in my head clamoured 'Are you kidding? You've got no chance! You'll make yourself a laughing stock!' and such-like. Yet I did it. At a time I thought Susan's Mum, Cheryl – who was already a firm friend of my Mum, and therefore likely to share news of my visit - was least likely to also be at home, I knocked on the door a veritable bundle of nerves. I barely let Susan say "Oh hello" before blustering into my rehearsed offer.

To my enormous surprise and relief, Susan responded favourably. I was secretly euphoric, though my euphoria was tempered somewhat by her request that we have our walk the following day, as I knew I'd hardly sleep that night through a combination of anxiety and excitement, and that a delay would increase the chances of everyone knowing by then...which indeed they did. So I felt even more self-conscious than usual on returning to Susan's home to collect her for our walk. On being invited into her room beforehand, I remember seeing her jewellery spilling out of a box and clothes lying around, including on the floor a black bra I could barely take my eyes off. I'd never been privy to a teenage girl's room before and, compared to my entire existence, it smacked of far greater sophistication.

The walk itself was, well, pedestrian. I made uncomfortable attempts at conversation as we took to the pavement along the busy main road outside the school grounds. Matthew had threatened to drive past with Mark and watch us, which made me feel all the more self-conscious.

My biggest problem was not knowing what else to do except walk. About 40 minutes later we were back at her place, by which time my Mum 'happened' to turn up to see Susan's Mum and, rather than face any embarrassing questions, I sloped off. Susan had suggested we write letters to one another and, once I'd returned to Stourback days later, that's what we did.

At last I had something thrilling and positive to occupy my thoughts. I was amazed that anyone other than grandparents, uncles and aunts wanted to correspond with me, especially a cute girl. I wasted no time in corresponding and would end each missive with 'Write back soon'. The big issue was whether to sign off with 'Love' and I chose the lighter option of 'Love from...' After a while I added X's for kisses, and when Susan reciprocated my imagination went slightly wild. I read each of her letters again and again, and sniffed them hoping for a hint of her scent.

Gradually I grew increasingly daring in what I wrote to Susan. That never meant sexually, just in terms of wanting to get together, go places and do things...and putting more X's at the end.

But when one of her letters was handed to me during Fr Anthony's daily delivery over breakfast in the St Anselm's refectory, it was snatched from my hand, opened, passed down the table of laughing lads as in turn they read bits aloud in mocking voices. It ended up pinned to the House notice-board to the amusement of an even wider audience. I was utterly mortified.

When half-term came, Mum arranged to take Susan and I in her car to go shopping. I just sat there in silence, ignoring Susan, wanting to shrink into a shell. We never communicated again after that, and she must have been mystified at my sudden change towards her, maybe wondering if something in her last letter had caused offense. I could not bring myself to explain – not to her, not to Mum, not to anyone. The fact was the prospect of becoming a bigger victim at school outweighed the delight of exchanging letters or spending time with Susan.

My entire existence was now influenced, if not dominated, by a bunch of bullies. There was one simple way of escaping, and that was just to leave Stourback. Mark's five years there were now almost up, not that that made much difference to me. I wouldn't have minded attending the local comprehensive – the kind of place public school folk, including my father, looked down upon. Unless I was incredibly unlucky or most of Britain's male teens were like my Stourback contemporaries, I assumed I'd be happier at virtually any other school, or home-tutored by my parents at Cardinal's. The relationship between them was now frequently turbulent, and Dad remained difficult to say the least, but their home was like a womb to me, and I still had an umbilical-like attachment to it. So it wasn't about looking to leave school to booze and womanise like many lads of my age. I wasn't a lad in that sense. I was a boy still needing his Mummy. It did occur to me that by then I had a legal right to quit school if I so desired, as my eldest brother had done so several years before. But I faced predictable resistance.

"What on earth will people think of me if another of my sons becomes a quitter?" yelled Dad. "Your mother and I work damn hard day and night to send you to a top public school, and this is how you thank us? If you turn your back on this education, this opportunity, what hope for you in the future? Useless child! Why can't you be like Mark? Leave if you want to, but don't come crying to me when you can't get a decent career."

On the surface Mum, as ever, appeared to be trying a more reasonable strategy, yet I detected determination in her. "But you've only got two years left – that'll whizz by in no time - and it would cause so much disruption if you did go. Please don't." I realised she was now needing this son to stay at Stourback, otherwise her then only justifiable access to my Housemaster would be denied. And as I viewed her as my only ally in the World, bar my dog, I couldn't do that to her. I could happily let Dad down, no problem, but not Mum.

That year, 1977 when he was 77, Grandpa died. So Mum, devastated again, took me and Mark to stay with an understandably bereft Grandma in Worthing. Strange how I was in the same House at the same school as Mark and very rarely saw him there, yet we were sometimes stuck with one another on holidays. One lunchtime during this holiday, Mark was telling me how the famous American singer Mama Cass had died a few years before reportedly from a heart attack when choking on a ham sandwich. I chuckled, and grandma gave me a severe telling off explaining "It's no laughing matter. You should show respect. Your poor Grandpa died of a heart attack." That made me feel terrible, and again misunderstood – wasn't it obvious I hadn't meant any harm? But then of course she was grieving heavily. So much so, in fact, that she couldn't bear hearing the bath taps running as Grandpa had died when they were full on in preparation for his evening soak, and Grandma had to break the bathroom door down when she saw water flooding under it.

13.

WARY OF THE SIXTH FORM

The last two years of school were spent in the Sixth Form studying for the big exams: A'Levels. You moved out of dormitories and into rooms – a shared room for the penultimate year and a single one for the final year. You were also usually appointed a Captain. That was a pupil of a certain level of authority within your House and, if you were deemed to have particularly special leadership qualities, of the entire School. At the end of the previous term, there had been the traditional speculation within St.Anselm's as to which of the Fourth Year would be made Captains. Jimmy Hales told me he thought I would be and, if he didn't actually explain why, I got the impression his theory was based on the fact that I didn't drink, smoke or take drugs...unlike most of the rest. Yet when I returned for the Autumn '77 term, a list on the House noticeboard revealed that everybody in my Year had been made a Captain except me and Stephen Banks.

To people in the outside world at any time, this would have seemed completely insignificant. To me within that little world which was everything to me then, it was an enormous blow. I tried to pretend it didn't matter, but it certainly did. It was a massive slap in the face from Fr.Anthony, whose task it was to make these appointments. This was presumably him reinforcing his earlier claim that I lacked integrity for showing what he considered disloyalty to some of my Housemates. Yet since when did they show an iota of loyalty or decency towards me? And he a Catholic Priest who'd made a vow of chastity yet was not just having a sexual relationship, it was with my mother, and I'd kept the secret about their illicit liaison. It occurred to me that this humiliation might also be aimed at Mum – suggesting that she too might be lacking integrity in giving in to...him. In which case the pot was indeed calling the kettle black.

The exclusion of Banks and myself entailed other messages and consequences though. The most common reasons Sixth Formers failed to attain such promotion was for fairly serious misconduct of some sort, yet we not only hadn't ever committed such offences, we were the least likely in St Anselm's to do so. I'd been led to believe that the most law-abiding should be rewarded. The majority of others did everything they were not supposed to do, and often brazenly in full view of Fr Anthony. Where was the sense or fairness in that, and what example did it set?, I pondered. If Banks and I were being punished for being weak, could not the character of boys who indulged in drinking, smoking, drugs, bullying and so forth be questioned too?

Even I knew then that schooling should have been about protecting pupils, and helping them developing their strengths. It was obvious Banks and I were lacking in many ways, and it must have been incredibly obvious that promoting all the Year except us was weakening us much more, not least because it was literally putting us in a weaker position than everybody else. We were already disadvantaged from the others in terms of character, confidence, etcetera, and this was not only kicking us while we were down; it was virtually an invitation to others to kick us too. It felt like I'd fallen victim to that prank of having a label like I'M A DICK, TAKE A KICK Sellotaped to my back. And, sure enough, that's what happened...psychologically at least. Juniors were joining in too, such was my pathetic reputation. I hated being in that position and not having a clue as to why I was in it or how I could get out of it. Official confirmation had been given that Banks and I were inferior to our supposed peers, and consequently the butt of disrespect.

Despite my regarding this as the most serious in a series of setbacks, I was never going to react in negative or drastic fashion. I certainly did not consider suicide as 1) whether I survived or not, immense pain was guaranteed, 2) my persecutors would have won, and 3) I was determined that I would one day find happiness and satisfaction in later life. Although there was then not the slightest sign of it, I somehow believed positivity might lie ahead once I could escape this rancid institution and the toxic boys in my Year.

In my darkest days at Stourback, I spent time alone either hitting tennis balls against an outside wall in the school grounds or walking alone on the hills behind St Anselm's. It made me feel lonely, but then I felt that the majority of the time anyway even when I was in the company of others, including my own family. I was the only person I could be sure had my best interests at heart. While walking or practising tennis, I'd contemplate my unpleasant present and promise myself a brighter future, though I'd no idea how I might achieve the latter. What I did know was that in the meantime I still had a lot to endure, due to my unhappy unstable background, my rejecting father, brothers and Housemates, the relationship between my mother and the person – the Priest – who'd just shamed me, and my consequently mixed-up mind.

So at that late teen stage, when nearly all my contemporaries were blooming in confidence, even arrogance, I remained afraid of my own shadow. I would have liked to know how to be strong, cool, popular, etc, but for all its academic achievements Stourback taught none of that. Most of the staff were clergymen of limited experiences and horizons, many of them having attended Stourback themselves and ventured only as far as university before returning for the monastic existence. Yet they were widely regarded as wise men.

At weekends, films would be shown for staff and pupils in the school theatre-cum-cinema. One such screening was of the latest Paul Newman movie Slap Shot. Depicting the rougher aspects of American minor league ice hockey, it included a mildly intimate scene involving Newman and his female lead. That had reached the point where he was unclipping her bra when suddenly one of the Stourback Housemasters, Fr George Wendover, ran down the central aisle shouting to the projectionist: "Turn it off! Turn it off! We'll not have any of this filth shown here!" The film was duly terminated and everyone ushered out of the building. Many years later, the same supposedly learned Fr George would be assigned the task of helping an A-List celebrity couple solve their marital problems. Small wonder they divorced shortly after.

A perennial favourite of the Stourback Film Club was the Lindsay Anderson classic If..., set in a boys' public school, largely I'm sure for the storyline involving a 'pretty boy' as much as the climactic scene where rebellious pupils machine gun the staff to death. I was now aware that pretty boys were the ones considered most attractive to those who experienced homosexual feelings – themselves referred to at Stourback as 'benders', 'queers', even 'pederasts'. To my eyes, pretty boys were the boys who most resembled girls, which suggested what I suspected anyway: that if actual girls attended this school there would be little or no homosexuality here. Some who at least experimented in it at school went on to stay gay in later life, but by no means all. I doubted many, maybe any, would have gone gay had they not attended this single-sex Catholic institution.

In this, my penultimate year at Stourback, I was allotted a personal tutor, Father Thomas Jenkins. I visited him in his study several times, but wasn't sure what role he was supposed to play because he seemed far more set on discussing me personally than anything I was studying. It therefore occurred to me that, contrary to what I'd been led to believe, maybe not all Stourback Sixth Formers got given tutors and mine was simply provided as a fresh confidante. But surely Fr Anthony couldn't risk me sharing potentially reputation-destroying information with one of his monastic colleagues... Anyway, as I was at that stage feeling extremely let down by him, I was disinclined to open up to another.

Fr Thomas did seem approachable – kind-hearted and gentle and, well, more womanly than manly. Like a middle-aged lady in a long black dress.

I can't have been having a good day on our first day because I told him I 'kept getting things wrong'.

"Nobody ever gets everything right, no matter how much time on Earth they are blessed with" he replied. "Our Father in Heaven knows that none of his children here on Earth are perfect. Life is full of challenges but God…"

I couldn't let him continue. "I'm sorry but why bring God into this? This is nothing to do with God, at least not as far as I'm concerned. The father I can't seem to do things right with is my actual father who only lives 10 miles away on this very planet."

"I understand, my child…"

"Sorry but I'm not sure you really do. And I don't mean to be rude but I'm not your child either" I added, despite momentarily wondering if Mum's weakness for Catholic priests dated further back than I knew.

Mid-session on about my fifth visit, Fr Thomas unexpectedly told me to stand up and he complimented me on my height. "I don't like being tall" I told him, "I want to be a normal size!" "Oh" he said. "But it's such a blessing. You should be proud to stand out, handsome lad like you..." 'Handsome lad? No way will that ever be truthfully said of me', I thought, so gave a look of incredulity...but was then maddeningly unable to stop myself smirking with embarrassment, which may have encouraged him. "All you need is self-esteem" he explained with the surety of someone who could just fetch it out of a cupboard. "I could help you with that." Well, it was something I knew I needed, in spades, but also knowing he was a busy teacher let alone priest, I said "How would that work?" Fr Thomas rose from his armchair, stood close by my side, slid his left arm around my shoulders and whispered slowly in my right ear "I'm sure we can come to some arrangement". I wasn't sure what he meant by that, but I didn't wait to find out. I made my excuses and left, never to return.

Though I would always have my suspicions, it is possible Fr Thomas's intentions towards me were only honourable. No doubt that's what would have been argued in court had things ever come to that. I didn't witness any homosexual activity involving the Stourback clergy, but some you could sense were enamoured by certain boys. In my time at the school, at least one senior priest there quit to marry one of the Mums. Whatever their persuasion, making chastity vows clearly did not prevent natural urges rising, often to an overwhelming level. Of all the mistakes made by the Catholic Church, imposing nature-defying restrictions on its monks and priests was the worst ever and inevitably damaged many of its followers and its reputation.

Shortly prior to my arrival, a long-held annual debating contest between Stourback and the nearest convent school, St Martha's, was ended when two opposing contestants were caught having a near-naked feverish fumble in a broom cupboard during the interval. I never heard what became of the girl, but the boy was expelled on the spot. That was the price paid by every Stourbacker found in flagrante with a female, which occasionally occurred in Sixth Form rooms. Clearly heterosexuality was not just unacceptable but forbidden. Yet, if talk was true, homosexuality was commonplace within the school and basically hidden under the proverbial carpet. I often heard it said that if two boys were caught together, it was a case of 'Now, now, don't be doing that again, but we won't say anything.' A confusing scenario to say the least, particularly considering the continuation of the human race then depended on male/female intimacy. As if such issues weren't mindboggling enough for impressionable teenagers holed up in a single-sex boarding-school located in the middle of nowhere. Now even the once-yearly meetings with St Martha's were banned, the only females we ever saw on a regular basis were kitchen maids...and at least two of those got pregnant by pupils during my era.

The only outlet for the boys, except presumably for the few who did get girlfriends somehow and for the priests who didn't find women like my mother to have secret liaisons with, was masturbation. All that wasted sperm from so many that could have created armies of children! And all those years of internalising sexuality, which for me was coupled with the isolation prompted by persecution... Unhealthy to a disturbing degree, yet what I knew then to be normal.

The only 'sexy' non-celebrity women I saw were in pornographic magazines, which inevitably materialised from time to time. Oh, and one in a novelty pen owned by a Stourbacker which, when turned up or down, removed or restored the clothes of a tiny busty lady in a capsule of liquid.

I had no sight of an actual naked woman and then couldn't imagine ever doing so. I did once buy a 'porn mag' at a railway station, but only after watching the kiosk from a distance til there were no customers, raising my coat collar to cover my face as much as possible, securing the correct change in a sweaty palm, and speaking in the deepest voice I could muster in case my age was questioned by the newsagent. It was a moment matched in embarrassment only by buying condoms from a chemist a decade later.

In the first year of Sixth Form, Sex Education classes started. Possibly because my entire spirit was at that point so quashed, I'd lost the childish curiosity I'd had during dormitory chats and Blackfoot's unofficial lessons at Parkstone Prep. I can only recall one topic from the Stourback sex lessons: the general difference in ease and speed with which men and women orgasm, and how we guys should ensure our women were satisfied before ourselves. As the closest encounter I'd had with a woman by then was walking along a road with Susan Taylor for 40 minutes, not much of this made sense to me. The way my mind worked, I'd only have properly understood sex classes if a couple had demonstrated right in front of us or better still I'd been the male half of that couple. But of course had either happened, the school would have been closed down in an instant...which now makes me regret not thinking of that!

The only images provided to aid understanding were scientific drawings of male and female intimate areas. Were those shown as photographs or film presumably they would have classed as pornography, and I doubt many would have been returned to the teacher. That was Gordon Parks, who usually taught Latin. His sex lessons didn't last long. Rumour had it they were stopped when he made reference (to a class other than mine) to having sex with his wife on their kitchen table. I've no idea if that was true but, if it was, the axing of his lessons showed Stourback to again be attempting to shield us from reality.

14.

I GET TO GET OUT OF THIS PLACE

Sixth Form was supposed to be all about the preparation for and taking of A'Level exams, in three subjects. The choice for me seemed a foregone conclusion as there were three I'd always done well in: English, History and French. Had I continued that triple success at A'Level my future, university and career-wise, would have looked promising. But, without being given any say in it, I was told that instead of French I'd have to take Politics – a subject I'd never had the slightest interest in. Apparently my failure in Spanish O'Level led to the decision. My objections fell on deaf ears, so failure in one A'Level subject was assured.

A few tortuously long terms on and the following Summer it was Show Weekend – when the annual prize-giving ceremony took place and all the competing contributions were displayed in classrooms for parents and siblings to view. Only once or twice did I ever have anything exhibited, and that paled by comparison with other boys' creations. So there was usually not just no pride but some shame that another year had gone by and I still hadn't come up with anything of note. But Show Weekend always involved a series of events, starting on the Friday evening with a choral concert in the Abbey Church. That year Mum came with Matthew, his then girlfriend Mary, and (meeting me for the first time) her younger sister Tamsin. I can't remember if Mark joined us, or the girls' father Freddie who was a Stourback teacher with designs on Mum. The reason I can't recall is that, from the instant I was introduced to Tamsin, I was captivated by her. Throughout the concert, rather than face the performers in front of the altar, I kept turning to look at Tamsin. I thought my glances were subtle, so I was shocked when Mum mentioned my interest later that night. In fact, Mum, Matthew and Mary promptly arranged for me to take Tamsin round the school Show exhibitions the next day. It was embarrassing to think that everyone was suddenly trying to fix me up with this innocent lass, but that was superseded by the opportunity to spend a few hours alone with her.

She didn't disappoint. Tamsin looked delightful in a polka dot dress and had that glorious air of lightness and promise that an appealing teenage girl in early Summer exudes. So it was with proper pride that I walked her through the numerous classrooms and galleries displaying paintings, sculptures, woodwork, metalwork, and countless written projects. She was the epitome of sweetness in her smiles and comments, though I might well have appeared distracted to her because I was....by her.

Determined to make the most of this opportunity, I decided to ask Tamsin if she would write to me...as the situation with Susan had led me to believe that was the thing to do. I was paranoid that at any point my persecutors might spot us and destroy the situation, so at the end of our tour I led her to a quiet part of the grounds close to the tennis courts which was covered by blossoming trees and mercifully free of crowds. By the time we reached there, my heart was thudding inside me as I prepared to make my suggestion...expecting a rejection. Yet Tamsin responded positively and I was 'over the Moon'. Had we been starring in a musical, this would have been the moment when I'd take her hands in mine and lead her into a romantic waltz while we stared into one another's eyes. But that was never going to happen. I'd never danced in my life by then, and was so devoid of confidence that I wouldn't have even dared look direct at anyone for long, most of all a feminine vision of loveliness. And, fearing that any more time spent in my crap company might cause Tamsin to reverse her decision, I felt it best to quit while I was ahead. As I said goodbye and walked away from her that sunny day, I was practically doing cartwheels of elation in my head. Within a few hours I was composing my first letter to her, requesting she send me a photo of herself.

Rather than place the letter in the St Anselm's daily pile for posting and risk the chance of it being spotted, stolen, opened and exposed, I chose the safest option and put it into the public letterbox outside Stourback's Post Office. As the phone box stood beside that, and this was a rare moment when not only was it empty but had no queue outside it, I decided to call Mum. In no time at all, she warned me that if I was planning to write to Tamsin I should be very careful about the content of my letters because the nuns at her convent school were known to open mail addressed to the girls, and censor it. I didn't have it in me then to think, let alone write, anything contentious. I was deeply private and self-conscious, so the thought of my words to Tamsin being read by anyone else filled me with horror. Even Mum knowing that I was entering into this correspondence embarrassed me. And of course there were risks at my end too. I looked back at the letterbox and, after checking no-one was watching, tried to slip my right arm sufficiently far through the opening to retrieve my envelope from the top of the pile inside. But I couldn't reach far enough.

There followed several days and nights of worrying myself silly, half-expecting to be summoned to the Housemaster's study where I'd find him holding my opened letter to Tamsin, shaking his head and tutting before discussing my possible expulsion. No such thing occurred, thank his Lord. And mercifully I was even able to collect my mail from him prior to it being distributed in the refectory. Hearing back from Tamsin was worth any awkwardness and risk. It was a moment of great excitement as well as relief.

As with my letters to Susan 10 months previous, I came across to Tamsin more worldly than I was, and ended them 'with love' and eventually 'kisses' too. It was beyond exciting when she did the same. Yet I'd never have dared arrange to meet. Then one weekend I was leaning out of a St Anselm's corridor window when I suddenly saw Tamsin cycling along the road outside wearing (I've never forgotten) a blue Guernsey jumper and jeans. Then she slowed down and looked up directly at me.

The natural, normal, right response would of course have been for me to acknowledge her and gone down and met, and maybe wandered off down the road with her, hopefully to somewhere we could have been safely alone. Had I done so, maybe we would have spent time together, and who knows what that might have led to – I'm sure only in a harmless way.

However, I was not natural, normal or even right at that time…though my letters to Tamsin may have suggested otherwise to her. I was actually a deeply insecure, self-conscious, scared, troubled individual. And a significant amount of that stemmed from people with whom I was living in the building I was looking out from and she was looking up to.

So instead I immediately went into panic mode because I feared all hell would break loose if I was seen or heard talking to a girl, worse still the daughter of an unpopular teacher. So as Tamsin looked up, I disappeared inside the window as fast as I could and didn't dare glance out again for a good few minutes til I felt sure she must have moved on.

Just days later I got a letter from Tamsin saying she thought she'd seen me and asking if I'd seen her. I didn't know how to respond. My priority was keeping my head down and keeping myself from further persecution, but I couldn't tell her that. So I just never wrote back. The following holiday, while Matthew was visiting Mary (by now his fiancé), he suggested I join them and spend time with Tamsin. When I declined, he asked me why not and said Tamsin had been wondering why I'd ceased corresponding with her. I told him I didn't want to talk about it and left it at that. Strange, secretive, complicated fellow I was then.

It was as if I'd had two early chances at happiness, and let them both go through fear. I remember reading around that time that a man's sexual peak occurs at the age of 18. Terrible news – I was already 18 and hadn't even had a kiss on the lips let alone sex. Not even come close. Yet for about seven long years by then part of me, which when aroused influenced most of my being, was like a homing missile without a home ever in its sights.

It could almost be said that a saviour of mine at Stourback was Bob Dylan. He was definitely a much needed distraction. I discovered his unique music and Marmite voice when I was in Sixth Form, and it was a love that would never die...though sometimes be hard to explain. Unlike many Dylan fans, I wasn't drawn to his lyrics. As with most songs, a few words or lines here and there would occasionally strike a chord – like a horoscope can - but when a song is not written with you in mind, how much can you really relate to it? Never more so than then, my life was as far removed from Mr Dylan as any person. Yet his sound and songs somehow tapped into my personal zeitgeist like nothing else artistically ever could.

In the predictably arduous year of sharing a different room each term that meant also repeatedly hearing the preferred music of three other teenage guys, which were in order ABBA, Simon & Garfunkel, and Elgar. ABBA was the choice of Ron Dutton, which was surprising seeing as he was by then the House hard man and a lynchpin of the school's 1st XV rugby scrum. I was lying in my pyjamas on my bed trying to read one evening while he played their album Arrival over and over, when he suddenly said "Twiggshit, you weirdo! I've noticed you don't use urinals like everyone else. What's going on? You got some kind of deformity?" I gave him a weary look and slowly shook my head, assuming he might be aware of what had gone on in Year 2, but that was never going to be enough for him. "Prove it!" he demanded. "Show me there's not something seriously wrong with you!" He clearly wasn't going to let up, our room was four floors up, and you never knew what he might do when in a mood to intimidate and dominate. So I showed him. He stared as if in disbelief for the few seconds I allowed, and gasped "F***ing Hell!" but not for the reason he'd perhaps expected. I'd no idea why until weeks later a towel fell from his bulky waist to reveal beneath it what was best described as a button mushroom.

So one of the biggest benefits of finally getting my own room in my last year was playing what I liked when I liked, which was pretty much all Dylan. As was also being free to stick up pictures of my celebrity crushes. Above all at last I had a private sanctuary to escape to, even if I lived in constant fear of others invading that space. The sad fact is hardly anyone ever visited me, whereas most of the other boys in my Year led very lively social lives based around their rooms. They certainly had what I didn't. Finally I was a House Captain, but only because I had to be by then, and I never dared attempt to impose any discipline.

Once as I stood in line for the Stourback phone box at almost 18 years old, I caught my reflection in a small window above the Post Office door. Such was my self-hatred, I rarely looked in mirrors for longer than required moments to check my spotty face was otherwise clean, my hair tidy or tie straight, because I assumed I actually was as ghastly as most people seemed to consider me. Yet here I stared, immensely surprised to find for the first time in my life that I liked what I saw - not actually the sight for sore eyes I'd long believed myself to be. Shocked, I checked twice to ensure I hadn't made a mistake and set eyes on someone else in the queue instead. I remember having similar thoughts when the team photos were printed. There I was in the centre as Captain of the school's cricket third team: lanky, fair and, acne aside, really quite presentable. But how could that be me? I may have looked alright on the outside, but inside I felt a stupid, pointless victim.

Being away at public school hadn't toughened me up. If anything, I was more of a mummy's boy than before. My relationship with Mum had gotten closer, and I was glad of that, realising the extent to which my go-between role had become vital since my parents' move South. She couldn't keep away from Fr Anthony and even bought a house in the village where Parkstone Prep was, from where she could potentially conduct their relationship more easily.

I don't know whether she made that purchase because she'd heard Fr Anthony had by now moved on to the mother of another boy in St Anselm's, or whether Fr Anthony moved on because Mum had gone to all that trouble and expense out of desperation for him. Certainly, that affair took a turn for the worse from her viewpoint. Maybe he decided his relationship with God or this other Mum was more important, or he couldn't risk the inevitable scandal of getting caught out. I do know my Mum wanted it to continue though.

Yet soon it became clear she was succumbing to the advances of Freddie Marshall, the Stourback teacher who was father to Mary and Tamsin. He was married, but that wasn't going to stop Mum or him. I was more concerned they would become the talk of Stourback because he was something of a school joke being, to put it mildly, no oil painting. I was surprised Mum allowed things to get intimate between them. But he was very persistent, she was clearly lonely, and it was an obvious attempt to make Fr Anthony jealous, though I've no idea if the latter ever knew about it let alone cared.

On reflection, Mum was demonstrating a similar absence of self-esteem as myself. We'd been drained of that by Dad and his tyrannical hold on the family. They were still legally married. Maybe because of Mum's frequent absences, Dad was struggling at Cardinal's, not just at keeping the school together but keeping himself together. His family was breaking up as well.

It was then announced that Fr Anthony would be quitting as Housemaster of St Anselm's that Summer - the same time I was leaving, so just my luck!

The best company Mum now kept at her house was Lulu, my dog. But in those school holidays Jerry Jacobs, driving his first car, accidentally ran her over. The noise of sheer pain that emanated from Lulu as she was crushed by one of his tyres was hideous to hear. She was then laid in her basket in Mum's hallway, struggling to breathe and – I shall spare you the grim details – very obviously injured. I knew I should be beside her, holding her, stroking her, talking to her, in her hour of need, but cowardly me couldn't face it. Yet I knew that if I was the victim, Lulu would never have left my side under any circumstances. Instead, I stayed out of the way in the lounge, frightened yet aware Lulu must have been absolutely terrified as well as in agony. Mum told me the vet was coming to give Lulu an injection to make her feel better, but somehow I knew what that jab really entailed. Even though I hadn't been the perfect owner, Lulu had been the perfect friend to me – relentlessly loving and loyal when no-one else was – and her loss was hard to endure. After Mum's miscarriage, for me this was like having a second candle of hope snuffed out.

From what I could see, Mark was by now the only happy member of our family. As ever a cheerful, popular, relaxed individual, he endeared everyone who encountered him, starting at home where we'd all be riveted when he related his adventures, tickled when he told jokes and impressed when he did impressions. There seemed no doubt success was assured him whatever path he was going to take.

Dad always made it clear he wanted us to go to Oxford University like him...despite the fact that his own life fell apart while a student there. Cambridge would have pleased him too. It certainly seemed to be about Dad being pleased, or being able to brag about Mark to others, rather than anything else. To be fair, Dad was working in education and moving in the kind of social circles where offspring doing Oxbridge was as good as it got, feather-in-cap-wise. But Matthew had dropped out of school before taking A Levels, and neither Mark nor I got good enough grades. Mark would have fitted in socially anywhere, especially at either of those elite establishments where he'd doubtless have continued to excel at sport. Instead he ended up at The South London Institute Of Higher Education (aka SLI) at which you studied for Surrey University degrees. At the time, only one A' Level pass was required for entry. A big draw for Mark may have been that one of SLI's four colleges, The Dorothy Byrnes, was Catholic. It had grown out of a former convent school for girls and never quite shaken off its origins, because by the time Mark started at Dotty's (as it was affectionately known) there were about 20 female students to each male. Mark boasted that he was wolf-whistled at when he went there for his interview. And no sooner had he become a student himself than he was dating an apparently very attractive American girl whom I sadly never got the opportunity to meet.

A few from the Sixth Form in St Anselm's, Stourback, were now claiming to have girlfriends - perhaps truthfully for all I knew, though I'd never seen any of them with females who weren't family. Had I been able to take my situations with Susan and Tamsin beyond the letter-writing stage, I might have been able to claim two girlfriends by then. But I wasn't a regular guy in regular circumstances, and I'm not sure some of the others were either.

Most leavers talked of high-flying futures, probably with the help of their Dads, and I assumed the St Anselm's in-crowd at least would go on to dominate their respective industries like they had our Year in our House.

Some Stourbackers aimed to be soldiers, sailors and airmen. That, along with the priesthood, I would never have considered. After a decade or so stuck in boys' boarding-schools, why would anyone forego a life of freedom and adventure to return to being cooped up, bossed around, made to follow strict rules, and be largely estranged from females and loved ones? And of course the Armed Forces had the added high risk of terrible trauma and death. It did not make any sense to me...though I was mighty glad for the security of the UK that plenty of people were prepared to join up. I wouldn't have dared say it out loud, but I felt sorry for those who spoke of being prepared to die for their country, considering them misguided or maybe brainwashed. As far as I was aware, only a tiny per centage of the population expressed appreciation for 'those who died for us', there were only limited ways such appreciation could be expressed, and surely none of it could be felt by those it was aimed at if they were dead. History lessons I'd had appeared to repeatedly show that the loss of a person - even multiple people - made next to no difference in wars. So what a waste of that person's opportunity to exist, especially assuming we really do only get one life. And once that's over, they no longer have a country to live in and benefit from the success of - instead they probably have nothing at all. I was mighty grateful there was no National Service in my day.

None of my contemporaries mentioned careers I fancied. I'd no idea what job I was going to do, but I hoped it'd be more exciting than theirs. One thing was for sure, whatever path I'd take, however successful or busy I'd become, I knew I'd still secretly remember each and every one of my persecutors for the rest of my life. I'd make damn certain that, for better or for worse, they'd be the making of me and not the ruin of me.

No way I'd be keeping in contact with any Stourbackers, definitely none of my Year in my House – a feeling that was no doubt mutual. Rebels, bullies, drunks, druggies, and idiots ruled in St Anselm's because the Housemaster, my mother's lover, allowed them to.

Many of them boasted about things they were planning to do on leaving. The difference, confidence-wise, is they were full of it and I had none of it. And hideous though my spell at Stourback had been, these boarding-schools were all I knew and were like little worlds of their own which I'd gotten used to. Pretty much all I wanted at that point was to feel secure as the uncertainty of the big wide World beckoned my fearful self.

I'd then spent more than a quarter of my life at Stourback and even with the family discount it had been outrageously expensive to attend, yet I honestly didn't sense that the education it had given me was better than I'd have got in the fee-free state system. I liked to think that at most other schools I'd not have been distracted from my studies due to relentless disrespect, though I did wonder if a flaw in my character meant that was to be my fate wherever I went. What I had learnt more than anything at Stourback was that too many of its staff and pupils were warped and/or unpleasant. In my day there were a few day pupils who weren't attached to any of the school's Houses, and their comparative anonymity might have suited me, but then time spent at home would have been with Dad – a far from ideal alternative.

My last year entailed a lot of wishing away the time til I could finally leave.

I didn't say goodbye to anyone in my House, and of course they didn't say goodbye to me either. I assumed they swaggered off not giving a moment's thought to any damage they'd inflicted on me.

It's hard to express the elation and relief I felt when Mum collected me from Stourback for the final time. Before being whisked back to her home, I asked her to drive me down the road which cut through Stourback's considerable acreage, and back. At the far end, on the edge of the monastic forest, I saw a Public Footpath sign with the l deliberately erased so it said Pubic Footpath. A silly schoolboy gag, but I laughed and laughed and laughed as if it was the funniest thing I'd ever seen. I guess that was like a valve finally being loosened and five years of tension released in a burst.

15.

YOU SIR, WITH LOVE

Among the big benefits of leaving school was finally being free to make decisions for myself. My first was to head south straight away. The 11 largely unhappy years I'd spent in Northumberland unfairly influenced negatively my view of that county, if not the North of England as a whole, and I was unable to even appreciate its famous scenery like tourists did. I now wanted to be as far from it as I could get.

Leaving was liberating in many ways. I was no longer put down on a daily basis - except on my occasional encounters with Dad - and I didn't have to keep looking over my shoulders for someone unpleasant creeping up behind me. In fact, it was like a tremendous weight was lifted from them as the pervading sense of peril dissipated. But I was still very much a weak and fearful person who, for all his upmarket costly education, had not yet learnt to be a man.

The vast majority of people I was around til the end of my teens were male, yet I had not one close trusted friend among them. I doubted I'd ever quite trust members of my own gender again knowing what they were capable of. Yet I did admire guys who gave off an inner strength that the likes of school bullies wouldn't even consider challenging. And I got to thinking that they were the ones most likely to live a long time as they could probably handle most of what might get thrown at them. No idea why but longevity was fascinating me then. When Elvis Presley, one of the most successful solo entertainers ever, died at the age of 42 in August 1977, I wondered if he'd have chosen to give up all the astounding achievements of his reasonably short existence in favour of a long life of anonymity. At that time, I myself fantasised about fame and fortune – though I'd no idea how I might attain it – yet, had I faced the aforementioned choice, I'd have still gone for the longevity option. But whatever was in store for me, manning up appeared to be a necessity.

Around that time, I overheard a conversation in which it was stated 'You can tell how much of a man a guy is by the firmness of his handshake.' Up to that point I'd never given any thought to my own handshake, and now I did think about it I realised it was worryingly limp. "Like a wet fish" someone described it to my embarrassment. So that was it – I decided that from then on I'd only show a strong grip. An opportunity to debut my macho Luke-shake soon cropped up at a cricket match on, of all places, the playing fields of Eton. Back at a top public school, one of 22 men in a sporting encounter, inevitably I wanted to show the others what I was now made of. I gave each offered hand an almighty squeeze, and in return some winced, others moaned, and all commented. Had I only done it to the opposing side, it might have helped secure victory, but my focus was on convincing everyone that this was a strong male they were playing with...even though it wasn't really.

In 1979, the American country music star Kenny Rogers topped the singles charts with his song Coward Of The County about an apparently lily-livered young man who gets pushed too far by bullies and eventually turns and fights, knocking them unconscious. I was never the type to fight physically – I really was too much of a coward for that – but I determined to prove myself in a positive way one day, and ideally become admired to some extent.

Another thing I was now free of in the real world was being governed by Catholicism. I'm certain I'd never have willingly embraced any religion, but I'd been coerced since birth to adhere to that one. So, from 18 and a half, being properly able to think for myself, I dismissed it. I wanted to only think for myself.

Officially non-religious as I was then, I remained open-minded about the existence of a God. After all, who was I to tell anyone what the truth was? In my opinion, none of us could know for sure.

By then, bizarre as it may seem, the only thing I liked about religion was the resemblance archetypal images of Jesus Christ's face had to that of my sports idol Bjorn Borg then. Probably because I felt I was facing a challenging life alone, fighting my own battles, I was fascinated by singles tennis matches and at the time Borg was the master of those. An incredible athlete with an ice cool temperament who famously kept his feelings in check so was hard to read. Above all, he was a champion who won pretty much everything, including the hearts of young women the World over. The only thing I then stood a chance of winning would have been a contest to find a living contrast to Mr Borg.

I was now well aware that most religious people follow the faith in which they are brought up, just as other kinds of beliefs are instilled in them by the families and communities in which they are reared. Certainly, it was my father on Earth rather than 'Our Father Who Art In Heaven' who led me into Catholicism. For me to be convinced by something, even as a youngster, I needed infinitely more persuasive an argument than the fact that my Dad was a believer, especially a Dad who disrespected me and only demonstrated Christian values professionally, not personally.

The hypocrisy of my father's behaviour was also demonstrated by inhabitants of Stourback Abbey, the other major imposer of Catholicism upon my life. As it was reputedly the planet's top Catholic school, I dreaded to think what the rest were like.

By now spending increasing amounts of time in her Northumberland home, Mum had embarked on a new affair with another member of the Stourback clergy: Fr Malcolm Banks, who just happened to be Fr.Anthony's replacement as Housemaster of St.Anselm's. So I now knew two priests who broke their vows of chastity to get intimate with my mother. They had both spent most of their lives reciting The Lord's Prayer with the line ***Lead us not into temptation***, and preaching such issues to the likes of me, yet evidently found their own physical urges too strong. Though unlike them I was yet to experience intimacy, I was aware how powerful the desire for it was, so understood why they had been led into temptation. But that's not to say I forgave it in their cases.

Lord knows, perhaps literally, what others among the Stourback monks and priests got up to. Many gave the impression they, more than anyone, had the absolute answers to existence, which struck me as unlikely seeing as they'd barely lived outside their monastery...and clearly were far from all being paragons of virtue. Some even came across as egotistical when I'd always understood they were supposed to be the epitome of modesty. While all that was enough to put me off Catholicism for life, I was never a believer in religion anyway,

What I did believe was that, however well-intentioned it was on my Dad's part, being forced into not just religion, but a particular religion, in my early life was unjust. At such an influential stage, that singular school of thought with its own attitudes and answers to life's key questions was imposed on me to the exclusion of others.

Despite walking away from Catholicism as my teens ended, having had that faith instilled in me throughout my youth was to always make it hard to shake off. For the following decade or so, I felt like an escapee from an institution whose strong searchlights sought me out in the forest of life as I tried to find my route to liberty.

However, I wasn't so brave as to walk away from most of what I was used to. Having only ever lived in boys' boarding-schools up until I left Stourback, what did I choose to do for my GAP Year but...work in a boys' boarding-school. In that respect I might have been on a Dad-pleasing mission or, when contemplating other options, my ears still resonated with his 'I wouldn't do that if I were you' warning. He helped me get the job of Junior Master in a distinguished Middlesex prep school, Olivedale, run by one of his golfing Head friends. At least it wasn't Catholic.

Many years mixing with, and on occasion even standing in for, staff at my Dad's schools meant it didn't feel too strange switching from pupil to teacher. Also, Olivedale teachers tended to wear similar outfits to Stourback boys: jacket, tie, shirt, trousers, socks and supposedly shiny shoes, all in dull, plain designs and colours which made the wearers look more than middle-aged.

The pupils here were aged eight to 13 and they weren't going to worry me at 18/19 as one of their teachers. Pre-teens I'd come across in my limited world were generally not troubled or trouble, definitely none at Olivedale in 1979/80. This privileged lot didn't need to play up as they had everything they could have wished for. I never saw a single case of homesickness and they were so impeccably behaved that they'd fall silent to a handclap - no shouts or bells required. So mercifully easy really, though that did make me a tad complacent and slack.

During my first supper in the staff dining-room, I made the worst start imaginable, picking up the tomato ketchup bottle and shaking it hard, not realising its top was loose. The sloppy red ingredients splattered over Karl Yeltsin who, being a fearsome senior languages master with a permanent frown, was the last person I'd knowingly have targeted. A few days later, while talking to Catherine Relf, another Olivedale veteran, she berated me for having my hands in my pockets and leaning against a wall. I was well used to being told off as a pupil, but it stung more as a staff member. In those days, if ever my shortcomings were pointed out to me, I took it badly inside though tried not to show it externally. But at least that showed I cared, that I didn't want to disappoint myself or others.

Otherwise, following a lifetime of disrespect at home and five years of it at Stourback, it was strange being spoken politely to by others. These well-mannered pupils had to call me 'Sir'. Oh my, finally I felt some courtesy coming my way, albeit from little schoolkids under my supervision. Unfortunately, not having matured myself and with a father who still treated me like a kid, I often felt more like a pupil than a master. I'd find myself joining in the boys' conversations, jokes and games. One lunchtime in the refectory, the lad at the opposite end of a table from me began pushing and pulling it, and to the great amusement of him and the 14 or so other boys sitting either side, I joined in. Big mistake. Olivedale had a tradition of letting the teachers out of the refectory first after every lunch. As I exited the refectory that day the deputy Head, Neil Monckton, a humourless slightly sinister character, was waiting for me with a withering put-down in front of my other colleagues, including "I don't know why you're here". It was one of the biggest humiliations of my life.

On the plus-side, I found I could relate to the children in the classroom, and vice versa. I was only given the youngest to teach, but it was a pleasant surprise to find they hung on my every word, did what I asked, and even laughed at my jokes. Best of all, some even announced – as innocent children are prone to do – that they loved me. In the most innocuous sense, of course, and probably because they were living away from those they really did love. I was given notes, cards, pictures and assorted gifts telling me this. Not valuable gifts in terms of money, but priceless to me in the fact that they said what I'd never heard or truly felt (other than from my Mum) before.

The boys seemed to enjoy my classes more than their other ones and most did well in tests and exams. Yet, maybe because I knew it was unlikely I'd pursue a career in teaching, I didn't put much effort in to planning lessons and writing reports. Regarding the latter I should have known better from the injustice I long felt at one unfair word in one report when I was at school. The father of a boy in my youngest class sought me out on an Open Day to dispute something pretty innocuous I'd written. As I hadn't given it any thought, I couldn't recall why I'd stated it, and I barely knew what to say. A lesson for me in the need to maintain good standards and do right by people whenever possible.

Another first for me was earning money. A small salary of course, but I was then still years from mortgages or bills, and it was nice to not have to rely on parental handouts at last. No mathematician, I was no saver either. With each pay packet I wandered into the local town centre and splashed out on my two favourite things: sweet foods and vinyl records. I'd then lounge around in my tiny room, playing the latest Bob Dylan LPs – though unfortunately this was his born-again phase – while stuffing my face with sweets, cakes, tins of rice pudding, and bowls of Angel Delight.

My pokey little room was at one end of a short staff corridor high up in the school building. The two neighbours were Junior Matrons of roughly my age, but while I quite fancied one I didn't do anything about it. The stupid thing was: for all those sex education classes, unofficially at Parkstone Prep and officially at Stourback, no-one had actually taught me anything about relationships....and presumably, in Catholic schools especially, they'd rather sex was only obtained within a relationship. I hadn't the first idea how to approach women and talk to them, let alone attempt to date them. These young Matrons were friendly towards me, and being already used to male attention courtesy of their more regular upbringing, clearly found my withdrawn nature strange. But I just felt safer in my small cocoon.

One evening, I returned to my room after supper to find the exotic 18-year old daughter of the Portuguese couple who ran the school kitchen lying seductively in my bed wearing scarlet lingerie. At any time a year or so on from then, I'd have been in seventh heaven thinking all my fantasies had come true. But at that moment I was appalled and urged her to leave immediately, which she did. All I could think of was that my personal space had been violated and, from the gales of laughter emanating from along the corridor and other staff on the floor below, it was mortifying that so many were in on a joke at my expense. In my head I was briefly back at Stourback being tormented, though I soon gathered this was merely an attempt to try and work out what I was about. I doubt it left them any the wiser.

Sex and relationships were a confusing mystery to me. Olivedale's Head, Stanley Dresser, and his pretty wife Kate were often larking around behind the scenes with another attractive couple who were their closest friends. There were rumours of wife-swapping, but I saw nothing of that and I'm not sure I'd have known what it was if I did. Deputy Head, Monckton, however was single and shifty. Every academic year he personally selected a bunch of boys to live in his house rather than sleep in the dormitories. It didn't seem right to me, but this was a man with a self-importance and stern demeanour that put him beyond reproach. Rather than question him, I just wanted to impress him. To my mind, he was Olivedale's equivalent of my father - dark-natured and impossible to please. I was put in charge of coaching the 2nd XI football team and, having attended rugby union-playing schools myself, I instructed the boys to split into a two-line tunnel through which they could applaud the opposition off the pitch at the end of a match. Rather than be pleased, the watching Monckton shook his head and hissed at me: "This is football, not rugby. Not here please". So I never asked my team to do it again.

Again I felt undermined, and in need of appreciation. I was drawn to newspaper and TV ads featuring a famous bodybuilder demonstrating what he claimed to be the cause of his impressive physique. Called a Bullworker, it was a spring-loaded exercise device about three feet long which you either compressed at both ends or pulled at the cables along each side to hopefully expand your upper body. Thinking this might make a man out of me, I ordered one hoping it would be discreetly left in the staff quarters or ideally delivered to my room. To my horror, it was handed to me in the school refectory as I supervised a table full of 11-year old boys. I immediately hid it under my chair in the hope no-one would notice. But for the rest of that breakfast I faced a barrage of "Ooh, what's that sir?" "Why don't you open it now?" "Can I see?" etc. Then the last thing I wanted to hear: "Sir, is that a Bullworker? I've seen them advertised on telly. They're for wimps who want to be butch!" Red-faced and mortified, I couldn't finish my food fast enough, grabbed my obvious-looking parcel and dashed up to the privacy of my room to unwrap it and begin my quest to become Mr Macho...which never quite happened as mastering this mechanism alone was a big challenge.

Sunday nights at Olivedale were Dinner Nights for the staff. We were expected to spend it in the Dressers' own dining-room, making polite conversation. I was socially inept and could not cope with small-talk, so I only attended two and otherwise hid in my room or deliberately delayed my weekends at home.

Nonetheless, that academic year passed by quicker than any I spent as a pupil. It was an interesting and generally positive experience.

On the final day of what they knew was my final term, my class sang For He's A Jolly Good Fellow to me. I was blown away. It was like the icing on the cake of unprecedented appreciation for me. As if that wasn't moving enough... Stephen Pottinger, a boy so shy he usually hid his head under his desk lid whenever I went near him, now approached me in the corridor with his right hand outstretched and said "Goodbye sir, thank you sir". The courage I knew it had taken for him to do that brought me to tears, which I was unable to stop as I said all my farewells after the best year of my life by then...as it had been a father, brother and bully free one.

I wouldn't have wanted to stay on longer than that year though. Too many staff I encountered at my Dad's schools and here had gotten reliant upon the security and routine they provided and become stuck for life, never sampling more than a smidgeon of what the outside world had to offer. At 19, I had finally outgrown boarding-school bubbles and looked forward to expanding my horizons. But, as a final fling as it were, I accepted an invitation to tutor and teach tennis to an Olivedale pupil whose parents expected more from him. They were a rich, well-known-in-their-field family with a country house in countless Hampshire acres where they kept horses. Also staying with them then was a heavenly French girl in her late teens, aptly named Angelique. I had never seen a living creature with so perfect a face. It was instant infatuation. I totally lost my appetite. I didn't even want to eat sweets. I was just awestruck by her appearance. But I didn't for the life of me know what to do about it.

The daughter of the family and her French boyfriend invited myself and Angelique to a screening of the film Fame in London's West End. I saw this as my opportunity, and decided on a move I'd seen male characters in cinema scenes make on females they fancied... Never having had any encouragement from Angelique whatsoever, shortly into the movie I slipped my arm around her shoulders. She pushed it away. A few minutes later, I tried again, even attempting to stroke her head too. Same reaction. She was having none of it. I spent the rest of the film, journey home and stay with this family feeling humiliated and wondering what I was supposed to do instead. Angelique kept her distance from me. Ever since I've cringed and winced that I was so naive to approach the poor girl that way. It was excruciating, yet I knew no better. I guess I must, in my utter naivety, have been under the misapprehension that if you fancied someone they'd fancy you back. I couldn't have been more wrong. How different life would be were that the case, and were it like it was literally in the movies, certainly for me whose ability to learn anything required logic and consistency. With matters like that, as I hadn't learnt in my youth, I was clearly going to have to learn as an adult as I went along...usually from my mistakes.

I used to think my brother Matthew had made a smart move in leaving Stourback early in that he escaped the confines of public school and Catholicism to live a regular life, and above all because he attained invaluable experience of the opposite sex...and sex. Yet, when in the Summer of 1980, he married Mary, even completely inexperienced me knew their relationship had no hope of lasting. They bickered constantly, for starters, but above all they were way too young. The wedding took place in the Abbey Church at Stourback, and I used my role as an usher as an excuse to not even enter the building. In his remarkably relaxed speech, Best Man Mark cleverly quipped of Matthew, who shared my disinterest in religion (albeit little else): "How nice to see him back in church again!", though that would turn out to be the last time except for other weddings, and funerals.

The first girlfriend of Mark that I got to meet was not what I expected at all. She was named Isla and known as Skye, which was surprising given her lack of humour. When Mark brought her home to meet us – in the family flat at Cardinal's School - my parents and I envisaged a goddess befitting the hero of our family. Instead before us stood a very ordinary looking woman with protruding teeth, a pasty complexion, a dated dark bob, and a coy manner which a celebrated Lady would soon make famous. Mum and Dad were instantly all over her as they were always going to be towards anyone Mark was attached to. But while she made some effort towards our parents, she was from the outset odd towards me. It's hard to put her conduct into words, except ones such as 'devious' and 'manipulative'. More sly than Skye to me. Yes, she was very religious, but as with too many Catholics I'd met by then, she was clearly not a nice person. It didn't take me long to realise there was something not quite right about her too. Publicly she played the innocent to a tee, yet she wasn't just awkward, she was aloof, condescending and rude. I said as much to Mum after Mark and Isla had left that evening, and disappointingly she leapt to their defence.

"At least Mark's got a girlfriend!" was her retort – something I took as a hint that she thought me a failure or homosexual, or both. It's possible Mum didn't mean it as more than an off-the-cuff remark, but those six words would hurt me deeply for ages after, because they came from my mother, my confidante, probably the only person I'd ever felt close to up to that point. I thought 'How exactly does she expect me to find a girlfriend seeing as I only have brothers, I've only lived in isolated boys' boarding-schools and attended them as a pupil, and – almost entirely due to my family's treatment of me – I am devoid of any self-worth whatsoever? Anyway, it's not like you can just pop out, find a girl you like and bring her home (like cavemen brandishing clubs once did, according to legend). Definitely not in the remote places we've lived in.'

Such was Mark's status as the family idol, our parents immediately elevated his girlfriend to a position above me and Matthew. It was a case of 'Yes Isla, no Isla, three bags full Isla', while as always it remained 'No Luke. Not you. No chance.' Isla not only noticed it, she secretly gloated about it – her equivalent of Mark's '25 wins to me...' boasts when he and I were competitive kids. Like when you see a cheeky child pretending to be quite the angel in front of parents and strangers, yet when those backs are turned sticking a tongue out and/or giving a centre finger salute. I tried pointing out Isla's duplicity to my parents but they were having none of it. Rather, they insisted I "respect her". She was Mark's girlfriend and, as Mark was the Twigg equivalent of royalty, riffraff like myself were obliged to not say or do anything to displease him. So Isla got away with murder. To my mind, her weird conduct should have been nipped in the bud like John McEnroe's misbehaviour at Wimbledon around then should have seen him thrown out of the event the first time, then he'd never have done it again because he wouldn't have wanted to miss THE tennis tournament all players wanted to win.

At that point in time, Mark had it all – looks, confidence, charm, sporting prowess, the lot – and could probably have had any woman he wanted. Yet the one woman he wanted was awful Isla. I could only imagine that her appeal to Mark was her status as a devout Catholic and therefore as a virgin. It was surely never her appearance or personality.

Mark's misguided idealism showed itself in a different form as 1981 approached. He discovered that our parents would soon be 25 years married, and he felt that worthy of a special celebration. I knew it was the last thing they themselves wanted, and perhaps to put Mark in the picture aside from anything else they soon announced their separation. Dad would remain in the South of England while Mum would move permanently to Northumberland. I knew that was so she'd be close to Fr Malcolm, about whom she now thought and talked to me incessantly.

Mum soaked up the best-selling book and hit TV series of The Thorn Birds, released in 1977 and 1983 respectively, telling the story of a woman's affair with a Catholic priest. She even liked the coincidence that one of the main characters had the same first name as me.

Ironically, when parting from Dad, Mum decided to convert to Catholicism - to doubtless feel closer to her lovers, maybe better understand them, despite the fact that bedding priests went against all that religion stood for.

Dad was by now as morose as he'd ever been, constantly complaining about things he disapproved of. When he really wanted to make a point, he'd use exaggerated terminology like 'utterly despicable' and 'absolutely disgraceful' which the situations he referred to rarely were. One evening he returned from Wimbledon where he'd taken a group of kids from Cardinal's to watch the tennis. He was fuming because one of them had asked a former champion for an autograph, and she'd not only refused but told the boy to leave her alone. I tried to explain to Dad that neither he nor Jennings Junior can have known what was happening in that player's life at that time, even in the preceding minutes, and although she was an international star she was still only a human being with feelings. He wasn't having any of that. "Well, she showed no feelings towards the poor boy" he raged. "No, she was just downright rude. I'm going to write and tell her so." He duly did as well, and was even more livid when unsurprisingly she didn't respond.

On another occasion when he blew something trivial into a catastrophe in his head, Dad stormed out of a room shouting "Sometimes I wish I was dead!" Later, with trepidation, I told him I thought that a terrible thing to say...then waited for the inevitable backlash. "What would you know, you horrid child? You've not got the first idea what I have to put up with in life!" I'd heard such things from him umpteen times by then – and this 'child' would soon no longer even be a teenager - but they all still hurt.

Then Mum confided to me that Dad told her he had never loved her. Yet they were married for a quarter of a century. I couldn't imagine how that made Mum feel, but it made me very sad. Sad that she married him in the first place, sad that they were together all that time when she could have been with someone else who did love her, and sad that he would actually tell her that. What a wicked, heartless low blow. It was high time Mum and I both left him to stew in his own misery.

That Mum fared better than Dad after they separated neither surprised nor disappointed me. In fact, I was glad. I wanted her to be happy and him to be unhappy…because that's how he'd made me, and Mum, countless times.

Newly-single Mum made friends easily. One was a female aristocrat who, while only in her 40s, committed suicide. I was baffled as to why a titled lady with a lifestyle beyond the wildest dreams of most people would kill herself. Mum explained that her 'beautiful' friend had dreaded getting old physically, which baffled me even more. Such aspects of life never occurred to me then. For the first time I was looking forward with optimism and a determination to keep progressing and never giving up.

16.

FINALLY IN BLUE JEANS

When it was my turn to decide where to study for a degree, I hadn't achieved the required A'Level grades to do the entrance exams for Oxford or Cambridge Universities. I'd only have gone the Oxbridge route to please Dad anyway, and I'd got to the stage where I enjoyed displeasing him as I was no longer under his roof and therefore jurisdiction. Moreover, of all the universities in the World, those two would have most represented an extension of Stourback, and that was the last thing I needed. I had to stay out of that rut.

I chose to follow Mark to The Dorothy Byrnes College (aka Dotty's) at South London Institute (or SLI). Its ratio of female to male students obviously compared very favourably to Stourback, and would hopefully mean even I could finally get a girlfriend and Mum could never again knock me for not having one. If I followed Mark there in the hope of having him look after me, I must have inexplicably forgotten his glaring failure to do so at Stourback. But he and I now teamed up for two-bedroom student accommodation in nearby Putney Heath, and thankfully we got on better than we had when sharing a bedroom as kids. That was probably because I was marginally more mature by then. Only marginally, mind.

Our elderly landlord Terry was proud – some might say boastful – of the fact that he was a successful sculptor, that Ginger Rogers had once visited his studio, that a friend of David Frost lived next door, and that he (Terry) had a much younger girlfriend. However, he wasn't too pleased when his dog greeted me first and, after checking its name tag, I called out "Stringer! What a good name for a Springer!" Snooty-faced Terry sternly put me right. "That's not his name on the disc. That's my name." Oh Lordy, I'd put one of my clumsy Size 11s in it again.

I remained naive in the extreme. For example when, like my fellow Freshers, I was welcomed to the College by a young priest issuing instructions about a compulsory medical taking place the following day, I really did feel flashbacks to my nerve-wracked first week at public school. Until I was told this was actually a hoax from a student from Mark's year posing as a member of the clergy.

The next morning, as we Freshers all exited a large lecture hall after an introductory talk by the Student Union President, Celia Kelly, Concorde flew overhead and half the crowd stared at the sky in awe and gasped. Having worked in Middlesex the previous year, I was among those who'd seen the distinctive revolutionary aeroplane many times before. But that was about the only area in which I might have been considered experienced compared to the majority of other Freshers.

They all already seemed to me to be pretty comfortable in this new environment, as I stood alone watching them chitter-chatter away to each other. And in such an array of accents, which was a surprise to my ears after years of hearing almost exclusively 'posh' boarding-school tones. Different voices in terms of pitch too. Then I noticed how many around me had long hair...and it really dawned on me I was surrounded by young women – masses of them. There were a fair few guys around, but I wasn't looking at them.

For me, the highlight of Fresher's Week was that evening's coach tour around the sights of London. It was fun having the capital's landmarks pointed out with student humour. I sat in a double seat on my own, but unlike at Stourback I felt I was among friendly folk, maybe because they were mainly female. I was impressed seeing on the wide back seat of the coach a guy sprawled in a very self-assured fashion, sporting trendy clothes and a coolly tilted fedora, and with women either side of him hanging on his arms and every word.

The coach tour was followed by the Fresher's Disco. I was only a few months from turning 20 yet I'd never been to a disco before

- they wouldn't have been appropriate at the all boys' boarding schools I'd been at - so I'd never danced before either. Looking around me now, I didn't just sense I was the only inexperienced partygoer at Dotty's, but probably in the entire civilised world. And I couldn't envisage myself ever giving dancing a go, because it clearly entailed letting yourself go – another thing I'd never done before. Most guys I could see were clutching opened bottles of beer, and most of the women glasses of wine. I wasn't sure whether or not alcohol helped them dance, and I wasn't even tempted to find out for myself. Some here were naturally rhythmic, but the majority ranged from okay to utterly uncoordinated and I reckoned I'd rather not try at all than fit into the latter category. So a wallflower I was to be then.

As I literally propped myself up against an unoccupied area of wall, I was very conscious, self-conscious, of being alone while everyone else either already knew one another or effortlessly integrated. Judging by the fact that no-one was looking my way let alone coming up to introduce themselves, I wondered if I was just destined to be an outsider, if not invisible to most others. However, my eyes were swiftly drawn to a shapely lass across the room who I overheard being called Bridget. I glanced at her sporadically from my distance, but she didn't notice. I didn't know what else to do. I certainly didn't have the guts to go over to her. I wouldn't have known what to say or how to behave if I did. In fact, I didn't approach anyone present as, due to my past, I only anticipated disinterest or rejection. So, after half an hour, I slipped out of the party and walked home to my digs a mile away, stopping en route at a petrol station shop to buy a pack of cakes and immediately ate the lot. I was disappointed at my social ineptness, that I didn't have the nerve to even say hello to the likes of Bridget, and that I needed comforting by sweet food. The fact that pretty much every other student I encountered drank alcohol made them at least seem more mature and relaxed than me. There was I, in contrast, sober, anxious and insecure, and childishly reaching for sweeties to raise my spirits.

I thought about the guy in the hat on the coach, who I'd also seen charming ladies at the disco. I was fascinated because this outwardly confident, cocksure student had an unusual angular face atop a scrawny frame, and I couldn't work out what he had to hold these women in his thrall. It quite mystified me because, in every story I'd read or seen, only handsome macho men got girls.

Some kind folk occasionally said I was good-looking – and thank goodness I had that asset - but a lifetime of being made to feel ugly by those who should have loved me was entrenched in my psyche. So I wasn't yet feeling appealing, or most specifically like a man. I still felt like a boy, behaved like a boy, and dressed like a boy…a public schoolboy. And sounded like one too. Which meant that at SLI, where the vast majority of students were from very ordinary backgrounds, I stood out like a sore thumb. A few of the guys seemed to take an instant distrust – if not dislike - to me because of that. Ironic really because I'd hated my public school experience and wished I'd gone to 'normal' co-educational schools like them, partly as I'd probably then have also got into the dating game in my early teens. But no sign yet from them of the testosterone competition or unpleasantness so prevalent at Stourback. And I already sensed that here, if I was to experience difficulties, as these guys lived on campus and I didn't, it was unlikely there'd be problems between us, and I really would be able to walk away and have somewhere else to go. Naturally I'd rather they liked, even befriended, me. I loathed the thought that, if ever I left people I'd just been in the company of, they'd then say "What a jerk!" or something to that effect. At school I hadn't just suspected that was the case, I knew it was. I longed for people to think and speak highly of me, whether to my face or behind my back.

Lessons in socialising and conversation, and ideally relationships, at school would have served the likes of me infinitely better than Religious Studies or Latin, to name but two subjects I could happily have done without. Desperately hoping I might finally fit in somewhere, I tried hard to think of something to say to my fellow students. I reverted to a stock Stourback and Olivedale question: "What does your father do for a living?" That was all very well when the Dads were top politicians, captains of industry, High Court judges, celebrities, etcetera. But this lot were offspring of ordinary folk, and offended at my well-intentioned enquiry. What's more, with so many women among them, they quite rightly wanted to know why I didn't enquire of their mothers' occupations too. Anyway of course it wasn't as if I was proud of my Dad irrespective of what his job was.

My own insecurities aside, the overriding vibe here was casual. I was to study English and History for my degree, and the workload was ridiculously light involving only three lectures a week, three essays a term, and three exams a year. That was extremely helpful as it gave me much-needed time to devote to the education I needed most, in normal life...and the fairer sex.

The tutors bore little resemblance to teachers I'd had at school. You addressed them by their first names, which took some getting used to. My English tutor was very 'right-on' from his attitudes to his dress sense, and very Left-wing politically. Camp, sandal-wearing Steve I struggled to take seriously from the moment he said of a Dickens' classic: "It's obvious why he called it HARD Times", and what he's telling us about that character when he's touching that knob – it's clearly not just part of a door..." Was Steve rather than Charles not the sex-obsessed one? For all anyone of us present knew, maybe no such double entendres even entered Dickens' head. When I watched footage of Bob Dylan in his 1960s heyday being asked in press conferences about deep meanings behind his lyrics, I noticed he smirked and giggled. A mixture of embarrassment and amusement, I suspected, because he'd probably chosen certain words and lines because they rhymed rather than held any significance. But that was merely my theory.

Too shy to be sociable, and not actually knowing how to make friends, I initially spent much of my spare time observing others or standing in the College common room playing the trendy arcade game of the day, Space Invaders. Even doing that got me overthinking, as I always tended to do when alone – this time about what I'd come to call my Mind Games. I thought then how many forms of popular competition are representative of life itself, and wondered if that was partly why those competitions were popular. For example, Space Invaders required avoiding obstacles of increasing difficulty as you progressed to higher levels while striving towards bigger goals. Bagatelle / Pinball, which I'd watched and played in my Seventies childhood…I sometimes felt like that silver ball shot into a bewildering world where I was shoved from pillar to post. For those who don't go for the 'We choose our own parents' theory, the circumstances into which we are born are a Lottery. The board game Snakes And Ladders is of course reflective of life's ups and downs, of how fortunes can change for the better or worse depending on how the dice roll for you.

Occasional references to death which people made during my life thus far included 'When you're time is up', and that reminded me of boating on a lake for 30 minutes or whatever until the call of 'Come in No.9, your time is up' came. Perhaps I hoped my eventual end would be that simple and peaceful, and that it wouldn't come when I still wished I had more time.

The only way in which I contemplated suicide was in wondering whether people who attempted or committed it believed it actually was the end of everything, or if they thought their spirit might return in a new body for another chance at life. Using my game analogies, I viewed the latter like a Scrabble player putting their allotted letters back in the bag and hoping the replacements would give them more chance of winning.

Perhaps it was the term 'The Human Race' which got me thinking about the most obvious one, because I now viewed existence as a steeplechase – except there is no race or competition as such; just hurdles to be overcome in order for progress to be made. For as long as The Human Race exists, this steeplechase is ongoing. Each individual person starts the race when they are born, and finishes it when they die. The only official start was the beginning of The Human Race, and the only official finish will be the end of The Human Race. Depending on what you believe, the reward for participating in the steeplechase of life is the journey itself, or maybe to be found once your life is over.

All those plays and films I'd watch of a certain duration – usually a couple of hours – and now I was seeing existence like that. Humans were players in the play of life, with no set script, entering the stage at birth, having a limited time in which to perform with sets and scenarios and other cast members before exiting when our final curtain falls.

Most of my thoughts though were about members of the female species, and how I might finally land one to call my own. But I was befuddled as to how. Without guidance from a person or book, I could only learn from what I witnessed…which was precious little.

A youth spent with only brothers living in boys' boarding schools meant that I at 20 was merely at the stage most lads reached in their early teens: clueless about girls and forming relationships with them. That was embarrassing, mortifying at times.

Even a basic education in attraction would have made it a million times easier for lots of guys like me, I was sure. But as my school teachers had included many oddball bachelors, mostly members of the clergy who – ironically excluding those intimate with women like my Mum – wouldn't have known where to start talking about relationships and sex.

My Dad, who of course had gone to the same school when the prospect of such lessons would have been far less likely, was never going to be a role model in that department. Too many times I'd watched him trying pitifully to pull women. Those memories stuck in my mind not just because they were cringey, but because he'd done it in front of Mum when they were married - humiliating her. I didn't want to be a failure with the fairer sex like my father but I feared I might be.

There'd been a brief period in my early teens / my brother Matthew's late teens when he appeared popular on that front. As he was then scruffy, lazy and not very bright, I couldn't see any obvious allure...though of course I wasn't female, and I was his little brother. However, I did notice they seemed to like the fact that he rode a motorbike. Maybe to ensure they were aware he had one, he would rev its engine a lot in their company. If that was some form of mating call, it was not one I was ever likely to employ. Motorbikes were scary to me, fitting right into our Dad's 'I wouldn't do that if I were you' category...which may have been a reason Matthew got one. Neither could I see any appeal in the noise they made, nor why bikers often tended to make as much of it as possible as they rode them. How could the roar of engines get girls going weak at the knees? That was beyond me. The only loud I liked was when I turned my music up, and I definitely didn't 'do' danger. Besides, when women I now knew encountered the revving biker kind, they'd employ words like the one that rhymes with banker.

My other brother Mark, of course, had long won everyone – male or female – over with his stories, jokes, impressions...anything. But the key was he did it all with self-belief. Whenever I attempted to do the same, my lack of confidence meant I never got positive reactions like he did. However, here we both were at a College with such a majority of female students, it surely wouldn't be long before my luck would improve.

In my ideal world I'd just find a girl I fancied, walk up to her and, if she made it clear she fancied me too, I'd take her out on a date or straight to bed. No questions, no games. Yet I was finding the reality so much more complicated.

The age-old basic unofficial ritual whereby we humans glance at someone we are attracted to and hope they look back to confirm mutual interest...well, I needed that more than most, for extra reassurance. I could tell it was easier for confident men, but I wasn't one of them. Maybe the only real barrier was in my own head, which was choc-full of thoughts and theories, but also damaging self-doubt.

In my ignorance, I was convinced that one's ability to attract was determined by how good-looking one was. In most films, television and theatre shows I watched, the handsome leading man tended to land the beautiful leading lady. No person or book had informed me of key issues such as it's not about how you look on the outside, it's how you feel on the inside and how you come across. I looked okay but felt awful about myself, and came across as anxious and insecure...because that's what I was. I'd talk a lot – and a lot of sh*t – through sheer nerves. Rather than sweet-talking the ladies, I was more likely to put them off through inane chatter. I so wished I had the patience, intelligence and wit to say exactly the right things at the right time...like leading men did on screen. I overlooked the fact that those were actors spouting lines written for them, and how it was then all edited to add a flawless finish.

Maybe having absorbed childhood stories of dashing young men being so heroic as to win over beautiful women, I did believe it vital to impress those I wanted to attract. I watched fascinated when men, whether in real or fictional situations, would present women they were interested in with flowers, chocolates, wine or whatever. To me, it was clichéd and embarrassing, and suggested you felt you didn't have enough to offer personally, and were trying to buy love from the outset. And I also considered it an unwise move unless you were sure the attraction was mutual, as most students didn't have much money. I'd heard enough stories of pretty young things swept off their feet by ugly but wealthy men to know love could be bought...but my bank accounts got all too often overdrawn as it was.

There were lots of song lyrics written and sung by men overtly professing their adoration of women, which were they spoken in actual situations were more likely to have had the recipients running for the hills rather than swooning in gratitude. Also, I'd read in books and seen on TV and films that guys got the girl by being persistent. When I tried it, my persistent seemed more like pest, which was the last thing either I or the women I was keen on wanted.

Usually believing no-one would be attracted to me, I'd go out and try to attract. Really try. Try to amuse mainly, often making a fool of myself. I tried to amuse because I kept hearing that what most attracted females to males was a good sense of humour...though I doubted mine would ever be regarded as good.

So the likelihood was that, if I was to get a girlfriend, she would need to pursue me rather than the other way round. Indeed, I'd only been at SLI a few weeks when a girl from my English group made herself known to me with noticeable excitement. Her name was Sarah Rusk, she had a lisp, regarded herself as very religious and was therefore mightily impressed I'd attended Stourback, "THE Catholic School" she called it. Sarah was engaged to be married, as quite a number of these Catholic girls were on starting at Dotty's – though, as I'd discover, hardly any still were on finishing. Because of her betrothal I thought nothing of the enthusiasm Sarah showed...even when she asked if she could join me at my flat one evening "to listen to records". An even slightly older me would have jumped to a very different conclusion at such an invitation, but these were still innocent times for Luke Twigg.

I had supper with Sarah in the College canteen, during which I took a medicinal lemon drink for a sore throat, then we wandered down the road to the flat I shared with Mark...who fortunately was out. Sarah had brought a little stack of vinyl LPs, including one featuring the Bellamy Brothers' track If I Said You Had A Beautiful Body, Would You Hold It Against Me? Sarah stuck that on, then turned from the turntable and asked for a cuddle. My reaction? I threw up. Three times! Not because of the cheesiness of the record she'd selected; it was sheer nerves at being invited to get close to a female for the first time in my life. Yet as I stared in shock at the oversized pizza puddles I'd projected on to the floor, I didn't know what to make of it. Nor did Sarah. However, she not only cuddled but kissed me afterwards, which was a sure indication of her keenness because there can't be many humans willing to snog a mouth from which vomit had been emitted just minutes before.

Nerves as well as naivety were to rule, and ruin, relationships I embarked upon. As for the elusive Holy Grail of sex, well.... Catholicism and its clergy at Stourback had done their best to try and persuade the likes of me that that was off-limits outside marriage. Yet knowing that two of those clergymen had themselves been having non-marital, vow-breaking, intercourse with my own mother, and that both my Catholic parents had indulged in affairs, at least meant I saw through that. And such was the overwhelming power of sexual desire, any guilt trips in my head would have stood no chance against it.

Not so Sarah Rusk. Wracked by Catholic guilt more than the fact that she had a fiancée, she would never allow anything beyond passionate kissing – and that only from the neck upwards. On a unique occasion when I eventually got to lie beside her, the moment my hands wandered under her blouse and in the direction of her bra, she got positively shirty and called a halt to the proceedings. I remember thinking: "I've waited all this time to finally bed a woman and she won't let me do the deed. Damn Catholicism again!" And also: "If this is anything to go by, maybe females don't want sex like us males do, and will always need persuading to partake."

A tactic I learnt when wanting to lay with a woman, ideally for the night, was to say "I promise I won't try it on...I'm happy just to be with you, to look at you, maybe kiss you...nothing more". If they took you at your word, you'd then be expected to stick to it. For the first hour or so that was do-able, but after a while restraint became increasingly difficult. Then, if you broke your promise and made a move, you'd usually be turfed out of the bed, the room, and sometimes the relationship.

Sarah Rusk didn't fall for it, and ditto my next object of desire, Rosie Turner. We got off to a good start when, on my unusual choice of a first date at a Crystal Palace versus Manchester United match, she clutched my arm in the stands at Selhurst Park which sent right through me a personal thrill akin to what the home supporters showed when Palace fired the ball into United's net. But in the ensuing couple of months I never got to see Rosie unclothed either. She'd happily kiss, but there was to be no proper canoodling with her. Worse, a Scottish friend of Isla started circling her like a testosterone shark. Despite being my middle brother's long-term love, and a religious nut, Isla encouraged this theft of my fledgling girlfriend and I was left bereft. If I hadn't already had it with Catholicism, which she portrayed herself as a devoted disciple of, I definitely had now.

I wished some other guy would steal Isla away from Mark – anything to get us shot of her. Whether knowing that gave her extra motivation, Isla displayed conceit that she'd bagged one of the small group of male students, and a popular, handsome, confident one at that. Me being the introvert I was, I marvelled at the chutzpah oozing from Mark as he hosted student cabarets and led Dotty's rugby team's post-match bawdy singsongs in the bar. He was so sure of himself I couldn't imagine him ever getting his heart broken, only being the heartbreaker.

A skinny blonde student from one of the other three SLI colleges seemed more laid back and worldly. This was Sheena West whose blonde ringlets flanked a flat but pretty face that almost mirrored my own. The fact that she never seemed to be wearing a bra over her almost-as-flat chest, coupled with the way she looked at me in seminars, suggested a woman who'd been round the block several times before Sarah Rusk ever got to taking her B-Cup off in front of a bloke. In fact, Sheena's apparent sexiness scared me as much as it thrilled me. The more attractive I found a woman, the more I was frightened of them and the heartbreak and humiliation they could potentially cause me - in a 'the bigger they are, the harder they fall' kind of way.

Once I'd fixed a date with Sheena, I decided to seek tips from an older, female, student at my own College who'd proven approachable thus far. Advice about turning a date into a relationship, basically. "You need to ask her if she'll go out with you" was the advice. I didn't feel comfortable asking such a question – in fact, I hated the idea – but, hey, if that was what needed to be said, then say it I must. In the dread-filled 24 hours or so leading up to the date, I practised the line 'Would you like to go out with me?' time after time. And, as I waited anxiously to meet with Sheena, I kept wondering when the best moment would be to pop my question. Hoping to expunge all memory of my only previous cinema outing with a young woman (Angelique), I took Sheena to Hammersmith to see a silly horror film starring Susan George and Oliver Reed. It may not have been quite so terrible had I not spent the entire time worrying about THAT question. Which meant, rather than do something more romantic post-movie such as go for a drink or walk by the river, I hurried Sheena back to her College on the tube and, as we turned into the road where her accommodation block was located, I finally uttered the required words: "Will you go out with me?" They did not have the desired effect. Sheena stopped in her tracks, looked at me with bemusement and said "What???" Unwisely I repeated the question. "But we've just been out..." she pointed out, with perfect justification. I was stunned. Mortified. It was as if I'd opened a window to allow a fierce gust of wind to blow away everything I'd been hoping for. I couldn't think of anything to say to Sheena after that. Nothing coherent anyway. Certainly nothing that could heal the damage and paper over the mistake I'd made. Generously in the circumstances, Sheena asked me up to her room for a coffee, but by then I felt so livid with myself that I sloped off home after a few minutes assuming I'd completely blown it. The next day a mutual friend sought me out and asked what on earth I'd said what I said for. I explained I'd been advised to. I later discover that the student I'd taken advice from had little or no experience of relationships herself, and from what I can gather still hasn't decades on.

I often regretted what happened that night. If I was in a movie in which my character could go back to chosen moments in time and change things, that would be one of mine. Although I'd not done anything unpleasant or harmful, such was my absence of confidence that I didn't believe the situation could be salvaged, assuming that, as Sheena now knew what a naïve numbskull I was, her interest in me had now evaporated for good. I wished I had what it took to prove otherwise, but I didn't.

I almost had a chance to make amends a few weeks later. Not with Sheena, but with her best mate Julie who somehow also emerged as date material. Perhaps it was a plan they hatched to see if I really was that inept. Anyway, the Sheena experience had rattled me to the extent that I'd become fixated on how I came across. Ever since I was called 'boring' at school (even though only by one person), I'd got it into my head that that was because I had nothing to say, certainly nothing interesting. I didn't even try to explain then or anytime since that when I had attempted to contribute to conversations as a child, my Dad mocked me and shot me down in flames... And if my own father felt a need to do that... Then of course my nervous blurting was getting me into difficulties occasionally. But the 'boring' tag haunted me, made me fearful of silences – specifically that I might be the reason for them. Maybe others had nothing to say to me either and were bored. It didn't occur to me that it may have meant they actually felt comfortable in my presence and didn't need to talk. Cool, monosyllabic types scared me, made me do the opposite: gabble. All those Clint-style men of few words I'd watched on screen sweeping beautiful women off their feet, yet I continued gabbling at them like an anxious idiot and getting nowhere. What I certainly didn't want happening on a date was conversation dying. My ideal was easy flowing banter. The slightest breaks in chat were concerns for me, and needed urgently filling...even if with any claptrap. And then there was that old adage about the way to win a woman over was to make her laugh.

So for this evening, rather than rehearse a heavy proposal like with Sheena, I decided to tell Julie a load of anecdotes I thought she'd be amused by. I practised these stories too, even figuring a revision-style method of remembering them. Problem was I started reeling them off as we stood waiting for a frustratingly delayed bus to whisk us away (neither of us could drive, let alone owned a car), and by the time the bus finally did arrive I'd exhausted my entire repertoire, and Julie, in the process.

Presumably dates were supposed to be things you looked forward to, but I now regarded them as dreaded ordeals, sure I'd make an ass of myself and get rejected.

It may have been a blessing in disguise that I never got Sheena or Julie back to my place. If they weren't already convinced I was a sad dork, they would have been the moment they saw the giant poster at the head-end of my single bed: a home-made collage of press pictures of Lady Diana Spencer, my big celebrity crush at that time. How annoyed I was when, during the press-call for their engagement, Prince Charles awkwardly remarked "Whatever in love means". I remember thinking I'd take infinitely greater care of Diana if only she knew me.

Ditto, when I saw Sheena in an intimate embrace at yet another College disco I'd attended in the forlorn hope of regaining her interest, I was deflated to detect that the man in question looked like he didn't give two hoots for her...yet she was evidently smitten. I could not fathom why she'd prefer to be with someone who'd treat her like dirt rather than someone – ie.me - who'd treat her like a princess.

I was also bewildered when heavenly redhead Jen Church, who I did my best to win over, opted instead for a guy who so closely resembled a bashed up car that he was nicknamed Banger...at least I think that's why he got called that. Few would have disagreed that Banger was far from the handsomest bloke around, yet he exuded confidence, even swagger...and worse, as Sleazy put it so delicately, Banger got to 'bang' Jen Church and I didn't. How did he manage to win over this cutie I practically idolised? I couldn't compute it.

I sometimes thought I looked nice on the outside, but I didn't think I had much else going for me. In fact, I was sure I didn't. The likes of Banger not only absolutely believed he had every right to date a babe like Jen Church, he thought her lucky to have him.

From then on, if a girl I fancied preferred other men, I'd take a close look at those guys and see what they had that I didn't. That usually boiled down to comfort in their own skin, so that became my aim. But wanting it was one thing and achieving it something else altogether.

To my frustration, I was finding relationships complicated, unpredictable, almost impossible to attain. I longed to discover a formula for cracking them and knew I had to persevere.

The first sunshine of my first Spring at SLI, I sat alone on a bench on the lawn at Dotty's supposedly reading one of the set books from my English course. It was a literary classic I hoped might draw an attractive interested party, so I held it an angle that made the title visible. Incredibly, it didn't take long before a female student wandered over to me, though not in connection with Wuthering Heights. "Sorry to bother you" she said, "but I've seen you around occasionally and I notice you always wear corduroy trousers. I hope you won't mind me saying but they're very old-fashioned and I think you'd look much better in jeans." Pippa from Wakefield, it turned out, making an approach many would have considered cheeky, but which I found kind and courageous and very much appreciated. That weekend we went shopping in busy Oxford Street to buy my first pair of denims, enabling me to take a little step forward from public school stereotype to student stereotype. It didn't take long to find some – not nearly as long as it took me to get used to wearing them after a decade of cords and flannels.

While we were in the West End, Pippa told me she wanted to get a Memory Board. Feeling indebted, I immediately dashed into WH Smith and bought her a popular-at-the-time wall-mountable notice board (with a marker pen attached) on which reminders were written. But she didn't receive it with the delight I'd anticipated. The noise of London's main road of shops meant I'd misheard her wish for an Emery Board, a very different item I hadn't known the name of anyway. Trivial though that seemed to me, I think it put paid to any interest Pippa might have harboured. Our afternoon excursion was not the start of a romance or even a friendship. In fact, I barely recall seeing Pippa again after that, which suggested I wasn't the guy she'd hoped I'd be. No surprise there.

The best thing that could have happened to me at this stage in my life would have been for a well-meaning person such as Pippa to show me the ropes, to gently coax me out of my shy self, to turn me from nervous nerd into at least a semblance of a regular relaxed guy with some element of worldliness. I could imagine that being the subject of a romcom featuring a badly dressed stammering twit taken firmly in hand by a brassy dominant woman who won't take no for an answer. But in the real world people didn't tend to do that, and I wasn't sure if many other guys would welcome it.

So it was mainly up to me to watch and learn, from my own experiences and what I could see of others. And something I did notice, particularly being among the minority gender here at Dotty's, was that guys behave very differently in the presence of girls, definitely when outnumbered by them. Groups of male students would often be full of blokey bravado, especially when talking about certain females. Yet when joined by or within earshot of women they'd be much more careful and respectful. On one memorable occasion, a crude lad known as Sleazy was boasting to his pals about a pretty student they were admiring in the distance: "If she was my bird, we'd be at it all day and all night for weeks on end, and still she'd be begging for more!" He was then tapped on the shoulder by her best friend who was standing behind him and heard every word. "Oh yeah" she said, "Well I remember when you were dating Clare Miller, I used to see her out and about all the time, never looking satisfied!" Instantly Sleazy's mates laughed with her against him, and he looked so mortified I doubt he ever made that mistake again.

Had I analysed why I so wanted a special lady in my life, the main reasons would have been to prove I was capable of attracting, to have the companionship of someone who cared about me if not loved me, and most of all to provide me with what my entire being was now hankering for: a sexual relationship. But as ever I felt so utterly unworthy, assuming it was always going to be a case of women choosing to be with me rather than the other way round. I couldn't envisage myself sweeping any off their feet. And, like when nobody wanted to pick me for House teams at Stourback, I'd probably always be a woman's last resort.

Til the end of my teens, I'd mostly only seen women on TV and other sections of the media. Now that plenty of actual women were around me on a day-to-day basis, I looked at them a lot – with fascination and sometimes awe. Believing that women's intuition was far greater than a man's, certainly this man's, I was convinced they could sense when they were being ogled in person, even from behind. I imagined that was only a fraction of their radar awareness, reckoning that within a matter of moments they could assess a guy's emotional make-up...even from some distance away. Not unlike when the next decade saw Arnold Schwarzenegger's Terminator get a statistical analysis in his computer-brain the instant he encountered anyone.

I took to placing those I desired on pedestals and worshipped accordingly, which probably explained why I found myself unable to relax with women I liked. At least not until I was certain they liked me. I assumed that they must like me if they kissed me, but I'd feel nauseous with nerves until I secured a snog, at which point I calmed somewhat. Someone I unwisely shared this with sniggered "So women make you sick, do they?!" I made a private pact to not eat for hours before first dates, and certainly not while on them. Women who played it cool or confusing I was baffled by and usually gave up on, rather than bring shame upon myself.

Then, at the start of my second year at SLI, a female Fresher with evidently plenty of experience of men, not only appeared in my life but made it blatantly obvious she wanted to be a big part of it. I'd never known anyone so instantly and utterly smitten as Gloria before. She would turn up at my flat at all hours of the day and night, apparently needing to be near me. Yet she herself had a besotted boyfriend who, distraught at her transfer of affections, threw himself out of a car on a motorway in a suicide attempt that mercifully failed. The stupid thing was I didn't even fancy Gloria and, while quite flattered by her crush, I'd no desire to make her more than a platonic pal.

I just wished that the girls I did want felt like Gloria did about me. My Mind Games kicked in again. This game was Scissors,

Paper, Rock in which, on the count of three, contestants shape their participating hand into one of those objects. Paper wins over Rock as it can wrap around it, Scissors win over Paper as they can cut it, and Rock wins over Scissors as it can crush them. I was now seeing that in relationships: one person could break another's heart but then have their heart broken by somebody else. More than most, I imagined, this was a game I wanted to win. I didn't want to have my heart broken and be a bigger loser than I already felt. I must only be the heartbreaker, the victor in love. But I knew I currently lacked the required attributes, let alone girlfriend.

I was into music more than ever. Rather late to the Blondie party, it was their 1978 album Parallel Lines that I was now playing on repeat...sometimes while gazing at the Debbie Harry calendar on my wall. I slowly accumulated a collection of vinyl singles and LPs, including some of the classic albums most people owned at the time, including Rumours by Fleetwood Mac, Hotel California by The Eagles, Tapestry by Carole King, Desire by Bob Dylan, Band On The Run by Wings, and The Year Of The Cat by Al Stewart. The latter included a track called If It Doesn't Come Naturally Leave It. In that second year, a friend Nicola I consulted regarding my various failed attempts at getting any relationship off the ground quoted that title to me by way of advice. Yet so bothered and insecure was I regarding the dating game that no relationship came naturally to me...and I was sure I wouldn't want to leave it if it did.

Nicola also suggested I try not to wear my heart on my sleeve so much. Apparently, all my anxieties showed in my facial expressions and body language. But wasn't that just me being me, and wasn't it vital to always be true to oneself? Oh, this relationship business seemed so difficult and complex! I was sure I needed to devote more time to understanding its rules.

"Your sporting hero Bjorn Borg famously kept his emotions in check on-court, so his opponents didn't know what he was thinking" Nicola reminded me. "Be like Borg. Most women would opt for a man of mystery over a man of predictability anyday."

I didn't like the idea of relationships having a competitive element, though it seemed inevitable. I'd pretty much given up playing sport by then, except tennis, my favourite. Cricket matches didn't have much of a female following so being in a team, even if I were a star of one, wasn't likely to bring female attraction per se…in which case I wasn't interested. However, if you excelled at anything sporty, that impressed other guys (in the team and supporting) which in turn gave you some self-belief you could channel to hopefully pull girls. Besides, cricket matches took too long with too much hanging around, with other men, and I was too impatient with lots of things to do, chiefly being with women.

Somehow I found a doubles partner in slender blonde Sophie, whose backhand was almost as gorgeous as her backside. I immediately placed her on a pedestal. And when she told me she was a former beauty queen, that pedestal was raised even higher. Of course she had a boyfriend, and as he was a hunky policeman I immediately decided I was never going to be able to compete. That actually meant I didn't try, and we shared plenty of fun times together…though most of them consisted of me thinking naughty thoughts about her. That Summer she did a lot of sunbathing in her bikini on the College lawn. I lay on a towel beside her in full worship mode. When she asked me to apply her tanning lotion, I was ready to explode like a shaken champagne bottle. I sensed she enjoyed the flirtation and my admiration. An older me would have just taken her in my arms and kissed her. But back then my insecurities created a massive psychological barrier of not being good enough that I could not overcome.

"What the heck are you scared of? She won't bite!" I asked while giving myself a strong talking to. The answer was rejection – I'd had enough of that in my life already, and couldn't face much more. Even the fact that I only talked to myself about it was because I didn't trust anyone not to start mortifying 'Loser Luke likes Sophie' type gossip.

17.

SOMEONE TO WALK OVER ME

It wasn't until my third and final Year that things finally came good on the personal front. In the first week I was told that a very attractive blonde Italian Fresher named Luisa had taken a fancy to me. She was pointed out by mutual acquaintances from a distance and, when I said I liked the look of her too, they arranged for us to meet at a Dotty's disco. I still didn't have the guts to dance, but it hadn't escaped my attention that guys who did tended to have better opportunities to get girls. So it was a measure of how interested I was that I allowed myself to be led into the centre of the disco floor. There I battled both my self-consciousness and the loud music in an attempt to chat to Luisa while shuffling from side to side to at least be seen to make some sort of moves. Within a moment, her friends disappeared leaving us suddenly feeling very exposed. Fortunately the overriding feeling for me was excitement at meeting her.

It soon became clear that part of the attraction was our shared naivety. I managed to get invited up to Luisa's room later and, as I stood drinking coffee, she hovered around me flirting as best she could. I was way too short on confidence and big on fear (of blowing it) to make an early move on her, no matter what signals she was giving off. Weeks later she'd tell me that her College friends had recommended she ready herself for a first kiss that first night.

When our first kiss did happen, it was in distinctly less romantic circumstances. We'd agreed to go out for a day, somewhere in London. As ever, I knew I needed to get that kiss over with before eating, and I remember us standing on a concrete island waiting to cross the road on the south-side of Putney Bridge when we turned to look at one another and the moment felt right. Oh, how soft and sweet her lips were…even amidst the noise and fumes of traffic. Every opportunity I got from then on, I kissed her more. So glorious was it that I can't remember what else we did for the next six or so hours. In the evening, to my great elation, Luisa offered to spend the night with me – I didn't even have to ask. What a result!

Only a couple of weeks before I'd promised the couple whose house I was lodging in that I wouldn't have any girlfriends to stay. I was about to break that promise already but, despite usually being a rule-abiding person, it was well worth a slapped wrist – even an expulsion if needs be – just to make love with the loveliest girl I'd got close to by then. Not just make love, but finally lose my virginity. I was 21 and, as that was much later than most other guys claimed to lose theirs, I'd knock a few years off in future 'When did you first do it?' discussions. By this age, my virginity was like an embarrassing disease to get shot of as soon as possible.

Rather wonderfully, Luisa and I knew it was the first time for both of us. Which meant it was a tricky, clumsy experience, but still one I wouldn't have swapped for all the world. Neither the limited way I'd got my kicks in preceding years, nor the things I'd read and heard about love-making, none of it came close to these sensations, for me at least.

Yes, I'd attended a few 'sex education' classes at both schools – maybe I shouldn't have caused Blackfoot's to stop at Parkstone Prep as they might have come in handy now - but I hadn't absorbed much from them partly because they understandably didn't involve practising with a real partner. And, despite perusing a few 'porn mags' as a desperate teenager, I never watched a porn film with their presumably perfect sex to make me feel inadequate. Of course there was plenty of sex in movies and TV shows I did see – just not so graphic – and that made me feel inadequate enough as it was. Not only were those women often divine to look at, the guys managed to satisfy them within a mere minute or two…getting them in a state of ecstasy I could only dream of.

The next morning, I awoke early – well before Luisa – and just looked at her, almost as if I feared she'd disappeared and it had all been a dream. But there she lay, a heavenly vision, the rays of first light through the curtains enhancing her angelic appearance. I could not believe my good fortune. Good fortune I didn't believe I deserved. I'd never forgotten when my prep school crush, Georgia, had expressed a preference for fellow pupil Mike Trailer over me – it was rejections like that which I always anticipated, not bliss like this.

I would say it was worth the wait, but 10 years of frustration before that was surely way too much for most males. If it was the same for Luisa, we certainly did what we could to make up for that lost time, getting intimate at every opportunity, over and over until our bodies demanded we sleep, then starting again when we woke.

Luisa was the first person I got totally naked with. The previous Catholic girls had always insisted I literally keep it in my trousers. Of all the chronic shyness I'd suffered in my youth, what I'd been most self-conscious about in those early years was anything to do with sexuality or nudity. From about 12, I never wanted anyone seeing me unclothed. Yet with Luisa and I sharing an introduction to intercourse, and my being constantly aroused by her, I became the complete opposite. I'd happily be totally starkers when we were together and loved her seeing me like that as much as I did her.

Still reeling from the fact that I was now three years older than the apparent age of a man's sexual peak, I soon noticed that the drug-like desire to have more and more sex seriously kicked in once I'd experienced it.

Being to me beautiful and at long last the provider of proper physical love, Luisa went straight to the top of my highest pedestal. I regarded her as a Goddess, and totally overlooked the fact that she actually was a vulnerable innocent like myself. Awkward though our initial intimate encounters were, Luisa and I both said we felt like we were making love rather than having sex. However, we were aware our recklessness may lead to something undesirable at that stage in our lives: pregnancy. Luisa went on The Pill, which defied the Catholicism she'd also been raised to adhere to. On an early visit to her family's smart Surrey home, she had her washbag opened by her holier-than-thou mother and the offending tablets were found. The poor girl had everything but the kitchen sink hurled at her, and she was made to promise not to see me again or have sex with any man unless she was married to him. The parental threats disturbed her for a few days, then mercifully normal play was resumed and pills consumed.

If that's how her mother reacted at finding Luisa taking contraception, I dreaded to think what she'd have been like had Luisa gone home pregnant. I must admit that I quite wanted her to have a child by me, because I thought that would make me seem manly, and presumably my source of sensational sex would remain accessible for a lot longer if not a lifetime. Equally naively, I didn't envisage how our lives would change, probably forever, were that to happen. Young Luisa going through childbirth alone would have terrified me. I'd never witnessed it in person but on TV and film it always looked scary and agony, and I thanked Heaven men didn't have to go through that. Being in this first relationship, I became aware of periods and how difficult they were for women to deal with. I remember thinking 'I'd far rather be male than female. All us guys have to put up with is shaving'…then I realised women did too, and over a far larger area.

I'm not sure Luisa was any more convinced by Catholicism than I was, but she wasn't going to turn her back on it while having very religious parents who continued to exercise control over her life. But she did give me, as a token of her love, an inscribed silver bracelet she'd received on the occasion of her Confirmation – one of the three sacraments of initiation into the Catholic Church. I duly treasured that and occasionally wore it, elated it suggested commitment.

When I look back now on our first few months together, it's like the compilation of idyllic scenes sometimes shown in slow motion with dreamy music in movies. Thus far these were the best times of my life, and Luisa was the best thing to have happened to me, by a huge distance. The fact that she was Italian made her even more glamorous and exciting in my eyes. I'd never been to Italy but its food, football, fashion, and films alone had a high-class reputation even I was aware of. And Luisa always made an effort to look stylish.

Having a gorgeous girl on my arm, and in my bed, gave me a sense of pride I'd never known hitherto. Maybe it also gave a glow, if not smugness. Over a lunch in the College canteen, another male student presumably envious of seeing me sat with Luisa whispered to me "You fucking love yourself!" I knew better than to reply, but I thought to myself 'If only I did'. However, finally I had something to show everyone, especially my family, that I was attractive and could attract an attractive young lady. I wrote letters to both my parents asking them to pray the relationship lasted. I didn't pray or totally believe in prayer myself by then, yet my parents did which is why I asked them. A residue of Catholic brainwashing too maybe, or sheer desperation to find anything that would ensure Luisa would continue to want to be with me.

That's how I saw it, you see: that I was lucky – incredibly lucky, in fact – that Luisa liked me, loved me, and wanted to make love with me. There were definitely times, early on at any rate, when Luisa considered herself fortunate in having me as her first love. But I never considered that. I was just amazed she wanted to be with me, and was convinced that sooner or later she'd see sense and dump me. Sex with her, for me anyway, was such a superb experience, I dreaded ever being denied it. There were potentially other women who could enable me to have that, but back then my thoughts and desires were solely focused on Luisa. We were one another's one and only. Inseparable forever lovers, right?

The only person I felt safe confiding in was my mother, who herself was always itching to talk to me about her affairs. I remember discussing orgasms with her, not in a youngster-learning-from-a-parent kind of way but like close mates would. Perhaps this was her treating me like the daughter she'd never had…and maybe always wanted. At the time, it didn't cross my mind that a teenage guy having such conversations with his mother might be inappropriate, but I'd got so used to the lack of boundaries and respect from my family that it seemed normal to me.

As my first proper girlfriend, Luisa was the first I said 'I love you' to. It would have been more accurate for me to say 'I am totally and utterly bonkers about every little bit of you' and, though I'm sure she could sense that, I felt it wiser to stick to the standard three-word declaration for the time being. Doing that caused me almost as much anxiety as asking her out had, mainly for fear she might not respond in kind. She did, and it sounded even better in her accent…and better still in Italian: Ti Amo. I supposed I'd never been told it before because nobody did actually love me before, and maybe I should be grateful that at least I wasn't lied to in that respect. But now in the back of my head lurked doubts that Luisa really meant it, that I was worthy of it. I never imagined I'd mean much to anybody.

Dating Luisa had lifted my self-confidence sufficiently that I now danced with her when we attended occasional functions…though I also did so to ensure other guys didn't. But I was as far removed from John Travolta as was humanly possible, uncoordinated and self-conscious to the core. An indication of the extent to which my self-confidence remained in a fragile state came when we attended another student's 21st party. Struggling to relax strutting my stuff with Luisa, I was horrified to have the girlfriend of a friend point at me, mimic my moves and laugh her head off. I immediately stopped dancing, and never did so in front of others again. That wouldn't have won me any marks for courage from my own girlfriend, but again the fear of ridicule mattered more to me.

Occasionally Luisa would tell me about her life at an Italian seaside resort where her family had a holiday home and spent most Summers. In one such chat she talked of a previous love named Paolo with whom she'd been intimate to a degree that got my insecurities rising to the surface. I envisaged a smooth swarthy athletic cool guy I could never compete with. The straw that broke this camel's back was the time Luisa asked to borrow coins with which to make a call on a College payphone. She returned to her room in a noticeably unhappy mood, admitted she'd spoken to Paolo and had come away feeling sad about him for some reason. On hearing this, I immediately felt nauseous, dashed to the sink in the corner of her room and threw up twice.

Doubts were creeping into my head. At the very least I needed consistency from Luisa. A male friend in whom I confided at the time told me "If you want consistency, you're dating the wrong gender!" I didn't have enough experience to know what to make of that.

Luisa was my priority thought most of the time. For the Winter holiday of 1982, Mum, Mark and I joined Dad in Portugal where he was then running an international school. It was certainly a change spending the festive season in sunshine – a stray dog ran away with our uncooked chicken, for one thing - but all I could think of was Luisa back in England. Every moment away from her, especially at such a distance, was agony for me. I'd spent most of what little money I had on gifts for her. Officially of course they were Christmas presents, but on reflection they were also her rewards for being attracted to me, for loving me, for giving me my first proper experiences of sex fabulous sex. I'd have given her the Earth for all that…and I was secretly gutted Luisa only got me a pair of sports socks and a set of sweatbands. Selfishly overlooking the constraints of student budgets, needy me needed a more generous gift as it would have made me feel more loved. Now, just as I'd done almost since birth, the less I felt wanted the more I sought to be…and the less appealing that made me.

When I caught myself in the mirror at Dad's rented little villa in The Algarve, all I could see looking back at me was a worried face showing for the first time lines around the eyes. I was only 21 and had a thick healthy head of hair, yet suddenly I became convinced I was rapidly ageing and it was receding...and to such an extent that Luisa's interest would wane as a result.

Shortly after we reunited for the Easter term, Luisa told me she'd be appearing in a French play at SLI with fellow students on her course. I turned up to the first of the four performances to find she was not only the sole female in a cast of five but she had a kissing scene with the leading man. That was a lot for me to deal with. I'd never seen her do more than peck anyone else on the cheek before, and it was extremely uncomfortable viewing. A green-eyed monster emerged from within me. Even though I found the play boring and barely understood a word of it, I attended all the other three performances too, not to support her but to see how much she was into the kissing, and whether she was becoming enamoured for real by her leading man. I couldn't help but quiz her about it afterwards either.

It was horrible how jealousy took a hold and made me feel like it was weakening me, empowering Luisa, and threatening to wreck our relationship. I needed reassurance from her, which I didn't think was much to ask, but she didn't provide it. That made me think my suspicions were justified. Within days, my insecurity over Luisa had multiplied like a fast-growing cancer. I was in love with her but I was becoming obsessed with her and with losing her. And the more pressure from me, the more she backed off.

Then one weekend she went away without telling me where. I was beside myself with worry that our relationship was in danger of disappearing, but I pinned my hopes she'd just gone to stay with her parents to give herself a break. On the Sunday evening, she finally called me and said she'd been with her leading man from the play the previous two days and – to my utter devastation – nights. The coldness with which she delivered this information suggested she didn't give a damn for what we'd had, and almost that she wanted me to suffer.

Weirdly I demanded details about what they'd done together, not just to confirm they'd had sex but how and how often, and even how much she'd enjoyed it. I couldn't believe what I was asking...or hearing. To make matters worse she sounded proud when answering, not in the least ashamed or sorry. I tried to make her feel guilty, primarily that she'd destroyed the great situation we'd had. But in the back of my mind I was conceding 'If she thought it was great, she wouldn't have done this'. And I could tell that the more I attempted to prick her conscience, the more it made her feel trapped. I remembered well how Luisa had resisted when her parents had used Catholic guilt to try and stop her having sex, so I didn't hold out much hope of her giving in to my wishes here.

It soon became apparent that interrogating Luisa and being angry with her was not just getting me nowhere, it was making matters much worse. Still fresh in my memory was how my father's putdowns and general negativity had made me want to keep away from him as much as possible – who would want to be around that if they could avoid it? – and what I mostly wanted to do now was reattract Luisa. I then came up with what I called my Pond Analogy. That was about envisaging a child having their stray ball floating in the middle of a pond and wanting to retrieve it – the natural reaction may appear to be making waves but that will only push it further away, so the only real hope is to wait for it to drift back naturally.

But the more I thought about it, I couldn't imagine any way forward for Luisa and I then. I told her our relationship was over, and I sensed she wanted that declaration to come from me though it was obvious from what she'd done that she'd already decided that.

Even my indoctrinated thought process that always assumed I deserved negative circumstances had me thinking. All I'd done wrong was become insecure, jealous and overly keen – hardly a crime, and only borne out of a troubled early life, naivety, inexperience, and intense feelings for Luisa. Surely if she loved me like she used to say she did, she'd take all that into account and be kind accordingly? Nope, not a bit of it. She'd gone totally cold on me.

Going over and over all this in my head – convinced I no longer even entered hers - my conclusion was that either my failings were completely unacceptable to her or she was now sufficiently enamoured of this other guy. In desperate search of hope, ideally solutions, I took several students who knew us as a couple to one side individually and gave them the lowdown. Their advice varied from 'Forget her, she clearly can't be trusted', to 'You never know, she might soon come to her senses'.

To an extent, I felt as if my existence had met a bad end. I hoped for more sympathy and concern from those I confided in, but the main response with an unsurprised shrug was 'Sh*t happens!' and they moved on never to mention it again. It was then I discovered there's only so much interest others will take in your problems as understandably they have to deal with their own lives. Besides, it became apparent to me that the only person who really had the answers was Luisa herself. As every single individual in the World's vast population has their own likes, dislikes, preferences, tendencies and so forth, it is very difficult to apply general rules to people.

The ensuing weeks were hideous. I could barely believe that everything we'd experienced together had been demolished by Luisa. I'd got dropped and abandoned like something she'd decided to buy then changed her mind and put back on the shop shelf. The sense of rejection was as bad as I'd ever felt. The biggest issue for me was that not only was I now deprived of my sex source, I had the hideous constant thoughts of her having it with someone else. I couldn't bear that another guy occupied her mind…and her vagina. We'd only had each other before that, and I'd been under the impression that we belonged to each other exclusively. Not anymore. I was no longer entitled to that intimate access, to an Access All Areas pass. It was now another man's entitlement. Sure, with memories you retain access mentally to a degree - and neither she nor her new man would be any the wiser if I chose to access those – but I now knew only too well that nothing compares to physical reality. Aside from other relationship benefits like company, I'd become addicted to intercourse and more with Luisa, and it was difficult coping physically and mentally with it no longer being available. It was possible I could have had it with other students, but at the time I couldn't bear even the thought of being with someone else. If only she felt the same way. I was learning in the most painful fashion that, when you still want to be with someone, it's very hard to accept them being with anyone but you...especially loving and having sex with them.

I knew I had an enormous amount to learn as far as women and relationships were concerned. By then, most people I met of my age had much more experience than myself, already including Luisa who in my eyes was now an adult compared to the child I felt I still was. That saddened me as we were one another's first love. Anyone of any experience would have known that first relationships rarely went the distance. But in the fantasy dished out in my early years of Catholicism, young women devoted themselves to one lifelong partner, and I suppose that placed an expectation in my head. I'd been led to believe that marriages were sacrosanct...yet of course I should have known from my own parents that that was far from always the case. And now like them and the two priests my mother had slept with, Luisa was demonstrating that relationships were not sacred to these Catholics at least. Maybe they thought they could do whatever they wanted and always get their slate cleaned at confession.

In analysing every bit of the situation in my head for weeks and weeks, I could understand why some extreme betrayed people were driven to murder, thinking 'Well if I can't have them, I'll make sure nobody else will'. But my ultimate aim was for Luisa to fall back in love with me, and she certainly couldn't do that if she was dead. Besides, murder would probably have resulted in my spending the rest of my life in prison, and even in peak turmoil I knew I didn't desire that. I thought about at least harming the bloke she'd betrayed me with, even wondering if Luisa secretly wanted me to show myself to be a real man that way. But she was more likely to resent me for harming him and displaying my jealous side at its worst, and would choose him over me. My most depressing realisation was that, if it wasn't that guy Luisa had gone with, it would have been another, maybe numerous others.

Among the advice I received was inevitably 'If you love someone, set them free'. As well as loving Luisa, I now hated her – at least hated what she'd done and was doing. I definitely didn't want to 'set her free', mostly because if she wasn't with me she was presumably with him. I just wanted her to love me and me alone. However, I'd never actually do anything to even restrict her freedom. Whatever she wanted I had to accept, no matter how hard for me.

Luisa made no attempt to keep me as a friend. Initially that surprised me as we'd been one another's first loves and as intimate as two people could ever get. But then she had already moved on without so much as a glance back at me. And, typical of me then, my focus was only on what she wanted. It did occur to me that A) I would find it incredibly difficult to accept the inferior and frustrating status of friend having been her boyfriend, and B) I should not seek friendship with someone who had betrayed and disrespected me, and switched from beautiful love to callous cold-heartedness.

As to why it went wrong…I was thinking it must have been my fault; so many things were. I should've known better.

That nine months with Luisa had taken me from my greatest high to my deepest low. The high had been borne out of a naivety that love lasted forever like in fairytales, and the fact that it didn't – in this case at least - brought me down to earth with an enormous thump. I didn't consider that this might be about another previously sheltered person simply needing to sample different relationships while she was young. Nor the fact that, had we stayed together, in due course I myself might well have felt such a need. I focussed instead on the fact that my behaviour had blown it, had pushed Luisa away and into the arms of another, yet I'd not known how to prevent that. The negative person inside me who'd always regarded myself as lucky to date Luisa rather than the other way round, was now saying "Of course she dumped you – that was always going to happen!"

Being repeatedly declared a loser by my brother Mark when we were young was not a patch on this. That had made me determined to win at sports ever since whenever possible. But to me relationships were way more complicated than any sport. Sports had rule books. Relationships didn't. Yet I was now discovering there were general unwritten rules about relationships whereby if those involved in them behaved certain ways - did or said certain things in certain circumstances - there would be certain consequences. So burnt was I from my Luisa experience that I vowed to react differently in future, though that wasn't necessarily going to be easy due to powerful forces of nature like jealousy.

The constant profound pain of parting, blaming myself for that, envisaging Luisa sleeping with other guys now…it was ghastly. Well-meaning friends were trotting out the usual 'Plenty more fishes in the sea' line, but it was as if there was only one fish in my sea because all I could think about was Luisa. In my agony I'd look at letters and messages I'd got from her when she was seriously into me, and wonder what had made her go from feeling like that to apparently no longer feeling anything for me. Similarly I'd gaze at happy photos of us, and play music we used to like listening to together. That all gave me a sense of what I was now missing, but it wasn't a patch on what we'd had. I read Iris Murdoch's book The Italian Girl, hoping it would give me an insight into one, but it did nothing of the sort. In one of the daily tabloid newspapers kept in the library at Dotty's, I regularly looked to see what its horoscope predicted for Capricorns…and Luisa's star sign Gemini. But of course they were so general and gave me no genuine hope to cling to. I soon became convinced its author was making them up over her tea and biscuits each morning. The esteemed astronomer Patrick Moore made much more sense when he declared in an interview at that time "The only thing astrology proves is that there's one born every minute!"

I didn't go stalking or spying on Luisa, for fear of what I might find as much as anything else. Had I so much as seen her chatting with another guy, my fevered mind would have jumped to unhappy conclusions whether justified or not.

All that obsessing was exhausting, and I took naps to help me get through each day. Every time I was about to nod off, day or night, I hoped that my situation would have changed for the better when I woke up.

I couldn't countenance that she clearly thought so little of me. Now I was set on winning Luisa back, but could she forgive the way I'd been, like I was prepared to forgive her betrayal …which was surely the greater crime? Her fling was soon over, to my intense relief, and somehow we made up. But things between us were never the same again. Neither I nor Luisa respected me for taking her back.

In the Summer term, on a weekend when Luisa really was at home with her family, it was me who played away. I 'got off' with Amelia, another pretty student, after leading her out of a party at the Student Union building to the nearby pond where we stood looking into each other's eyes. Amelia then breathlessly told me something I'd never forget: "God, you're hunky!" It was good for my ego, but the subsequent snogging was witnessed by a couple of male students who threatened to tell Luisa if I stepped any further out of line. They clearly weren't aware Luisa had already done the dirty on me. It was too late for that relationship anyhow. I was leaving at the end of that term, whereas Luisa would stay on for two more years.

18.

SHE AIN'T PRETTY, HE'S MY BROTHER

Despite the fact that I was still only 22 and Luisa had been my first serious girlfriend, so shattered was my already delicate self-esteem that initially I doubted I'd ever have any others…certainly not as physically attractive as her. Even then I'd heard and read about men so broken by the devastation of first heartache that they'd never really loved again. I was determined that wasn't going to be me, that I'd continue to rise above all adversity I faced, whatever it was. Besides, I needed love and sex too much to go without for long. And this was my case of an ignorant innocent getting burnt very severely by their opening relationship, and learning that most couples in the real world don't actually live happily ever after.

In terms of my Mind Games, the Luisa experience had seen me drop from the top to the bottom of the Snakes And Ladders board. Because of the way that went after too short a time, in my head it counted for so little in terms of success that it might as well never have happened. All the confidence I'd gained from being her boyfriend had evaporated, and it was back to the relationship game equivalent of Square One for me. I was still at the start wondering how to move forward without a set of instructions.

Also feeling like a boxer barely alive after being absolutely pummelled for 15 rounds, I made a few feeble attempts to get up off the canvas…only to get knocked back down time and time again in my weak state.

For example, among a crowd of drinkers on Richmond riverside one warm Summer evening, I stopped a striking-looking lady striding past me and launched into a truly dismal attempt to chat her up. She said nothing in response, just looked at me as if to say 'Is that the best you can do?' and continued on her way.

At a friend's wedding, when I gave my business card to the cute assistant to the photographer, I actually said "Call me if you're desperate". Understandably, she looked at me with bemusement, and dare I say a flicker of disappointment. But she was nowhere near as disappointed as I was at having said such a pathetic thing. Yet I really did sometimes believe that the only way a girl like her would call me was if she was desperate. I also sensed **she**'d never be desperate and therefore never call me. And indeed she didn't.

I shouldn't have been trying when my confidence level was registering zero. In fact, I shouldn't have been trying full stop, as that rarely worked. Mercifully I occasionally got lucky, though at that stage not with a woman or relationship of substance, which was what I hoped for. I ideally wanted to be the type of guy who bowled women over, partly as I'd come to believe that was what we were ideally supposed to do. But in most cases I found it was women who chose whether or not to date me and/or have sex with me. They tended to be the decision-makers in my situations, which went against what I'd long understood the male role to be.

Some women I encountered refused to have sex until they felt confident you wouldn't lose interest, maybe even end the relationship, once you'd done the deed. It was a blessing my Mind Games were private because here was the most politically incorrect. The strength of my attraction for women would indeed noticeably drop once I'd slept with them, and I equated that to the way new cars were said to lose value the instant they were driven off the showroom forecourt.

I'd been alive in the 1960s and 70s but not awake enough to acknowledge the extent to which people had become sexually liberated in that time. I only recall 'having' one other virgin after Luisa. Otherwise one had to accept that other guys had previously slept with your woman. But by then I'd slept with other women. Such was modern life. Even the term 'slept with' didn't entirely ring true as it really meant 'had sex with'…although of course it might have entailed snoozing together too.

By an unfortunate coincidence, the devastating disease AIDS hit its horrendous peak just as I was becoming seriously sexually active. It mainly affected the gay community, but heterosexuals were also warned against unprotected sex, and multiple partners. Promiscuous bisexuals and the mishandling of blood in medical circumstances added risk.

When a sexual relationship between two people began you weren't just taking on that person, you were also taking on their history of partners too. Now my Mind Games related sexual partners to games of Conkers in as much as when you won at that you took on the number of victories the conker you slayed had. That situation only seemed safe then if both people had a negative AIDS test. But I couldn't bear the thought of being tested, as there was no cure for AIDS in those days so the result would basically state whether you were going to live or die...and the death was truly terrible…so selfishly I didn't want to know. That was probably the one thing that made me glad I didn't have it in me to easily get women into bed.

That Summer, I was resigned to being single. To my dismay, Mark was to marry Isla. I clearly knew next to nothing about relationships, but I did trust my instincts and they warned loudly that he was about to commit marital hari-kari. For one thing, she had no time for me or Matthew, even though neither of us had said or done anything to justify that. Matthew and wife drove the many hours from Northumberland to London for a weekend which began with a Friday evening dinner at Mark's flat. The traffic was unexpectedly minimal and they arrived 35 minutes ahead of schedule. Isla answered the door, barked You're early!" at them and slammed said door in their faces. She didn't tell Mark for 10 minutes, and he then let them in, stressed but uncharacteristically unapologetic. If I was them, I'd have left. But they'd travelled a long distance and were concerned at the differences in our family favourite. Not long later, I was having my flat decorated and asked Mark if I could spend a night in one of their three spare rooms. Rather than the instant 'Of course' he'd have got from me had it been the other way round, Mark explained he needed to consult Isla, and I was soon told "It's not convenient for us to have guests at the moment as we've a lot going on."

Isla wasn't a lot better with our parents. It was as if this icy individual was trying to alienate Mark from his own family. A friend I related this to said "Classic narcissistic trait. That woman sounds like a narcissist". I initially misheard it as 'Nasty cyst' which also seemed accurate.

Considering the way Mark had always been with me, the extent to which it upset me was strange, but the day before their wedding, I sat with Mark in his car tearfully begging him not to go ahead with it. My pleas of course fell on deaf ears. Neither of my brothers was ever going to pay heed to anything I had to say, certainly not to alter a major course of their lives once their minds were set. Mum, the only other person who was finally seeing Isla for what she was, privately admitted "She'll be the death of Mark". But nothing and no-one was going to stop this union. I was driven to the event by the two most senior nuns from Dotty's who were delighted that this student couple were making the ultimate commitment. I kept schtum, not wanting to spoil their day and conscious that they wouldn't have been aware what Isla was really like. Not yet anyway.

While I was 100% certain that Mark was wrong to marry Isla, I was bewildered as to why he - being such a well-loved, self-assured, confident type - would wed an obviously unbalanced and unpleasant person, let alone with such a plain appearance. She was extremely manipulative and had him under her spell, which was loaded with Catholic guilt, but surely that wouldn't entice him up the aisle, would it? The only explanation I could come up with was sex. He'd been with Isla for several years before they tied the knot, and so religious was she that premarital intercourse was totally out of the question. I once walked in on them when they were kissing, and she immediately darted away from Mark to the other side of the room as if deeply ashamed. Those several years were in his early 20s and, as a red-blooded bloke, he must have been fit to burst by their wedding night. Having had a couple of other girlfriends by then – including the work colleague he dated during his three-month break from Isla - he presumably was not a virgin himself, though I didn't know or dare ask. I can imagine his desperation to finally have what Isla had so long denied him…though the odds on him then being disappointed might well have been short.

I had been right about Matthew's marriage. Within 18 months, his wife went off with their lodger and it was all over. He was now marrying again already and, while wife No.2 seemed more promising, I wasn't convinced this was a move he should be making either. But this time I kept my thoughts to myself. After all, as both my brothers would probably have argued, what did I know considering my only relationship had ended in failure after only nine months?

While I slightly envied both my brothers for settling down, for finding partners to share their lives and support them (if that really was the case), I didn't want the women they'd chosen and I didn't want children. Being fathers had clearly given them a different perspective on life to me, even more than they'd always had.

The only up-side to my becoming a Dad that I could envisage was that it would make me feel more manly and mature, but that was massively outweighed by the worry (which never seemed to end for parents I knew) and the cost. I could barely afford to fund my own bachelor lifestyle, so supporting offspring as well seemed impossible. Besides, how could I work peacefully at home, to earn the required extra money, if children were there too rightly needing my frequent attention? I would only have wanted to be the best possible parent myself, and ironically the way my parents were with me meant I was damaged and would probably need lots of time alone to work on that.

But I disliked being on my own – I regarded that as a failure – and I was not content in my own company, all probably because

I'd long been led to believe I was not a nice person. Not being in relationship meant my not having much self-esteem. I was sure I'd be happier and more secure within a relationship - aside from anything else, that would mean that to some degree I'd be wanted. I needed those I wanted to want me, to validate me. So if I didn't have a girlfriend, I'd often be on the hunt for one.

I already believed becoming more manly would get me girlfriends, and now I sensed that getting girlfriends would make me feel more manly. But for now I was little more than a wimp. I wouldn't have gone on vacation alone, and anyway I was under the impression that people were suspicious of men holidaying on their own. When attending events, particularly parties, if I ever had to make a solo appearance I'd feel like an unwanted lost soul and seek someone – anyone – to talk to. I was always convinced I was of no interest or consequence, thinking 'Nobody is going to want to converse with me…'

So, rather like a novice at skating convinced he'd always fall on his face and be ridiculed if he so much as tried to step on the ice, I looked to others to prop me up. If I could secure the company of a friend, the safety net that provided gave me sufficient confidence to attempt to be sociable. This was especially the case at drinks dos at which I felt awkward and usually left early, whereas at house parties if I found someone else willing to chat away in a quiet corner I was fine for hours.

On my plus side, the extent to which I was now largely accepted as a person by people at this College enabled me to begin to find my feet, hopefully creating a base on which I could build and flourish in due course. Finally, I was managing to make others laugh or express admiration for more than my appearance. Admittedly I was depending on others to give me approval, but hey it was a start. I sensed my foundations would probably always be vulnerable, but they were at least stronger than they had been before in my life.

Against all my expectations, I made two proper friends at Dotty's: Billy and Glen. Solid gold guys who'd continue to see me through countless ups and downs post graduation. Ever after we'd enjoy laughing at pranks played during our student days, like when I convinced Billy that Sarah Rusk's father was deaf so, when they met, he shouted loudly at a very alarmed Mr Rusk. And the occasion when Glen discreetly put a microphone by the window of Banger's room so a noisy night of nookie was broadcast on tannoys around the entire campus until ballistic staff put a stop to it. I could go on, but maybe you had to be there like we were. I'm so glad I was.

19.

LIVE WITH A THIRD DEGREE

As a young person, both schoolboy and student, I took lots of photographs. That partly satisfied my creativity and artistic streak. And as the years went by, the more I became aware that I was capturing moments and particularly people in time...freezing them at those points for as long as those images would last, ideally always. To me, only popular music could come close to retaining memories of specific periods in the way that photos or film footage did. I stuck my meticulously labelled photos in albums for future reference but I myself never wanted to be stuck in the past, especially as that had mainly been an unhappy place for me. No, while I was keen to keep those photos as a reminder of what I had experienced, I wanted to move forward and find what I had always wanted: security, love, excitement, etcetera.

Talking of stuck...it was noticeable how many former students still hung around Dotty's after they'd left – in some cases literally years later. Admittedly mainly males seeking to capitalise on the large ratio of females in what was clearly an easier environment to exist in, let alone get girlfriends and sex in, than most of the outside world. For an alarming number their student years really would prove to be the best of their lives. They were my best years up to that point, but if I had my way there'd be plenty of even better ones to come wherever future paths would take me.

Among teachers' numerous roles was convincing pupils of the importance of positive things, like being polite and competing fairly at sport. To many teachers, their prime objective was getting their pupils to pass exams. At Stourback I was made to believe the grades I got at O' and A' Level were vital. It was true in as much as A' Levels dictated whether you not only went on to university but also which level of university. With a Degree there was an element of that too. Lecturers instilled in you that the choice and quality of your future career depended on the standard of Degree you got, the basic being a Third and the ultimate a First. This generated pressure within us students to succeed, and the issue consumed many of our thoughts and conversations.

So I left SLI believing that most people I'd encounter in the following years, especially potential employers, would want to know what type of Degree I got and maybe also what O' and A' Level grades. As it turned out, in my entire life post-education, no-one ever enquired of my school exam results, and only one person asked if I had a Degree...but not what type of Degree. Knowing that made me feel somewhat conned, especially as teachers are judged on the achievements of their pupils, but no doubt they'd still argue that pupils should only be encouraged to perform to the best of their abilities.

When it came to choosing a career, I knew I needed it to be creative and different. I couldn't envisage regular jobs interesting or satisfying me.

My existence up to that point – living in and attending educational establishments - was familiar, safe and predictable. I hadn't exposed myself to serious risk or adventure. I'd stayed within limitations. Dad's catchphrase 'I wouldn't do that if I were you' had been a big influence. In my earlier restricted world, Dad and his words ruled. All the negativity he and others had hurled in my direction in over two decades meant I was either going to fail miserably, believing I really was as crap as they said, or I was going to at least try to do well. For me, the former was never an option. I didn't need motivating to succeed career-wise. It was ironic that by putting me down they motivated me to do well. There was no harm in being ambitious whatever the reason, but ambition was one thing and actually making it happen was another.

In my teens and twenties, I just wanted 'to be someone', like Marlon Brando's character in the film On The Waterfront did. I'd always felt like a nobody and I wanted to be somebody. No-one else ever seemed to think I'd amount to anything, and I thought that by becoming 'somebody' I'd prove them wrong, I'd show them, I'd have the last laugh. I felt that was paramount. Yet I didn't know how to go about being a 'somebody' or what kind of a somebody I wanted to be, let alone could be. By a 'somebody', I suppose I assumed 'somebody famous'. It was, after all, famous people who were a source of fascination, attention, and often adoration, to most people...including my Dad. I believed that if I achieved fame, there was a chance that he, my brothers, my other detractors, and girls who'd dumped me or were never interested, would look at me in a different light and actually be in admiration or regret.

The famous people Dad admired most were stars of sport and music, and funnily enough those were my ideals. I was born in the early 1960s. Crucial for the football fan in me, that was the decade in which England won The World Cup. And crucial for the music-lover in me, that was also the decade of The Beatles. England's failure to win a single soccer competition after that made even greater legends of the '66 squad on these shores. And surely nothing in the arts world anywhere would ever match 'the Fab Four'. Ever since they split in 1970, virtually every millisecond of their life together had been assessed and analysed. 'Oh, to be THAT significant!' I thought.

What early piano lessons taught me more than anything was that I had no talent for reading or playing music. When I also learnt in due course that John, Paul, George and Ringo never read music either, it was little consolation. I was never going to sing or play any instrument to even a reasonable standard if I lived another 200 years, yet by the time The Beatles were all around 30, they'd created countless tunes which most of the World's population knew and would never forget.

Achievement within a certain age became an obsession of mine. I noted that Brian Epstein, who'd not only discovered and managed The Beatles but also other internationally successful artists such as Cilla Black and Gerry & The Pacemakers, had died at 32. Jimi Hendrix, Janis Joplin, and Jim Morrison were only

27. James Dean, 24. To have your work, your face, your name... known around the globe when still so young was to me an incredible dream. I didn't want to die young though – but to achieve young and rest on those laurels into a ripe old age...to have people forever expressing appreciation at my achievements. I'd never tire of that because surely each would help cancel out all the times I was told as a child I was rubbish, and horrid, and I'd never make anything of my life.

Okay, the determination engendered by my early detractors didn't render me altogether without realism. The Beatles, Hendrix, Morrison, Dean, and the '66 squad were just a tad absurd to aspire to. Mind you, in the former case alone, who'd have guessed that a quartet of working-class lads from Liverpool could have gone so far? Truth is I'd have been pretty satisfied had I simply been able to write just one well-known song or best-selling book. I fantasised about being in a bar in remotest Australia and hearing a composition of mine wafting from a radio there. Or seeing someone sitting on a beach or a train somewhere reading a novel I'd written. Scenarios like that would have made me feel at least SOME degree of significance.

I did wonder how common the desire to 'be somebody' was, and whether it was most common among those like me who'd been rejected, put down, persecuted, etc, and whether bullies didn't have that need because they'd 'been somebody' as youths at school or in their local community.

Although I wasn't conscious of it at the time, three tiny sparks were ignited in my youth. When I was 13, my cousin Sam had a letter - protesting about a particular novelty song topping the singles charts - published in a leading music paper. For him to get something printed in a national publication seemed to me quite an achievement. On a public school Careers Day designed to get us thinking about possible paths to take, my brother Mark was in a group visiting the local newspaper. What he later related really caught my interest, as did the metal printing plates he was allowed to bring back as souvenirs. And in my darkest days at Stourback, a caricature I drew made it into the school magazine. It wasn't displayed prominently and I suspect very few among the modest readership paused to notice who the artist was. But for a boy who felt worthless, this was still an achievement, as someone actually valued something I'd created enough to publish it. There was the name of insignificant me in print – tiny print, but print nonetheless. That sowed a seed. I wondered how I could make it happen again. It occurred to me that the one career which combined my above average ability at writing, and to a lesser extent drawing, with having my name 'out there' was 'The Media', more specifically journalism. Maybe after a youth spent unnaturally internalising too much I needed a profession which required me to speak out. Perhaps subconsciously I envisaged myself popping out of the TV, radio or even the pages of The Times as my Dad was absorbed in it, and going "There, I've got your attention now!"

At Dotty's in those days, the routine was that graduating students met staff from the Careers Department during their last week. When I was asked by them what I fancied doing for a living and I stated journalism, the disappointing response was "Too competitive!" "I don't mind competition" I explained, but to no avail. "Think of something else" I was urged. The advisor would not entertain the possibility that I, perhaps any SLI student, might make a success of journalism. At that point, I wasn't sure whether I would or could, but I felt strongly that it should not be dismissed out of hand like that.

I actually had an alternative career up my sleeve: teaching. But as I'd been literally born and brought up in schools, as well as attending them as a pupil and being a junior master in my GAP Year, I wanted to at least give journalism a shot, because for one thing it was so different to my Dad's profession. And, as no friends or relatives were journalists, I knew I could never be accused of being given a leg-up to any extent; I'd have achieved it all off my own bat.

When I declared to Dad for the first time my interest in journalism, maybe specialising in sport, he liked the idea. Not having studied journalism, I'd no clue how to get into it. There was a cricket columnist for The Times called Duncan whose writing Dad enjoyed reading, so he contacted him asking for advice. Duncan kindly agreed to meet me. When I called him to make the arrangement, it transpired that he only lived about 150 metres from my student digs – an extraordinary coincidence that struck me as a kind of destiny.

Duncan gave good advice, but understandably he couldn't give me work or a job. Then, in another twist of fate, a real possibility opened itself up to me. Bernard Lacey, a student who'd left Dotty's the previous Summer returned one day telling of a course he'd just completed in broadcast journalism. He played an audio tape of himself reading the sports news, and he sounded so professional – a great contrast from his normally laid-back Brummie tones. It immediately made me think 'That's it...I'll become a sports newsreader...that'll impress people, especially Dad the big sports fan...and it may conceivably lead to me being 'someone'. Who knows?' So I decided I'd subscribe to the very same course.

The broadcast journalism course didn't have a vacancy til January 1984, but I wasn't going to waste the intervening period. I'd been told a few times that the best route into the profession was through local newspapers. So I went to the nearest one, The Surrey Bugle, walked into reception and asked to see the Editor – not knowing any better, nor any other rank of job within the press. When I said I was hoping her boss could help me get into journalism, the receptionist looked rather horrified. "You can't just come in here and ask for the Editor!" was her snooty response. "I'll call him but I don't imagine for a minute he will see you." Her contemptuous attitude turned to shock when, in due course, the Deputy Editor came to see me and, once I'd explained myself, he asked: "When can you start?" He was only referring to a short spell of work experience, but I was equally dumbfounded, not just due to negative receptionist predictions, but more those of the SLI careers advisors who'd disregarded journalism as 'too competitive'. After briefly pausing and checking behind me to ensure the Dep Ed didn't mean somebody else, I nervously offered "Monday?", to which he responded "Be here 9.30" and promptly disappeared back up the steps.

Typically, I was there well before 9.30am that Monday, just so grateful to have the opportunity. The dull grey open-plan office was populated with largely dull grey staff. Though I didn't yet know them, they seemed harmless and pleasant...which, if true, was going to be preferable to the groups of people I'd found myself landed with hitherto in life – my family, my school contemporaries, and my neighbours.

The Dep Ed sat me at a desk with a much younger work experience lad, plonked a pile of the paper's back issues on it, and told us to look through them.

Other than local historians or councillors, I couldn't imagine many people finding much to fascinate them in their local rag. But I did as instructed for 30 minutes or so, then walked across to the Dep Ed's desk – the Editor had a separate room – and asked if there was anything I could do, whether that involved making cups of tea (which I wouldn't have minded) or having a go at reporting (which I really wanted to do). His response took me aback. It was a discrete thumbs up accompanied by a whispered "Well done!" I'd no idea what he meant, again fearing a case of mistaken identity, but smiled as if I did. I would eventually learn he was congratulating me on showing initiative – a crucial quality for an aspiring journo. The schoolboy also on work experience remained firmly in his seat with those old editions in his mitts for several days afterwards. He never did get up of his own volition, but eventually he was given something to do out of sympathy more than anything else. For all I know he might have gone on to become a Media giant, but I doubt it.

As was tradition, I had to learn the ropes as a junior news reporter covering everything from council meetings and road traffic accidents to local shop openings and cats stuck up trees. One day I arrived at my desk to find a yellow Post-It note bearing the message CALL MR C LYON. I rang the number provided and wasn't really listening when the lady who answered said "Hello,

Chessington Zoo", which anyway wasn't surprising as that was on the 'patch' I now shared with a proper reporter. "Could I speak to Mr Lyon?" I asked. "Very funny" the lady replied sarcastically. Assuming she'd misheard me, I emphasised "Is Mr C Lyon there please?" The now rather irritated response was "Do you not realise we get this several times every day? I suppose you'll be calling back to speak to a Mr G Raff or P Cock..." The penny dropped, as did my face as I realised I'd been pranked and several Surrey Bugle staff were watching my embarrassment in fits of giggles. But, rather than see this as some unpleasant initiation ceremony, I was soon chuckling too as it was a harmless trick and I'd totally fallen for it.

Being in that newsroom reminded me of being in a classroom at school anyway, except with me a lone pupil among staff. These adult experienced journalists behaved sensibly and worked hard for the most part – this was how they earned a living after all. Sometimes I couldn't stop myself from acting or speaking immaturely. But I was on a mission to succeed which now brought me to my senses when necessary.

For me at that point, the most mundane task of turning a press release into a story required my greatest efforts and concentration. I may have been the only person who felt privileged to be there, to write articles (or at least attempt to then) which would have my name in a newspaper...albeit just a local one. Having for two decades previous considered myself a waste of space, this was quite a triumph personally.

I knew instantly that news reporting was not for me. I had little interest in serious issues like Politics, even on a local level. I already wanted to write feature-length articles. Encouraged by the ease with which I'd landed my work experience, I approached the Features Editor to express my interest. As various British pop artists of that time, including Boy George, Kajagoogoo and A Flock Of Seagulls were setting extraordinary trends in hairstyles, I was set the task of seeing how local hairdressers were coping with increasingly bizarre requests. So the following morning I headed off first to a barber shop on Kingston riverside. I was about to enter unannounced when I suddenly had a crisis of confidence. 'What if they don't want to speak to me?' I wondered. 'What if they hate the press and tell me to f*** off? Do I really want to risk being humiliated?' Beside me was a bus stop with a double-decker approaching and it occurred to me I could just get on that and get out of this potentially scary situation. Then I thought 'I tell you what, I'll go into the salon and see how they react. If they're friendly, I'll persevere. If they're hostile, I'll catch the next bus, disappear home and forget all about it.' Mercifully for me, the stylist I spoke to was charm personified, aware unlike me of the free publicity he'd be getting. I dread to think how I'd have fared career-wise had he slammed his door in my face.

It was with that first feature that I first noticed the work of the sub-editors, primarily tasked with cutting the words into the available space in the paper. For my debut I'd worried my socks off trying to produce my best work, and I was aghast that someone else would be allowed to chop and change it. All too soon I'd discover there were plenty of power-hungry subs who relished playing God with writers' copy (the journalistic word for text). 'The thing is with sub-editors, it's their personal opinion', I'd think, 'Why should my opinion matter less than theirs?' But, as was pointed out to precious me, it was their job.

Sub-editing aside, the resulting feature was well-received. I then threw myself into every opportunity at The Bugle, and within a fortnight I was offered a job. I didn't take it, as I was booked on the broadcast journalism course, but it felt great to be wanted. Finally my life looked to have an up, some kind of potential.

Sure, I'd ideally liked to have been a professional footballer or tennis player, or best of all a successful songwriter. But getting articles bearing my name published in a newspaper, and being offered employment during my debut, wasn't a bad start considering my history. It was one of those rare moments up to that point where I was actually quite proud of myself. Proud and pumped up.

20.

LADY LADY, NAY

In Autumn 1983, while waiting to start at the broadcasting school, I got a job as a sales assistant in Laurence Grays, a leading London department store...in their bed department. I hadn't requested that department; they assigned me to it without explanation. It was fairly new and didn't attract many customers – about half a dozen on an average day, and many of those were browsing not buying, or lost looking for the loo. So for most of the time I'd sit around doing nothing. Occasionally I'd wander over to the beds on display and straighten any sales signs or suchlike which might have been moved by the rare viewers and testers. Then I'd sit back down again, twiddle my thumbs and daydream about a more interesting career ahead or the girls I fancied laying with me on these luxurious mattresses. One was curvaceous Helen from the neighbouring China & Glass department but, for the sake of both our jobs, we snuck into the store cupboard instead for passionate kissing sessions when no senior staff were around.

For customers who wanted to try the beds, there were plastic protector mats bearing the manufacturer's name. One day an American woman was having a try-out when she turned to me and said "My husband is about the same size as you and, as I ideally need to test it with him and he's not here, would you mind lying down beside me?" I duly obliged, only for her to then explain: "Trouble is my husband keeps rolling on top of me..." "Madam" I said, "there's only so much I'm allowed to do in this job..."

Another time the long tedious days were lightened was when two well-spoken Barbour-wearing young ladies were surveying what was on offer, while chatting in low voices, giggling, and sporadically glancing at me like a couple of guilty schoolgirls. As shoplifting from a bed department was out of the question even for muscle-bound giants, I wasn't worried. "Excuse me, how much is this?" one of them then asked when checking out a pricey boat-style wooden bed. While I was searching for the answer, I overheard her friend whispering "Look, you know you can't afford it...let's get out of here!" "Not yet" Girl One whispered back, "I think he's rather cute". As I was the only person, let alone male, working in that department then, I was aware she meant me. But I pretended I hadn't heard, and to be busy, as the pair then strolled up to my desk. Girl One had a request. "Would you like to join us for tea?" "That's very kind of you, but I'm afraid I'm only allowed to use the staff canteen, and customers aren't allowed in the public restaurant" I replied truthfully, flattered but not gutted as neither woman set my pulse racing. "Too good for us, then? Suit yourself!" she said in what I liked to think was mock annoyance as they got up and left. Within an hour, the phone on my desk rang for one of the few times in my tenure. I picked it up and heard a familiar female voice say "It's me, Tara, I was in earlier with my friend...would you like to come for a jacuzzi at my place down the road in Knightsbridge?" I gulped, then again politely declined. "Oh, but I'd really like to hang out with you..." she explained. "Well, I'm here all day five days a week" I pointed out, welcoming relief from the monotony if nothing else. "Really?" replied Tara. "Then I'll come in and see you!"

She was as good as her word, and more. Most days at some point she'd turn up, perch on the divan beside my desk and chat away about nothing in particular. Dare I say her favourite subject appeared to be me, and she didn't hold back. "What I most want to know is" she told me one afternoon, "...what is the man in the bed department actually like...in the bed department?" Something in my gut told me to never let her find out, and I never did, though that didn't stop her persevering.

Unsurprisingly, Tara's frequent flirty appearances soon came to the attention of Mr Kitson, the near-retirement manager of not only my department but Carpets too. Aware that I had precious little to do as it was, he took a dim view of my not at least appearing to apply myself. Kitson told me to call a halt to Tara's visits, and wasn't convinced when I told him they were her idea and not mine. His plan to get shot of Tara involved moving me to Ladies Separates on the floor below where I was put to work folding sweaters. The women in that department showed only contempt for this token male in their midst, and drove me round the bend by repeatedly playing Lionel Richie's Dancing On The Ceiling (which they knew I couldn't stand) on their sound system. Once, while sorting a pile of fetching blouses, I heard the screech of coat-hangers being parted on a clothes rail, and looking up I was greeted by Tara grinning manically and saying "Found you!"

It was beginning to get unnerving. I had made sure to only let Tara see me at work, but one evening as I exited the staff entrance there she was waiting for me. I made my excuses and escaped, then actively sought the help of Mr Kitson to rid me and the store of what was resembling a stalker. I was back in Beds (the department, not the county), and next time she turned up she got escorted out of the building, mercifully never to visit or contact me again.

I was relieved, but at the same time curious to know: Why would this woman go to such lengths to win me over when I showed virtually no interest in her, yet women I pursued with vigour showed no interest in me? It appeared there was nothing more seductive to women than a man who didn't care. I didn't 'get it', and worse I didn't learn from it.

One Saturday lunchtime in mid-December, I popped down the road to briefly visit a guy I knew who was working in Harrods. On returning to Laurence Grays, I kept an appointment with Personnel on a high floor when I heard a distant but loud boom. I've no idea how, but I instinctively knew it was a bomb – a fact confirmed within a short time. I was to find out later, it had exploded outside the very door of Harrods I'd exited less than 20 minutes before – a sobering thought. I was surprised, and unnerved, that Laurence Grays wasn't immediately evacuated, but maybe they felt we were safer inside the building. Back at my desk, I saw out of the windows scenes of chaos and upset in Knightsbridge. Then into the bed department walked Annabel, a fellow sales assistant I'd befriended. She was in a state of shock and, on meeting my gaze, burst into tears. Within a year, her father would call her into his bedroom and shoot his brains out in front of her. Life was starting to take on very different perspectives to what I'd been used to in boarding schools.

My main aim in the aftermath of the Harrods bomb was to call my mother, to reassure her I was okay. I did that at the earliest opportunity on leaving work. The moment I heard her voice from Northumberland, I began crying while trying to talk. "What do you mean you're okay? Why shouldn't you be?" was her response – she hadn't by then seen or heard the news.

Those were otherwise thrilling times for me and I lived life to the fullest I liked it to be. But in the rare moments when I paused to take everything in, it dawned on me how close I'd come to being a victim of that terrorist attack which killed six people and injured 90. I even thought 'I wonder had I died, would I feel anything now or would every bit of me have simply switched off the instant it exploded?' And also 'Would Dad be glad I'd gone, or sad and wished he'd been kinder to me?'

For very different reasons, I would never forget that year's Laurence Grays' staff Christmas party. The massive majority of sales assistants in that store were female, and many of them attractive young women I was keen to get to know. So I was disappointed to be placed on a table full of men – plenty in pin-stripe-suits who were either destined for a career in The City, or simply looked that part. I spent the first few minutes enviably looking at the other tables where girls galore were already having the time of their lives, laughing and joking and generally getting into the festive spirit.

"Would you like a bevvy?" asked the chap on my left, gesturing towards the hundreds of bottles lined up for everyone's consumption. "No thanks, I don't drink" came my customary reply. But then, maybe because of what being confined to an all-male table constituted for me, I soon thought again. "Actually I will, thank you." I can't recall what he offered me, or indeed what anyone else offered me subsequently. Wine, beer, spirits...I had a bit of everything in the hope it would provide me with some of the joy the women surrounding us were evidently experiencing. Or, more to the point, some of the women themselves. I soon realised it was working.

Much of my adult life up to that point, when I'd encountered women I fancied, I'd found myself gripped by anxiety. Although I dearly wanted to come across as relaxed, devil-may-care, even debonair, my face only reflected fear and worry. When attempting to win women over, I'd think 'I've got her chatting, so I must be doing well!' But I rarely was. In fact, even by then there had been a string of dating opportunities I'd scuppered by talking too much or carelessly through insecurity and anxiety. I was a 'fools rush in' fool. I still had this 'thing' in my head that they were like 'Right, amuse me...show me what you've got!' I'd then try to do just that. Silly naive me would perform as it were with the aim of receiving their smiles, laughs, compliments - just as I had as a child attempting to please my parents. When my efforts weren't appreciated, I was dejected, sometimes mortified. Even when I got the desired reaction, it was temporary and superficial. They'd chuckle unconvincingly and I could detect their insincerity.

But here now, at the Laurence Grays Christmas Party of 1983, was a different me – the me I'd long wanted to be. My anxieties and inhibitions, usually heightened on such occasions, were gradually diminishing, disappearing. I actually felt empowered. No more Mr Pent-up Scaredy Cat, and in his place a young man at ease with the World. I was smiling and laughing as I brazenly approached, entertained, enchanted, even captivated the hottest girl I could find at the party: Lucy from Hosiery, someone I'd usually have considered way out of my league.

Judging by the expressions of delight on her delectable face, I was faring remarkably well with Lucy. But apparently judging by my own complexion, I was displaying signs of nausea. Maybe there was still a soupcon of nervousness inside me. Definitely there was an unprecedented level of alcohol inside me – different types of alcohol as well of course.

"You're going to be sick..." she observed, pulling me to my feet at a moment when it would have been wiser to leave me well alone. I hurled, and hurled and hurled. Unfortunately we were standing beside a display of stack stereos in the Hi-Fi department which was hosting the disco that night. At least two got sprayed with diced carrot and worse. I hoped they were wiped down before customers were allowed back in.

I then feared that with my vomit was expelled Dutch Courage. For a while I remained uncharacteristically confident. However that did diminish as I sobered up. So the carefree me that Lucy from Hosiery witnessed initially was gradually reduced to my usual self, quivering in the presence of a good-looking woman.

Predictably it wasn't long before Lucy made her excuses and left. My Mind Game was now Angling and I'd gone from catching a whopper to watching it wriggle off my hook and slip back under the water. Unlike the fish, I was then gutted.

Nothing was going to put me off though. Good or bad, it was all part of my self-education on women and relationships, of making up for lost time spent at boys' boarding-schools, and of proving myself as a man. It wasn't about finding Miss Right at that stage as I knew I was light years away from being settling down material...if indeed I was ever going to be.

The extent to which alcohol changed me for the better that night, especially relaxing me in front of a girl I fancied – the situation that probably mattered most to me then - was a revelation. Oh, the amount of occasions in the preceding few years when I could have done with that absence of anxiety. Yet I had to weigh that benefit up against the fact that it made me sick – the worst physical feeling I knew. So I wasn't likely to reach for booze every time such encounters cropped up in future. Besides, I remember someone telling me around that time that an alarming number of people who were tee-total in the first part of their lives and then took up drinking became alcoholics. Bearing in mind how addicted I felt towards sweet foods, pretty girls and sex, I could imagine falling under the spell of alcohol too. And, if anything was going to get me into it, the seismic event I was about to experience might be a candidate.

21.

GOODBYE TO JEAN

When I left College in the Summer of 1983, it became necessary for me to find new accommodation. I moved all of about 1000 metres, from one road to another and from one loft room to another within Putney...only this one was much smaller. The landlady, Fiona Fennell, a seemingly embittered divorcee in her 50s, was often to be found wandering round her terraced house in matching cream silk lacy underwear. With her witchy face and lumpy body, this was not a pleasant sight and put me off cream silk lacy underwear on women from then on. However, she did enjoy her job in television production and occasionally showed a benevolent streak.

Mum came to stay for a night or two, and Fiona kindly allowed her a proper guest room. During that visit, Mum occasionally had to stop while walking because of her Angina. On a trip to the shops in East Sheen, she came out with: "There's something you should know…I don't think I'll live much longer". That was quite something to be told casually en route to a chemist. I poo-poo'd the comment, and Mum urged me to take it seriously. Yes, I could clearly see she was troubled by the Angina and I was well aware that heart disease had claimed the lives of her father, mother and brother. But, as far as I was concerned, this was my mother and she was immortal.

That Autumn, when she was back home in Northumberland, Mum suffered a heart attack. I was told in a phone call, probably by one of my brothers. They both went to visit her in hospital, but I remained in London...no doubt still sure she'd be fine. But I was the only one who joined Mum at her home that Christmas. As she was still in delicate health, at her request I slept beside her in her bed in case she needed any assistance in the night. We talked a lot, not so much about her health but mainly of her feelings for Fr.Malcolm and

Fr.Anthony. Although illicit relationships with these Catholic priests may well have contributed to her stress and anxiety let alone high blood pressure, they were evidently also giving her happiness, and a distraction from her deteriorating physical state. In her living-room, I noticed the photos of my brothers and I were no longer neatly tucked into their frames, but almost hanging loose from them. On closer inspection, I saw that our pictures were now simply being used to cover over new ones of Fr.Malcolm. Yet the disguising was so poorly done that it was as if Mum wanted people to see what was underneath, to have her situation out in the open.

On Christmas Eve, Mum had what appeared to be another heart attack, albeit milder than before, and again she was whisked off to hospital. I honestly can't recall what I did during that festive period. I'm sure celebrations were virtually non-existent though Mum returned home within a few days.

At around that time, Mum had taken to doing what Dad's Dad, Grandman, used to do – standing and waving at us when we (her sons) left at the end of our respective stays. She got off her sick-bed to do this from her bedroom window that late December when I was taken away in a taxi. That sight would stick with me forevermore.

I went back to London, began my Broadcast Journalism Foundation Course and a promising social life. One evening that January, I was at a dinner party in Kensington when the topic of conversations happened to turn to funerals. I explained that not only had I never been to one, but that I would never go to one even if either of my parents died. I meant it too; death was a big taboo for me.

Following that dinner party, I spent the night with one of the female guests, and the next morning returned by bus to my digs in London SW15. No sooner had I opened the front door than I was ushered by my landlady into her kitchen where stood Mark and Dad, who'd never previously visited. The instant I looked at Mark, he just said "Mum's dead" and we melted into a tearful hug. I don't remember Dad joining us in our embrace, and it must have been difficult for him wanting to support our grief but being only too aware that he had caused his former wife far more misery than joy during their time together, and probably contributed to her going to an early grave. For Mum's sake, I wished she'd never met Dad. But then I wouldn't have been born, and I didn't wish that.

When Dad, Mark and I drove up to Mum's house in Northumberland where we were joined by Matthew, I kept thinking about the framed photos of Fr Malcolm in her lounge and how awful it would be if the others found them. Now that Mum was gone and I was perhaps the only person left carrying her secret, I felt a responsibility to protect her memory and even reputation. On arrival, I snuck into that room first...and found to my surprise that the family pictures were back as they used to be. But when I looked inside a drawer of Mum's desk, I found a love letter she'd been composing to Fr.Malcolm, sitting atop a bunch of correspondence between them, but I didn't have enough time to read or hide the evidence. I said nothing of it to my siblings, not wishing to tarnish their memories of Mum now we'd lost her. For the first couple of days they barely left her home, perhaps stunned at her sudden departure.

Otherwise of course the house was pretty much as it had been when I'd stayed there over Christmas a few weeks before. Except now I knew Mum would never be there – or indeed anywhere – ever again. I had a desolate thought that, were Mum still alive, she'd be continuing to enjoy the freedom of her home and beyond, but instead now she was lying motionless in a morgue miles away, along with other recently deceased. I half expected a call telling me "I know this is weird but I'm in this steel drawer and it's cold and lonely..." Part of me wanted to go find her, hug her, maybe give her a blanket or other comforts. But most of me knew perfectly well that all I'd find would be a dead body, and no way would I want to see one of those, even if it was my mother. Dad offered to take Matthew, Mark and I to 'see' Mum. I declined without hesitation. The others went, and Matthew admitted years later he regretted it as he couldn't get that sight of her corpse out of his head, and he'd rather only remember the smiley loving mother we used to know.

For that stay, I was also offered the opportunity to sleep in Mum's bed. Either this was a thoughtful gesture towards the vulnerable youngest son, or because none of the others fancied sleeping there. It was, after all, the bed on which she'd died only a few days before. And, though I'd slept in it with her a mere month before, it was too disturbing to contemplate now. Instead I chose to put a mattress on the floor of the least-used room in the house: the dining-room. I was privately terrified Mum would show herself to me in some sort of spirit form, but I felt that if she was going to be haunting her own family fresh from leaving this life, this would probably be last on her list of areas in her own home. Not once in our shared lifetime had I been scared of Mum, yet now she was dead even just the thought of seeing her again was deeply disturbing.

Someone who claimed to be in the know with such matters once told me: "If you ever see a ghost, you should say to it 'What do you want?'" I knew that if I ever saw one, even if it was that of my own mother, I'd either be rendered speechless or be screaming and running away rather than endeavouring to engage it in conversation.

It might have been that same someone who also said: "If you don't want to see ghosts, you won't." That hadn't proved true in my early childhood, but mercifully Mum didn't reappear to me posthumously. It occurred to me that, if she wasn't 'in spirit', maybe she'd gone straight to Hell for her affairs – if not for the infidelity aspect, for the fact that her lovers were Catholic priests.

Within the first two days of that week, Mum's closest friend Brenda turned up at the door unannounced. It occurred to me that, if Mum had made anyone else privy to her personal shenanigans, it would have been Brenda, yet I doubted Brenda would have known I was in on it too. I invited Brenda inside, but she wouldn't enter – politely claiming she wanted to leave us to grieve in private. To an extent it was an opportunity missed, but we wouldn't have been able to talk freely in front of the others anyhow.

On the (Wednesday) morning of Mum's funeral, her newspaper of choice, The Daily Press, was delivered as usual because we hadn't gotten around to cancelling it. Dad fished it out of the letterbox, glanced at the front page, gasped and tossed it across the room urging me to take a look. The main headline was Jean Comes Back From The Dead. Although it referred to the story of a woman who'd suddenly returned to her family after such a long disappearance that she'd been written off completely, it was a freaky coincidence considering my mother Jean was newly departed.

Mark then revealed that his watch had stopped at the moment Mum died. We found out the time of her passing from her devoted friend and neighbour Elsie Watkinson who'd been present...and I realised it was exactly when I had told the dinner party in Kensington that I wouldn't attend even my own parents' funerals.

There was actually no chance of me avoiding Mum's funeral. Even though the No.1 bond that kept our family as united as it could be had gone, the rest of us were sticking together to help us all through this unpleasant period. And, irrespective of the fact that I was now setting out on my own career path, I still felt and was treated as a child within this clan. Thus Mark's mother-in-law and aunt-in-law were assigned to me during the funeral.

It was held at the chapel of Parkstone Prep. The first thing I noticed on entering was a wooden coffin on a metal stand in front of the altar. So there was my mother, the woman I'd known, loved, larked around with, been hurt by, listened to, confided in...the lot...for 23 years, now stiff as a board inside a box. But this was nothing compared to what I would witness next. Three priests paraded in to conduct the ceremony – Fr.Phillip, the school chaplain, Fr.Anthony and Fr.Malcolm. The latter two went about their job without the slightest indication that this was in any sense unusual, awkward or – and this is what I found hardest to accept as I knew the limitless depths of Mum's feelings for them - emotional. I don't know why but it got me thinking about John F Kennedy and his brother Bobby reportedly showing little feeling following the mysterious death of Marilyn Monroe who they were both believed to have been intimate with and possibly complicit in destroying. Not that I thought these priests had done away with my mother to save their reputations, though all sorts of scenarios swam around my mind during her funeral.

I ignored the well-intended attempts of Mark's marital relatives, with their Catholic regalia of black veils, rosaries and bibles, to take care of me, even hold my hand. Instead I stared out of a side window rather than watch the hypocritical performance that was being played out on the stage before us.

Something I distracted myself with was what I privately titled Mum's Statistics. As a frequent watcher of sport on television, I couldn't help but notice that when matches ended, or players' participation in them ended, viewers were shown all sorts of analytical statistics. Now Mum's life was over, all the things she'd done were for a completed number of times, whether travelling abroad, drinking champagne, having sex…anything. Those statistics didn't matter to anyone, but they made me realise there's a limit to everything in our lives.

When the service was over, I joined Dad and Fr.Phillip in a car to the crematorium. Mum, like her brother and parents before her, had chosen to be dispatched that way. As I watched her coffin disappear on a conveyer belt through small red curtains, I knew she'd shortly be burnt in a raging furnace til there'd be nothing left of her but smouldering ashes. It was a ghastly thought. I wondered if her having slept with members of the clergy would mean she'd feel every horrendous sensation of being roasted to oblivion, and made to somehow spiritually live in a state of permanent regret. I definitely did not wish any suffering upon her myself. I just hoped, if she was now in a form which still experienced feelings, that they were not painful but peaceful and positive.

In Mum's defence, I'd been taught that God created everyone and everything, so should she be blamed for her actions? Was God not responsible for making her that way, and for the circumstances into which she'd got herself with a bad husband, sex-starved priests, the loss of all her original family, and so on? So if Mum's soul made it to the Pearly Gates and St.Peter were to be in possession of the full facts and truly fair-minded, might he have let her through? Or indeed did all that exist and happen, or was it really just lights-out from the moment of death? In seeking contact with her brother after he passed, Mum evidently believed in an afterlife, and a posthumous reunion with her lost loved ones would surely have been her ideal scenario.

Back at Parkstone Prep for the wake, within minutes I went outside and sat in Dad's car alone to avoid fuss and further hypocrisy. Had I known how to drive then, I would have done so...to somewhere private. I just wanted to be left alone, yet several well-meaning relatives tapped on the window to ask if I was alright. I think they expected this 'baby' of the family to be an emotional mess. Yet I didn't cry – not from the moment Mark told me the news of Mum's death until we talked about her on the fifth anniversary. For some time after the funeral, various 'loved ones' expressed concern that I'd not been seen in tears, several even suggesting that was "not healthy". They meant well, but to me it was nobody else's business. And, when I attempted to analyse it myself, I realised I felt a sense of completion with Mum despite her premature departure. We'd done so much talking in her last few years, either in person or over the phone, that I believed rightly or wrongly that no-one else really knew us like we knew each other.

After a while, I got out of Dad's car and wandered down the road to Mum's house to take advantage of my time alone there to hide her correspondence with Fr Malcolm. But the bundle of letters – including the one she'd been in the middle of writing to him - had gone. I had no idea who took them. I wondered if Brenda, or even Fr Malcolm himself, had because Mum may have given them a spare key, and they may have assumed no-one else was in on the secret. A few days later, I wrote to Brenda and asked if she had taken the missing mail and photos, but I never received a reply. Not long after, I heard through other sources that Fr Anthony had left the priesthood and was marrying Brenda. Lord knows what Mum would have felt about that. If, as I suspect, she'd have felt betrayed and broken-hearted, it was probably a blessing she never knew.

Talking of photos, Matthew, Mark and I now wanted ones of Mum to remember her by, and it was sad how few we found. She'd shied away from cameras, usually dissatisfied with the way she looked. Yet now she was gone we'd have settled for any of her, such was their rare importance as surviving reminders. And I was fully realising now that photos of anyone are a record of their existence, and usually long outlive the people pictured. I'd been a prolific photo taker since the late 1970s, and naturally none of the people I'd captured at any time had been exactly the same since, making those pictures all the more precious.

Mum had made friends easily and was much liked and loved. I wasn't aware of anyone disliking her – she wasn't the sort to offend anyone. So there was inevitable sadness among those who'd known her. But it struck me that, because she wasn't well-known, as with the vast majority of people her death would largely go unnoticed. She'd spent over half a century on this planet, and half of that as matriarch of our family, yet it was nothing like when a monarch died and there was a period of mourning, condolences sent from around the World, and so forth. Here there was just a little funeral and a wake, some cards and calls expressing sympathy, and that was it.

There was no body in a grave to visit. All that was now left of Mum was an urn of ashes, which would soon be placed near those of her original family members in the memorial garden of a crematorium in Surrey. But I would never feel that they themselves were there and that there was anything to be gained by visiting. Among those who were buried, there must be some surviving relatives, lovers or friends so utterly grief-stricken that they can't cope with knowing their deceased is now confined to a coffin six feet underground. My imagination envisaged the dead still with feelings, above all horrendously claustrophobic and lonely and unable to do anything to help themselves. So I concluded Mum had made a wise decision getting rapidly exterminated by fire.

Instead of a gravestone, my cremated mother merely merited a metal tag bearing her full name and dates of birth and death, and that was to be attached to a bush for a renewable time period at an extortionate cost. Mum's legacy would be the impressions she'd left on those she'd crossed paths with, including us her three sons. Had it been me who'd died then in my early 20s, I couldn't imagine there'd have been any genuine mourning or missing.

Within 24 hours of Mum's funeral, I was relieved to return to the capital to resume the broadcast journalism course. My father and brothers went back to their jobs. Everyone just got on with their lives. Life carried on as if nothing had happened. At least that's what I thought. I didn't think about what long-term psychological effects losing my mother so early might have on me. I'd been devastated enough at my first relationship ending badly after nine months, yet Mum had obviously been a mighty significant part of my first 23 years on this planet.

Of all the people from my life who were now dead, Mum was the one I'd known best and been closest to…and the one whose departure made me most realise I too would die one day. The loss of various relatives since I was eight had indicated as much, but such was my overflowing energy, enthusiasm, fascination and so much more that I could not imagine my life ever ending. And that my body would then have to be buried deep underground or at sea, or cremated. It was all so ghastly, particularly because I couldn't imagine ever not having the feelings of a living person. If I really did have to die, could not there then be more pleasant options?

This was when I started taking notes about not just my existence but existence in general because even now this – literally the matter of life and death - was never talked about in my circles and hadn't been even during my long period of education. I wondered if that was because there's enough to think about in everyday life as it is, and it's hard to get one's head around anything beyond that. Yet, while most of us and our lives seem so ordinary, it is really extraordinary for all of us.

Here's what I wrote at the time:

There are two main elements to us human beings – one is physical, and the other is spiritual. The physical is the human element, and the spiritual is the being element. The physical/human element, the body, is given life and operated by the spiritual/being element, the spirit. The time that the spirit exists in your body is limited. When your spirit first inhabited this body your existence as this human being began, and when your spirit leaves this body your existence as this human being ends. A human body cannot survive without its spirit. Whether or not the spirit can survive without a body, we human beings don't yet know for sure and may never know.

Human life existed long before you arrived on this planet and will hopefully continue to exist long after you die. The length of your existence will be just a tiny spec in the passage of time. You joined that time-passage at the moment you were conceived, and will leave it at the later moment you die. You cannot stay on forever; you can only take a temporary ride. It's also an eternally forward-moving ride. Every moment you're on it, you are a moment closer to your end, constantly sucked towards that in an inescapable vacuum. There is no going backwards.

That's the deal, whether you like it or not.

It seems strange that as a human being, particularly one born in a civilised nation in the latter half of the 20th century, the deal that is being human was never explained to me, especially during my early life. I was taught things like manners and good behaviour, and subjects such as Mathematics and Geography. But, when it came to the nature of human existence, I had to discover for myself. And I found that strange because I cannot imagine anything more important to be aware of in life than life itself.

It is not as if we human beings are born knowing what we are any more than we arrive in this World aware of where Africa is, who Julius Caesar was, how to tie a shoelace, etcetera. Perhaps it has been believed that the true nature of life – particularly its delicateness and brevity – is too ominous, or even disturbing, for a young person to cope with. But people can die or be affected by the death of others at any moment or age. And I had grown to believe that an incomplete awareness of life leads to a lack of appreciation of the value of life. Besides, are the stark realities of life so frightening when we have no choice? As I say, the deal is what it is, whether we like it or not.

As a youngster I'd desired my brother Mark's qualities and abilities, yet I hadn't truly taken in the fact that he like all of us would die one day, taking all he then comprised with him. Also I'd fervently wanted my favourite football team to win, yet they'd been competing for ages prior to my existence and would hopefully continue to do so long afterwards.....so did their success in the 1970s really matter as much as I felt it did then?

Even if the deal had been part of my education, I suspect I might still have found difficulty in coming to terms with it, particularly the fact that not long ago I didn't exist as this person at all and one day I won't anymore.

Like most people I expect, I view life in three definitive stages: young, middle-aged and old. As a young person, I was comforted by the potential of two of life's stages ahead of me, but I hardly ever contemplated anything before my existence or beyond my youth. I felt immortal. And I have most of my life since, despite often being reminded that a human life can of course come to an end at any age.

I never even questioned my existence in my youth. And, although I've nearly always known I didn't truly exist as this person before my birthdate of January 5th 1961, somehow it's seemed as if I've been around for a far longer time, perhaps even forever...though presumably I can't have.

When we live it's as one amongst countless people, and in one short life among countless years. Yet despite each human life being exceptionally brief in terms of all time, the living person has a different perspective than anyone able to observe the length of their one existence in the full context of time. For example, the Roman Empire is literally ancient history to people now, yet it's hard to envisage us being ancient history ourselves one day.

Time itself is the constant reminder. However, although I often check to see what time of day it is, I rarely consider that every moment which passes, passes straight into history and won't come back again. And, of course, with every moment which passes my life is getting shorter. maybe I don't consider it because I don't wish to, and maybe that's because there's nothing I can do about it.

Every day we are surrounded by things that symbolise our situation – such as seeds sprouting, blossoming into flowers which then wither and die, and dough created to make bread which is edible and appetising for a while before turning mouldy and rotting away.

The ageing process of human beings and its influence on our capabilities and appearance is probably the most poignant, and certainly the most personal, reminder of our temporary state. We are changing and ageing all the time. Fortunately, it is a slower, and therefore more subtle, process than it is for flowers and bread, but many (presumably all who enjoy life) would argue it's not slow enough. If we live long enough, the looks and abilities which developed when we were young will diminish. The older I get, the more I'm conscious of the phrase 'Make the most of life, you're dead a long time'.

I happened to have been born and raised in the UK during peacetime. If ever I felt sorry for myself, it was important for me to bear in mind that I was extremely fortunate to not be from a place of poverty, conflict, tyrannical regime, and suchlike. Compared to most people, I've been very lucky...so far.

22.

ON THE AIR AT NIGHT

The intense but intensely enjoyable training to be a broadcast journalist was now an ideal distraction for me. There were about 20 of us on the course, including a few obvious high-fliers who I felt instantly inferior to. One was paired with me on a reporting exercise at the Miss Great Britain & Ireland beauty pageant then setting up shop in the ballroom of a top West End hotel. Somehow, we managed to persuade the current and soon-to-be-former title holder to do a little interview and, from the moment her delightful presence appeared before us, I was as anxious as I would have been had she agreed to go on a date with me. Seeing the sheer panic I exuded, my oh-so-confident colleague whispered in my ear "Don't worry, I'll write a good question and give it to you". After I nervously stuttered to this angel known as Rose a couple of corny enquiries of my own, I was handed a slip of paper and immediately launched into the words it bore: 'Do you fancy a f***?' Mercifully, I just managed to stop myself before the second f-word and miraculously turn that into "flutter" - as in 'bet' on that evening's event - and as she was from an Irish family fond of horse racing it didn't even raise either of her immaculate eyebrows. How relieved was I? Amusing for the other guy, and maybe to me now, but a potentially disgraceful incident at the time. I was reminded of the conclusion I'd come to at Stourback: trust no-one and make your own luck.

With the ratio of females to males at Dotty's so high, there had been enough of them around there for me to make dating blunders and still have some interest to fall back on. In the subsequent everyday world I inhabited, I found women less accessible and less attainable. Though I'd have to concede that my biggest barrier was my own psyche.

One lunchtime during my training course, I popped into a cafe on Charing Cross Road and, as I sat there alone eating sandwiches, a striking young waitress came to tidy my table and gave me the kind of glances I'd only seen women give in the movies. I returned them, along with awkward smiles, but immediately lost my appetite and couldn't think of anything to say that I didn't think would put her off directing those big brown eyes my way. So I remained silent. Same time next day I returned, and the next, and the next, for a fortnight or so, and each time the same exchange of looks occurred in complete silence as she tended to whatever table I was on...despite my hardly having anything to eat due to nerves. Perhaps she expected me as the male to make the first move, but I never did bring myself to even say hello to her. I likened it to one of those frustrating dreams when you know what you want to do or say, but you don't or can't. The unconfident cynic in me wondered if she did this with other men to keep them coming back in to the cafe. Ironically it was the butterflies she gave me which put me off eating and drinking, so I barely ever bought more than a bottle of water which didn't really justify occupying one of their tables.

When it came to the section of the broadcasting course that required each of us students to interview a celebrity, I showed a degree of gung-ho determination that surprised even myself, driven by my need to succeed no doubt. The broadcasting school was sat in the heart of theatreland, and I decided to pursue the leading ladies of two of its then most popular plays...somehow sure I was more likely to get a positive response, and ideally interview, than if I tried the leading men. Not a thought to any official approach, I merely telephoned the Stage Doors of the venues concerned and asked to speak to the stars I sought. Next thing I know, I'm put through to the familiar rich voice of June Fleet and she suggests I pop round to see her in Shaftesbury Avenue the following evening 90 minutes before curtain-up. I did just that and, despite robotically reading each of my carefully prepared (in felt tip) lines from a clipboard that I clutched with sweaty shaking hands, this distinguished lady ended our encounter with a heartily delivered "Jolly good questions!" Three typically generous words from Ms Fleet which meant a vast amount to this awkward student in need of any encouragement he could find.

So encouraged was I, in fact, that I then tried Penny Hampton, her co-star in the then hottest TV sitcom, who just happened to have been my teenage dream of a woman. That call was also put straight through to her dressing-room, at The Strand Theatre, and suddenly there on the other end of the line was the blonde bombshell whose publicity photos alone could make not just my blood pressure rise. A similar response too: warm, kind and "come by tomorrow night at 6". Fear of my father's wrath had long made of me an overly punctual person, and for this meeting with my heartthrob there was no way I was going to chance being even a moment late. I set off on the 20-minute walk no less than an hour ahead of schedule. Consequently I reached the theatre ridiculously early and, even though it was snowing, I wandered around outside waiting for my appointment...and waiting, and waiting. When the time eventually arrived I was sent backstage to Miss Hampton who recoiled on shaking my hand. "Oh my goodness, you're freezing!" she exclaimed. I hadn't noticed; I was already deep into fantasyland. The actress then invited the journalist to join her on the bed in her dressing-room - of course not to lie down for what my wild imagination feverishly desired, but to politely sit and conduct the agreed inquisition. However, sitting just inches from my idea of feminine perfection, and on her bed, I was all aquiver anyway, so again it was a good thing I'd prepared my questions beforehand, bland as they undoubtedly were. Overwhelming nerves meant I was speaking as shrill as the then celebrity choirboy Aled Jones sang, snow and all. My divine interviewee must have thought I had been inhaling Helium or was just eccentric, though plenty of men then would have tripped over their tongues in her presence.

I had managed to attain and conduct interviews with these two revered ladies despite not finding the courage to even introduce myself to a seemingly interested ordinary cleaner in a cafe. Maybe my professional self was to be braver than my personal self, and good thing too because if I lacked income as well as guts I wasn't going to be much of an attractive proposition for anyone.

It did occur to me how most people I knew displayed a fairly equal amount of good and bad abilities and assets. Which meant that, if we are all created by God, dividing everything up like that is one incredible achievement. I myself, for example, had height, reasonable looks, an ability to write and a good eye for taking pictures, yet I was useless at Maths, had a weakness for sugar and lacked confidence and courage. There were times I wished I had more plusses - an Oscar Wilde talent for quick-wittedness for example - but I knew there were also plenty of people on Earth who'd love to just have what I had, so I should only ever be grateful not regretful.

Shortly into the training course, in order to obtain some knowledge and experience, I secured some evening shiftwork at a major independent station in London, MCR (which stood for Main City Radio), looking after guests and filtering calls for the phone-in programmes. It entailed anti-social hours and relying on unreliable public transport, but I didn't mind a bit as it was great fun. Most exciting was meeting and occasionally spending time with the famous presenters and guests – many of whom I'd grown up watching or listening to as a sheltered youngster in the wilds of the North.

Just over a decade after seeing comedian Kenneth Williams looking in a shop window on the Tottenham Court Road, one evening at this radio station very close to there it was my task to take him from the foyer to the newsroom for an interview. But, due to his extreme shyness and the fact that there was a party in the foyer that night, I was warned it was doubtful he'd even enter the building. So, as instructed, I stood in the giant front window waiting to welcome him. On explaining to a curious party guest what I was doing, she said "A nice-looking young man might be just the bait to reel him in…" – something that hadn't occurred to me.

Having been aware of Kenneth Williams all my life, and particularly remembering how awestruck I'd been as a kid when Mum pointed him out to me on that trip to London in the 70s, I was surprised how relaxed I was with him now. In fact, when with such celebrities for professional reasons, it felt pretty normal to be around them. And rightly so as they were all human beings like the rest of the population, including myself. But unlike most other people they had a status that set them apart, and that often made those entering their world behave differently. The key was to simply see and treat everyone, famous or not, the same. But with some in those early days, their celebrity and the reason(s) for that had tended to be what I saw and responded to first and foremost. It occurred to me that this was what I'd become like with women I was attracted to - awestruck and treating them like VIPs.

Maybe it was that deep-rooted 'I am unworthy' thing I couldn't get shot of. After all, they were coming in as sought-after guests, and I was just assigned to look after them. One time the difference in status was especially interesting. Walking down a MCR corridor, I suddenly noticed a disc jockey heading towards me with Dexter Troupe, the dormitory captain from my first year at Stourback who was now a rising star of the West End and a hit movie, and absolutely oozing arrogance. As they approached I got in an anxious state – which I wouldn't have done were he not now famous - yet I was inexplicably determined to speak to Troupe. "Hello. Do you remember me from school?" I asked, practically trembling. He coolly looked at me, put fingers to his chin not-sure-I-do style, then giggled with his DJ pal as they kept on walking. Of course he would have recognised me, having spent three terms living in the same House, let alone sleeping in the same room, not that long previously. But as he'd already attained a level above me in terms of fame and success, I evidently had a weird need for my existence to be acknowledged by him…maybe so from then on I'd have a kind of 'Troupe still recognised me even though he's now a celebrity!' string to my bow. But he'd made out he didn't, and I felt a fool for having bothered, almost allowing myself to be a Stourback victim all over again. 'I should have left well alone' I told myself for literally years after, but that sadly applied to too many awkward incidents I got myself into.

Around that time, I walked past a then retired British tennis star, aptly near Wimbledon, and without thinking I said "Hi, how are you?" He was perfectly polite back, no doubt used to strangers greeting him. But as I walked on, I realised that of course he had no idea who I was. His was just such a familiar face to me that my instant assumption was that we knew one another. I decided then that the definition of a celebrity must be that they are known to lots of people. How many people is incalculable. I guess 'far more people than are familiar with the average person' might suffice.

Another night MCR's guests included a leading palm-reader from the USA, who'd just arrived in the UK to promote a book. No sooner had I led her from foyer to newsroom than almost the entire editorial staff surrounded her asking to have their palms read. It reminded me of scenes from biblical dramas when Jesus is surrounded by cripples and lepers begging him to heal them. The lady explained she was struggling with jetlag, had only come in to do an interview and had neither the time nor the energy to respond to all these requests. I was effectively just a freelance office-boy then and not in a position to tell staff to leave her be. So I stood quietly and embarrassed (for her) at the back of the room as journalists and secretaries continued to crowd the poor woman. But I was taller than everyone else present, and to my surprise the palm-reader looked up, straight at me and said as if there was no-one else around "You're psychic!" I was shocked, and a bit horrified, which must have shown in my face. "Don't worry" she reassuringly added. "It's a great gift. Use it wisely" – the sort of advice I'd heard given in martial arts movies.

I expect that lady returned home to the States within days and didn't give me or what she told me a second thought. But I never forgot. In fact, she might have awakened something within me. Just weeks later I took a girlfriend, Caroline, for a little holiday on The Isle Of Wight. We stayed in an old house in

Ventnor and, on our first evening as we sat eating in the living-room there, I could sense the spirits of two people sitting in armchairs opposite us. It put me off my food, and I told Caroline that I wanted to go for a walk. "Why now? You said you were starving, and I went to some trouble putting this meal together!" I thought it best she didn't know the truth or she might be disturbed by it, but Caroline was a journalist too and by nature we are curious and persistent creatures. "Come on, tell me what the problem is?" she asked...and asked...and asked. The fact was she had a right to know, she clearly wanted to know, and I didn't want to lie, so.... "I think this room – if not this house – is haunted" I explained. "I get the sense there's a couple of people sitting on that sofa opposite." Caroline went pale, and angry. "Why did you tell me that?!" she wailed. I couldn't win. We didn't use that room again. Years later, I learned that the Isle Of Wight is the most haunted place in Britain.

I'm not sure my IOW experience qualifies as a psychic one, but I was to have plenty of them in due course. Such as the time I viewed a property in Wimbledon and told the estate agent I felt a very uncomfortable vibe there. When I mentioned it again and he realised I wasn't going to be buying, he pointed to the beam above our heads and revealed that the last occupant had hung himself from it just weeks before.

An aspect of life I've always loved is how wonderful things can suddenly occur unexpectedly. Bad things also occur of course, and I don't love those, but fortunately I've had far more positives than negatives happening out of the blue. The personal surprises have meant the most, and those have mainly entailed meeting women I've been instantly attracted to. My favourite occurred one afternoon when I went to a major publisher to interview an author about a new diet book. After an hour or so, I was about to exit via the lift when I looked up at the book's publicist Melanie to say goodbye. I'd only spoken to Melanie once briefly earlier, yet suddenly and inexplicably I felt an overwhelming sadness at leaving her. For the following few days, she and that moment were on my mind constantly. We'd agreed that, once I knew when my interview with the author was to be broadcast, I'd let

Melanie know so they could listen in. When I rang and re-introduced myself, she said "It's okay, I know who you are", paused, then added in hushed tones: "And I hope you won't mind me saying, but I can't stop thinking about you". I got goose bumps galore. "I've been thinking about you a lot too" I replied in all honesty. This was a magical moment, but could it be true love? We met up and had a heady spell of passion, but it was too much too soon for me and what started as a promising romance was sadly short-lived, which I long regretted.

Meantime, back at the radio station.... Once I'd completed my training, I was granted the opportunity to work in the Main City Radio newsroom as a freelance journalist. The rates of pay were poor and to get any of my interviews, reports or features on air for even a minute or two required hours of editing in a windowless booth, but it was thrilling to be at MCR full-time and I couldn't get enough of it. This was a top, trendy station, and whenever I took one of their chunky Uher tape recorders out and about for reports and interviews, I was proud to show the station's highly recognisable logo off on the exterior of the bright red protective carrying case. One morning I was sitting on a tube train with the Uher on my lap when a vaguely familiar young man leaned towards me and asked "Wasn't I at school with you?" It was indeed a lad I'd been at Stourback with and, though he wasn't among those who gave me a hard time there, it was quite satisfying to find him impressed when I told him about my new career.

One of my earliest radio reports was on an old lady conned into allowing a young robber posing as a meter reader into her flat where he then stole her life savings from the cash box she hid in her airing cupboard. I got the story in a taped interview with the poor woman but, when I played it to the hard-nosed News Editor on my return, he wasn't happy. "Where are the tears?" he asked. "We need to hear her sobbing. The story lacks impact otherwise. Go back and keep interviewing her til she cries." When I realised he was serious, I reluctantly returned and did exactly as instructed, though even after some time and probing she still didn't get emotional, and I felt terrible at imposing upset on an already delicate pensioner. Then I remembered a technique I'd seen TV interviewers employ in such circumstances whereby they'd ask things like 'It must be really upsetting for you…' and 'I can't imagine how heartbroken you must be…', and indeed that super-sympathetic approach finally got her choked up. Admittedly, the resulting audio was indeed more powerful.

I remained a very nervous and unconfident individual, always feeling inferior to the other people at the radio station. I thought of them all as serious talent and myself as just fortunate to be in their vicinity, let alone a colleague. My blurting still occurred occasionally too.

MCR's Friday night talk show host Sandra Wood was a highly-strung chain-smoker. My task was to take care of the celebrity guests before and after that programme. One of them, the internationally-famous actor and drinker Ben Hunt, one night proved tricky for Sandra to interview – monosyllabic mainly. I'd only recently learnt in training that the key to getting full responses from interviewees was to avoid closed questions – those beginning with 'Do you?' 'Can you?' 'Will you?' etc – and instead ask things like 'How do you feel about..?', 'What was it like…?', 'Please can you describe for us...?' and so forth. During the after-show drinks, Sandra was bemoaning to a few of us the poor responses from this particular guest when, while trying to be smiley and light-hearted, I just came out with "Well, if you will ask questions that can be answered with yes, no, or maybe..." She said nothing, I carried on with my duties of seeing the guests off, then left for the weekend. The moment I returned the following Monday, Sandra sought me out requesting a private chat with me in the privacy of a sound-proof editing suite. I couldn't think why, but she immediately reminded me what I'd said Friday evening and totally laid into me with smoke coming out of both ears and both nostrils, as well as literally from her mouth. I don't think I've ever seen anyone so angry at me. Yet until then I'd not given my comments a second thought. I could now see how it appeared to her to be insolent and unprofessional, as she put it, and I apologised profusely. But I couldn't help thinking A) I was right. B) I clearly hadn't meant any harm or embarrassment. C) How many people are so quick to blame and attack without considering what in a person's personal history might have made them act or speak in a certain way.

Sandra's fury shook my sensitive soul to its core, but I guess I'd shaken hers with what she'd perceived as a pop at her professionalism. I was now mortified yet she probably had been all weekend.

I kept my head well down in the newsroom after that as I'd no idea how many other staff she had shared her opinion of me with. Not long later, the station's Showbusiness Editor asked if I'd like to meet him for a drink. I accepted, despite not knowing his motive. As we sat in a nearby wine bar, he tried to talk me into leaving MCR, suggesting I'd be better off learning the trade in a smaller station. Quite something coming from someone I'd barely spoken to before. It was possible Sandra had put him up to it, but I also wondered if this man wanted me out because he himself felt professionally threatened by me. For all my failings, I was highly creative and keen, had potential and the advantage of youth over him. The fact that a stranger saw fit to say such things to me indicated I still gave off a doormat vibe, easily walked over. However, I couldn't rule out the possibility he may have had a point and was genuinely well-intentioned.

I did then apply for a job on a West Country radio station, as a sports reporter, only to discover that a guy I'd trained with was also up for it...and got it. In the call telling me I'd been "unsuccessful on this occasion", I was informed that it had come down to the two of us and he'd got the nod because he could drive – a vital asset for working in rural Cornwall. I didn't mind as I couldn't imagine enjoying a career in the countryside at this point. But never wanting to lose out again due to that disadvantage, I immediately booked driving lessons. My eternal disinterest in the likes of Physics and Mechanics meant I was no natural. In fact, at the end of my first lesson, the despairing instructor said to me "I don't think you'll ever pass your Test", but as ever that only made me more determined and I passed first time...albeit after 42 lessons.

There was probably nowhere in Britain more challenging to drivers than London, so while it could be considered a baptism of fire, I suppose it also meant that taking a car most other places would seem easy in comparison. One of the first bits of advice I'd been given on moving to the capital was "When you're in a taxi watch where it goes, because those shortcuts will be invaluable when driving yourself." That did indeed prove a great tip once I was behind a wheel myself.

Regarding the Cornwall rejection, I was philosophical thinking 'Maybe I am supposed to stay in London after all'. And in fact I was slowly being given more work to do at MCR including reading the sports news while the Sports Editor was on holiday. That was the fulfilment of a wish I'd had for a while, and it happened to coincide with a new presentation trend whereby newsreaders introduced themselves at the start of bulletins. Announcing "I'm Luke Twigg..." made me squirm every time. Disliking myself included my name, and I'd seen film of AA meetings in which the words "...and I'm an alcoholic" were traditionally added.

Those were the dying days of posh voices ruling the airwaves, and my public school accent went down well. It could have been the beginning of a bright career in broadcasting, but an old problem returned to haunt me: my childhood tendency to laugh in serious situations.

When recording reports and features, especially to tight deadlines with an engineer and/or producer handling the proceedings, I'd frequently get the giggles. So tense did I feel at such times that the slightest thing – which most people wouldn't have even noticed – would set me off. And once I'd started, I sometimes couldn't stop myself, like a speeding car clipping something then rolling over and over and over off a hillside. This resulted in multiple takes and everyone, most of all me, wishing I would get a grip.

My nerves inevitably multiplied when I was live on-air, to MCR's very large listenership. On most bulletins I struggled terribly to keep it together. I tried various methods of restraining myself, such as clenching my stomach muscles or placing my hands around my cheeks and forehead to create a kind of visor to protect me from distraction, but they both cramped my voice projection.

The sports news followed the news, the presenters of which constantly demonstrated a professionalism and calm that never wavered even when urgent stories were handed to them. They must have been baffled as to why I was allowed on air as I was so clearly uncomfortable. One innuendo-prone camp newsreader called Colin was highly amused by my obvious nerves, and would deliberately say silly things to get me giggling. One time needing the ruler with which we cut the paper of our bulletins into order, Colin said "Pass me 12 inches of pleasure, darling!" And when a horse named Wee Willie Winkie was his 'And finally' story, Colin turned to me during the jingle announcing my sports news and said 'Wee Willie Winkie? Why didn't they just call it Small Dick?!" Barely worthy of a snigger maybe, but not to the laughter tinderbox I'd become, and he knew it only too well. I've no idea how I read anything after such remarks.

I lived in constant fear of giggling mid-broadcast while reading a serious story...worst of all, involving a tragedy. I knew then that I had no future as a presenter on radio, and definitely not on television where there was no hiding place visually as well as audibly.

I'd actually wangled myself a meeting with a top presenters' agent at that time, and after an amiable chat she said very astutely "I can imagine, if you were ever broadcasting live, however calm you may appear on screen, internally you'd be a bundle of nerves – like a swan on water, seemingly serene from above and agitated below." She was spot on. I couldn't even envisage myself ever escaping my anxieties, or being able to smile when I was unhappy inside as was imperative for presenters. I guess at least this showed how honest and straightforward I was, but it was devastating to have to ditch a dream career due to nerves - a huge blow to my only realistic path to fame. But I knew it was better for me to never be famous than become infamous for corpsing while addressing an audience.

Something else also convinced me I was not cut out to be a broadcast journalist. In the fake newsroom I studied in at the broadcasting school, and the real newsroom I now worked in at MCR – both of which were male-dominated – was a testosterone-charged 'We must be the best' mentality, as if breaking the biggest stories and landing the most exclusives was a matter of life or death. It was reminiscent of the uncomfortable blood lust I'd had as a fast bowler in cricket at school. I got the impression that if you weren't prepared to give every ounce of effort towards the cause you should forget it and go home. I was more inclined to now go home.

Not many aspiring journos would have been content with where I'd got to by then, and indeed I wasn't, but having basically been told in my youth that I'd achieve very little with my life I had low expectations. And, due to how nerve-wracked I was, no choice.

I got a shot at scriptwriting for a sports TV channel, though that didn't turn out to be nearly as exciting and varied as being a radio journalist. I'd spend many hours composing witty and/or fact-filled nuggets to be read out before and after each programme, then mid-afternoon a voice-over artist would waltz in, take my scripts into a booth and swiftly record them all. Maybe it was just me feeling inferior again, but I found him a smug git, and frankly I resented the imbalance of our jobs, especially when I discovered he got paid four times more than me yet worked little more than two hours a day to my nine. I was a trained broadcaster with some experience in a major radio station, of course. Writing links for a barely watched channel seemed to me increasingly dull and pointless and I couldn't bear being in their office at the top of an old building in Soho. Plus, the commuting to and from Central London was often frustrating and occasionally unpleasant. I felt full responsibility towards a firm paying me a decent wage and understandably expecting a professional performance in return. I began to get ill. There was an almost trendy debilitating condition at that time known as ME, and I was convinced I'd got it. I took so much time off work that understandably – and genuinely to my relief – I was fired.

On reflection now, perhaps that scriptwriting job and that building gave me unhappy associations with being away at boarding-school. Just as I hid away in our family accommodation in schools we lived in when I was a kid, I knew I wanted to work from home where I felt secure, could be my own person, and wasn't overly beholden to others. But how was that going to happen?

Realising that if I was to have a future in journalism it could only be in print, I got back in contact with The Bugle, the local paper where I'd done my work experience and been offered a job. Luckily, they were still interested in taking me on. The office was a nice easy commute involving a drive through Richmond Park, and the work there was a cinch compared to the radio and TV I'd experienced.

When Mum was alive, I used to telephone her on a regular basis, sharing almost all my news whether it be good or bad. And for literally years after she died, whenever there was something I wanted to talk about, my first thought was to call her…before realisation kicked in. It took a lot of adjusting to the fact that Mum was now gone and could not be contacted again. Not in the traditional ways of the living anyhow. I did wonder whether the interest she'd had in spiritual matters may have helped her remain in my universe in some form. Perhaps the coincidental headline of The Daily Press the day of her funeral was some sign. Yet even if it was the case and Mum was in a position to guide me, I did not want to know. I had never gotten over, let alone forgotten, the middle-aged head-shaking woman who spooked me as a baby. Maybe that had been some kind of warning my mother would be dead at 51, perhaps even a representation of her spiritual self. I'd never know. But that was the extent to which I allowed my mind to dwell on her.

Back in the sedate surroundings of The Bugle, one afternoon I was at my desk staring into space while trying to compose an article on a typewriter when a senior reporter sitting nearby asked "How often do you think and talk about your mother?" I was taken aback, but told her how it was "I think about her from time to time but I never talk about her". "Well, you should" she replied. I looked at her, confused, and asked why. "Because, like most mothers, she presumably made a huge contribution to your life and, as she only passed away quite recently, it's wise to think and talk about her a lot because if you don't all your grief will build and catch up with you one day."

I did then try thinking about Mum more, but, other than my brothers to whom I rarely spoke, there was barely anyone I felt right discussing her with. And while I'd enjoyed plenty of times of great affection and fun with her, I honestly didn't look back on those years with enormous fondness or wished she was still around. Maybe sub-consciously I'd not forgiven her for my having to serve the full five years at Stourback in order to aid her affair, making me her go-between in an illicit relationship with an unprincipled priest, and being privy to her intimate secrets. There was also her occasional insensitivity. Dad made derogatory remarks on a daily basis, so I expected them from him. Mum was generally a big-hearted type, so when she came out with what I perceived as hurtful comments they seriously stung and I never forgot them. To the super-sensitive youngster I'd been, the most harmless comments were crucial, never more so than from parents. All rather sad really, because the good times with Mum outnumbered the bad times, but generally those early years were unhappy for me and I felt my parents were both heavily responsible for that. Of course I was glad they gave me the opportunity of life but I was probably just a result of them having sex one time - they wouldn't have aimed to create me in particular. And because I hadn't felt truly loved by them, I didn't truly love them...certainly not in the way most people I encountered loved their parents. Even less so my brothers.

Perhaps I even resented Mum for leaving this life when she did, though that was hardly her fault. I did wonder if she was aware of my feelings wherever she now was and regretted that. But the Mum thought that most frequently entered my head as the years and decades rolled on was how much she missed by dying in her early 50s. In the ensuing decades I'd imagine her being aware of events, like weddings and births, involving those she'd left behind and saying to herself something like 'How incredibly sad I didn't live to experience all that and share it with them.'

My brothers and I each inherited about £13,000 from Mum. I decided to put mine down as a deposit on my first property – a flat in Chiswick. The traditionally solid investment of bricks and mortar seemed the best way of respecting and protecting her legacy. Although religion hadn't been a part of my life for five years by then, my decision was influenced by the Parable Of The Sower. I knew that I needed to invest the money so it would grow for me, and that if I didn't invest it I'd soon spend it unwisely. There was even an element of the phrase I'd heard said of Jesus Christ: 'He died so we could live'. My inheritance from Mum enabled me to get a foot on the London property ladder, something I'd never have been able to do had she remained alive as, like Dad, she'd needed all her savings to live on.

With my stronger than ever perspective on the temporary nature of life, I realised that although I now owned a property it wasn't going to be mine eternally because there was a time limit for each of us on Earth. I had a mortgage, which made me feel quite grown-up…but only quite. Fortunately, it was a modest mortgage of £30,000 because, having hated Dad's scrimping on heating when we lived in the frozen north, I was determined to always have my own home as warm as I wanted. It was also satisfying to now afford almost limitless sweets, records and other things I'd been restricted or prevented from having as a kid.

For a while, Dad was noticeably kinder to me, presumably concerned how I'd fare without Mum. But he still couldn't help his true self emerging on occasion. When I showed him my flat for the first time, I was especially proud of its unique Stavridi stained glass window on the second of its three floors. "You had to go for something out of the ordinary, didn't you?" he pointed out. "You couldn't just get a regular place."

A rather bohemian girlfriend, on staying with me in the new flat, pointed out I'd taken to curling up in a ball in my bed when sleeping. I'd have been amused had she likened me to a hedgehog, but she said "That is the foetal position and suggests you might be sub-consciously attempting to return to the womb". Not a topic I wished to contemplate at the time. But I was having recurring dreams of a place I somehow knew to be Mum's former home although it didn't physically resemble the house she actually used to live in. In fact, it didn't resemble any house I'd ever seen in 'real life'. It was situated on two levels in some sort of indoor passages, not unlike a disused section of a shopping mall. When I went inside, opening doors and window shutters to let in light, it was pretty much how I (in my dream only) remembered Mum had left it. But then I'd discover many further rooms that I wasn't previously aware existed. My main thought was that this would add to the property's value when sold, yet I never did get to a point of sale as each time I either walked through the house or looked at its exterior I then woke up. I didn't understand the point of that dream, or another one I sometimes had as an adult which entailed a canal packed with warships of varying kinds, and from somewhere within there I'd have to reluctantly take a scary aeroplane flight. Most frequent though would be nightmares involving an anonymous ill-meaning intruder entering my room, and I'd wake calling out for help. I was no dream interpreter, but my early life had been full of occasions when my personal space was invaded, and it seemed there was fear and angst still within me.

Whenever I'd had nightmares as a youngster living at home, Mum would come to find out why I was screaming then advise me to turn my pillow over...as if there was peace, even happiness, to be found on the other side of it. I never stopped doing that, and I don't recall having another nightmare post pillow-flip though of course I've no idea if it was that which did the trick. Whether it did or not, there was comfort in continuing something Mum had taught me, particularly now she no longer existed.

23.

PAPER WRITER

I could have shrunk back into my shell on The Bugle, and had a distinctly mediocre career as part of me liked being under the radar. Returning to local press seemed a step backwards – back to the drawing-board - but I had a plan. I could get away with minimum effort here, and I had plenty of justifiable reasons to be out of the office on stories, interviews and other assignments. Young, energetic, loving the work and keen to make my mark, I was happy to work long hours. So discreetly I did occasional night and weekend shifts on national newspapers. Those shifts paid very well compared to what I was earning on The Bugle. But of course I'd only had four months' training as a radio journalist and I was not prepared for the stress and demands of daily tabloids. It was a whole different level of journalism…and of pressure. You'd be expected to work on several stories at a time, to tight deadlines, and with editors giving you grief if you didn't deliver. In the days when The Daily Call editorial was a gigantic open-plan office on Fleet Street, a news editor once bellowed "Twi-i-i-i-gg, where is your f***ing story?" so loudly that half the staff turned and stared at me. I wanted the ground beneath their dirty brown carpet tiles to swallow me up. And putting me in a frenzy only ensured I was even slower in completing the job.

When one morning I arrived for a shift on a different tabloid, Tomorrow, their Diary editor told me he had good news and bad news for me. The good news was I'd be going to Harrods to interview the immensely popular TV and radio presenter Paddy O'Hara who was there to promote his latest book. "The bad news is you're going to tear his wig off" he explained. I was shocked, particularly as he then revealed a plot as to how it should be carried out with the help of a fellow reporter. Wet behind the ears as I undoubtedly was, even I knew that ripping the hairpiece off any person, let alone one as distinguished as this revered broadcaster, was an appalling act and literally a crime. So I refused. "You want to be a journalist, don't you?" was the Diary editor's arm-twist. "Er, yes, but that's not journalism, that's assault" I argued, privately proud of my defence. I agreed to interview O'Hara but not scalp him. A more senior colleague was assigned to accompany me saying he might do the dastardly deed...but he didn't. He hovered behind O'Hara as I quizzed the genial Dubliner on a variety of harmless topics. So mercifully he returned home with barnet intact, and we returned to the office without a stain on our characters...although without a strong story. A few lines from my interview appeared as a pathetic tale in that Diary the next day under the headline The Irish Jig Gig. Weeks later, O'Hara passed me at BBC TV Centre and gave me a withering look and, while I couldn't blame him for assuming it was my fault, trying to explain it wasn't was probably only going to make matters worse.

On another shift, I was ordered to rummage through the dustbins of a showbiz star then dying of AIDS. It made me feel like a scumbag. There were times too when I'd be told to 'doorstep' various celebrities (which entailed standing outside their house hoping they'd come out and talk) in the midst of controversies. I was being turned into a nuisance, not a journalist. It wasn't my style at all, especially having endured five years of deep unpopularity at school.

One Sunday morning at The Daily Call, in an attempt to avoid distractions and stress, I snuck into an empty side room to work there. After a while I looked up from what I was doing to see several editorial staff laughing at me through the window. Seeing the bemused expression on my face, they did exaggerated impressions of me typing in plodding fashion with one finger. I must have appeared extremely amateur, if not a fake. But I didn't mind their mocking. Unlike at Stourback, I could tell it was done with good humoured amusement, and because I chuckled with them the teasing stopped. I'd learnt that lesson at least. I never learnt to type properly though – my one finger was fast enough for me.

Having realised after a promising start that a career in broadcasting was out of the question, I now sensed that I didn't have what it took to work full-time for national newspapers, not the daily ones anyway. Neither did I want my future to be on the likes of The Bugle. Often to be found on the editorial staff of local papers were loyal but lazy types who'd happily spend their entire careers there, never seeking or achieving anything more dynamic. Not me. I was ambitious and wanted to achieve on a prominent platform, but again I knew not what or how.

I got scared and depressed, and sat in my little flat perplexed as to how I could get anywhere career-wise. I knew I was depressed because I noticed myself thinking and talking like my Dad long had, bemoaning my fate, blaming others, and so forth. Since I passed my driving test, I'd become particularly aware how so many people did not have the same manners and standards that had been drilled into me in childhood. For example, when I'd slow up or stop to let other vehicles through first, I'd expect a signalled acknowledgment, and whenever that didn't come I'd be annoyed, often hooting at the drivers. It was the kind of thing that, when my life was not going well, really bothered me.

At one point it all got too much. I had what would probably be called a mini breakdown. This included envisaging the inside of my brain like a computer graphic – an undulating shape-changing expanse of mesh stretching into infinity. I also recall crying in my Dad's presence, him staring rather than offering a hug, and just responding with "Well, at least you now know how I've felt most of my life."

I was never depressed in the same clinical sense as Dad, but I used to get down about my own loneliness and chronic failure to make friends and get and keep girlfriends. That got me down partly because it made me too like Dad. Infuriatingly in some ways I was his clone. He recognised it in me too. Neither of us could hide easily our disappointment at our similarities. I'd go so far as to say there was unspoken resentment between us over them. So now that he appeared almost pleased I'd also had a taste of depression, suddenly that was the spur I needed to get a grip and back on track. Otherwise I faced a future of frustration and underachievement like my father, which was the opposite of what I wanted.

As luck – or who knows what else - would have it, Class, a glamorous glossy magazine, promoted their imminent launch on telly and a friend watching suggested I contact them. Their reporter who took my call told me they'd be specialising in interviewing celebrities and, if I knew any, they may be interested. Knew any? I was living in Chiswick, an upmarket neighbourhood popular with celebrities, largely due to its proximity to the then BBCTV Centre.

I interviewed a local actress – who happened to be hot at the time – and that went down well so I was offered other celebrities, and surprisingly soon some superstars. Suddenly, miraculously, I had the journalistic opportunity that suited me best: I'd be freelance, based at home but working for an international publication. I'd be recording interviews for transcribing, accuracy and legal security, but not for nerve-wracking live broadcast. And I could still earn a good living. Just what I needed.

With all those warnings from College still ringing in my ears about how tough journalism was to get into, and knowing my only short training and high-level experience was in radio, I did feel something of a fraud now and occasionally wondered if I might get found out and dropped.

Working in radio and during my brief stint as a TV scriptwriter, I never encountered any concerns about the quality of journalism and its providers. But I soon discovered that many people had a low opinion of print journos and/or were suspicious of them...of us. In a popularity poll, press reporters (mostly from the tabloids) would rank very low along with estate agents and traffic wardens. As a specialist interviewer, I noticed some celebrities found us useful and used us accordingly, while others – often those with something to hide – despised us and wanted us wiped from the planet. They forgot the extent to which press coverage helped get them where they were in the first place and continued to give them a public profile and promote their projects.

Trust between celebrities and the British press was then at an all-time low. The former were fed up of having their words twisted or taken out of context by the latter, and the public doubted they could believe what they read. So Class magazine was an excellent solution. They only wanted nice, positive, unchallenging interviews, usually written up in Question & Answer format to avoid any chance of them being misquoted or misinterpreted. So celebs and publicists liked the likes of me as they thought us kind yet capable of getting coverage. Quite honestly, any fool could conduct and write those interviews, so it didn't matter that I hadn't had the right training or was occasionally awestruck by who I was talking to.

Interviewing rich and famous folk now I was always excited, never afraid…though on reflection it would have helped if I had been. As with my school exams, I hardly did any preparation. I'd treat these early interviews like casual conversations, and if the celebrity concerned seemed to enjoy the chat and my company, that was good enough for me. I honestly expected the entertainers to entertain me, to regale me with funny anecdotes – not out of arrogance, but because I'd grown up watching TV chat shows like Parkinson and remembered my Dad being impressed by the relaxed rapport Parky got with most of his guests. Little did I know then that the guests had been grilled beforehand by researchers for their best stories and topics. Ironically, too many years later, I watched Parky explain that the key to a successful interview was preparation. If only I properly prepared then when the biggest names talked to me…

Some celebrities needed persuading to give interviews, and I'd attempt to charm them, though not quite to the extent I sometimes tried to flatter women into my bed. Fortunately for me, unlike with any other publication I worked for, Class magazine didn't seem to mind what their featured celebrities said in interviews. They could be as bland as they wanted, and promote whatever they wanted, and they'd still get published. What's more the celebs were allowed to approve the text, headlines and photos if they so desired. If all that wasn't enough incentive, there were serious fees paid to them too – fees which increased for sought-after interviews, photo-shoots inside their homes, exclusive access to weddings and other glamorous star-studded events, and even pointless ones like marriage blessings and baby showers. With a lot of them, Class didn't need to pay anything because hardly any other publications were, and none to the same extent.

Class's priority appeared to be just having these celebs on board, and being able to boast about that. If they did get a talked-about interview all the better, but those were few and far between. Most other national magazines, and every national newspaper, required their celebrity interviews to have a new and newsworthy angle and be revelatory. So prior to conducting interviews, journalists would trawl through the celebrity's previous ones to ensure they didn't go over old ground, or if they did that they got a new take on it. After those interviews, commissioning editors would ask what 'lines' we'd managed to get. This was not a reference to Cocaine, though in some cases that might not have been beyond the realms of possibility. These lines meant storylines, new angles – the strongest of which you'd place earliest in the resulting article 'to draw the reader in'.

Class magazine's policy of positivity, fawning even, to the rich and famous seemed on the surface – and to the cynical national press – to be absurd, and was mocked accordingly. But it actually proved to be a brainwave, as Class swiftly became the go-to publication for celebrities and VIPs in search of safe publicity and easy money. Even those who rarely if ever talked to journalists now gave in to this unique publication. Its popularity suggested that Class's readers, like its bosses, prioritised who the celebs were over what they had to say. And, for a lot of them, the pictures mattered much more than the words.

Thus Class rapidly became a sensation. I found myself working for the biggest audience I'd had, and not just meeting but interviewing the great and the good...and occasionally the not so good.

It didn't escape my attention that I was now effectively writing portraits of the famous after drawing them as a youth during Art classes in which the teacher had talked about her journalist sister doing celebrity interviews. I'd inherited my parents' fascination for well-known people, regarding them as interesting and important unlike myself. And with only four British TV channels and far fewer media outlets of any kind then, celebrities seemed enigmatic, awesome high achievers.

One of the advantages of being established as an interviewer was that, if there were any celebs I liked and wanted to meet, I was usually able to arrange an interview with them within a day or two, often in their homes too. That was a thrill and a privilege...in most cases.

If I'd been told as a kid that many stars I watched on TV then I would meet as an adult as part of my job, and occasionally get to know, I'd have been beyond excited, if I could even believe it. Some I was thrilled just to be acknowledged by, let alone welcomed into their homes for interviews and sometimes hospitality. Enjoying a great chat with the gentleman singer Roger Whittaker in the lounge of his sumptuous mansion, I remembered listening to his hits on the radio during prep school Art classes, and now thought 'How did this happen?' I had plenty of pinch-me moments.

It is said that, when someone becomes famous: 'It's not them who change, it's the people around them who change.' I often found that to be true. I changed too. I was fine when working with celebs, once I'd got used to it. But often when I met them socially, I'd still find myself slightly star-struck, awkward and blurty, through feeling unworthy (as a person, but interestingly never as a professional) of their company. It must have been strange for certain stars who, having found me pretty together for interviews, then encountered a nervy version at parties and events. I privately compared it to my Dad being excellent at handling masses of other people's kids during term-times and crap with his own kids during school holidays. But actually it was what I noticed in most people unused to being around famous faces: allowing the celebrity a sense of superiority or projecting it on to them. For example, if a celebrity made a joke, they usually got a much bigger laugh than any non-celebrities would were they to make the same joke, even if the latter told it better. It was similar to the ever-positive reactions my Goldenboy brother Mark got to his quips compared to mine during our shared youth.

As Class magazine was trusted by celebrities, so was I as a regular contributor…essentially for getting them positive publicity. Some would allow me to interview them repeatedly. A few said I was the only journalist they'd work with, though that was neither practical nor possible. On rare occasions I'd hang out with them and even become friends. In those cases, I'd ask them not to tell me anything 'off the record' because, although I would never betray their confidence, if it did then appear in the papers they might assume I had. I didn't want them even wondering whether I'd let them down. I liked to think they appreciated I was an honest sort anyway, but I soon learnt that they never really wanted you to be totally honest. For example, if you were interviewing them about their latest book, album, tour or whatever, even if it wasn't to your taste you couldn't tell them that or they might end the interview, and any dealings with you. Yes, some egos were THAT delicate. You just had to say it was 'great' and wish them well with it, whatever you privately thought. Visiting entertainers' dressing-rooms after performances I'd disliked was weird. When I walked through the Stage Doors, it was as if I was suddenly under some spell of sycophancy. I'd greet these presenters, actors, comedians, musicians, or singers with a string of clichés like "You were wonderful…it was terrific…haven't enjoyed myself so much in ages…" even when I thought the complete opposite.

Playing back interviews, which was of course necessary for writing them up, I'd be embarrassed at my impressed reactions – the most cringey being 'Wow!' – when the celebrity concerned was telling of their projects and achievements. Winning the Nobel Peace Prize, finding a cure for cancer, solving World poverty or walking on the Moon might merit Wows, but not appearing on TV shows, having books published or being awarded an MBE.

I admired performers their guts to go on stage or live on television in front of audiences – partly because I knew I couldn't - though a fair per centage were natural-born show-offs. Some in interviews would describe what their colleagues were doing as 'brave' or 'courageous', and I'd politely nod in agreement but privately be thinking 'You need to go see members of the emergency services at work or armed forces on the frontline, then you'll know the true meaning of the word brave.' I felt that, in the comparatively cushy life of showbusiness, some people needed to get real. Nothing they would ever do workwise could be as important as what people upon whom lives depend face on a daily basis. Medics, ambulance drivers, police, etcetera, deserve celebrity and the privileges and perks that go with it way more than performers and presenters do. Acclaim and awards given to actors baffled me. In the great scheme of important occupations, contributions to life, I couldn't see why people pretending to be other people merited such recognition. The vast majority, after all, were merely speaking words they hadn't even written. Yet some names I met clearly regarded themselves as among THE most important people alive, and unfortunately were too often treated so...sometimes by me, I'm ashamed to admit.

Probably influenced by my Catholic upbringing, I'd wonder about the extent to which people can justifiably take credit for their talents. Sure, plenty work hard to make the most of their abilities, but aren't those talents/abilities – even the inclination to work hard - just gifts they've been blessed with? If that is the case, shouldn't these people simply be regarded as fortunate rather than brilliant, and therefore less deserving of our admiration? I definitely didn't have a high opinion of myself, but I accepted that like everyone I had my fair share of gifts – though then I'd have swapped any to be a natural with women.

Having long assumed that pop and sports stars were to be most envied, I now observed their older selves struggling to match the thrill of their heydays and now larking around for laughs while increasingly in danger of becoming a mockery of who they used to be. Yet no two days doing what I did were ever the same, so I began to think it preferable to be a celebrity journo than a celebrity in many cases. Though I did envy the ease with which the famous could earn big bucks simply by attaching their names to products, campaigns, and even books they didn't really write. And, if they played their cards right, that should ensure their financial security. But too many celebrities I read or heard about, and sometimes now talked to, struggled to maintain stability and happiness, particularly in their private lives despite their fame and wealth. Which confirmed what I'd suspected: that more important than any occupation or status, was personal satisfaction and contentment. I was now beginning to believe that to be the most desirable asset of all.

The people representing most celebrities were often prone to excessive fawning. Being employed by them, they may have considered it part of their service...or required to be retained in their employ. The fact is I was also dependent upon the celebrities to earn a living. I needed them far more than they needed me. I needed the income interviews provided me with far more than the celebrities needed the publicity I got them. I required their permission to let me talk to them, and it was me asking about their lives and not the other way round. I had to always be polite and diplomatic towards them though some were sometimes dismissive and rude towards me. At times I likened myself to a hungry dog waiting for scraps of food to be dropped by celebrities from their lavishly laid tables as they feasted.

It was similar dealing with Commissioning Editors on newspapers and magazines. It was up to them to decide whether or not to buy my work, so they were in the powerful positions and I was powerless. A few took advantage of that and messed me about, knowing I'd be unwise to complain as they'd then stop taking my stuff. I just had to silently rely on karma serving justice for me, and probably others they screwed over.

Freelancing for me basically involved submitting ideas, stories and interviews to Commissioning Editors, which to me basically resembled throwing ideas at a wall and hoping they stuck. If ever I got yesses and found myself in demand, I felt good about myself. If I got rejections and work went quiet, I felt rotten. My job entailed rejection on a daily basis, and that was often hard to take. On the other hand, at any moment on any day someone could put something my way workwise, and fortunately that did happen sufficiently frequently for me to believe I would survive self-employment because I was somehow being 'looked after' spiritually. Newspapers and magazines were ever hungry monsters needing to be fed, so work was there to be had if I applied myself sufficiently.

I could never have imagined I'd get paid decent money to ask questions I'd have liked to ask many of these 'stars' anyway. Only a few times did the phrase 'never meet your heroes' ring true for me. Of the countless celebrities I encountered, I'd never forget which ones had bad breath, poor skin, obvious surgery, or a sense of superiority. One or two had most if not all of the above. Only about 10 were condescending, dismissive or downright rude towards me. Yet I was one of the nicest celebrity journalists working for the nicest publication in the UK. I didn't feel I had much choice other than to take poor treatment on the chin, if I wanted to complete the job and therefore get paid. But inside I'd be slightly resentful thinking of them 'All the advantages you have in life and you still can't be a decent human being. Money and fame certainly can't buy class.' People would occasionally ask me "What are celebrities like?" as if they belonged to a unique race. "They're just like any other section of society" I'd answer. "Most are nice, some are not."

I discovered that even celebrities have heroes who they'd name-drop if they met, knew or worked with them…sometimes as if they themselves weren't impressive enough. Perhaps to emphasise their familiarity with these big names, they'd refer to James Stewart as Jimmy, Robert De Niro as Bob, and The Everly

Brothers as The Evs, and suchlike, yet that only succeeded in making me cringe.

Interviewing people younger than myself, especially much younger, made me feel I should have done better. As an adult I was less impressed by talent and achievement, whereas as a child I'd often been in absolute awe of it. Thus, I was most interested in those I'd admired when I was growing up. I almost made it my mission to interview stars from my youth – in particular the 1970s, the hardest decade for me personally. A few had since left the limelight and were surprised to receive my interview requests out of the blue. It was as if I wanted to revive their popularity, as a way of thanking them for the light they brought to my dark days. Their stars may have dimmed by the time I caught up with them, but what they meant to my existence made me awestruck in a way that even A-Listers who'd emerged since could never do.

Twice I interviewed Nadia Comaneci, and each time I looked closely at her thinking (unbeknownst to her, of course): 'So you're the person who, as a child, made me feel inadequate!' But it occurred to me that, as she was best remembered for having gained 'Perfect 10' scores as a young Olympic gymnast, there must have been plenty of people around the globe who felt inadequate compared to her at that time – not least her fellow competitors. Of course it wasn't really Ms Comancci who made me feel like that; it was my Dad making her seem superhuman and me useless trash. If he thought better of me knowing I twice got to spend time with her, even got paid to interview her, he never said. But then that wasn't in his nature.

I once requested, via Perth cricket ground, an interview with Dennis Lillee, the Australian fast bowler I'd so revered in my teens…again partly because my Dad had been a fast bowler. When I got no response after several weeks, I forgot all about it. Then one Saturday morning my home phone rang and it was Lillee himself wanting to know more about my request. What words I could reply with probably made little sense, such was my shock and amazement at having him call me personally. He said he'd ring me back if he decided to do the interview, but he never did. That didn't bother me though – it was enough that for a few minutes he'd been aware of my existence and spoke to me.

It was 1970s pop stars that meant the most to me. The artists whose hits, piped through the feeble earpiece of my transistor radio under pillows in the dormitories at Stourback, provided a little bit of light relief from my then otherwise tortuous existence.

Spending several exclusive hours with Donny Osmond was emotional for me, remembering how I'd felt finding a broken copy of Puppy Love on a fencepost in bleakest Northumberland, when he'd been the most desired person in existence at the time I felt the least desired. Yet he told how he himself had a domineering Dad and gone through a confidence crisis once his teen heart-throb period was up.

I suppose when you do anything for long enough you learn techniques or tricks to improve. And I noticed that Donny, David Essex and Cliff Richard would, on being introduced, listen for your first name and repeat it back to you during interviews or conversation. As they were aware, it made you feel good that they knew and spoke your name – particularly those of us who regarded celebrities as superior beings.

Fascinating for me was meeting and interviewing female celebrities I was bowled over by in my female-deprived youth. In those early days, I assumed I simply fancied them because I found them physically attractive – their faces and figures, as much as their talents and success, would be what captured the attention of my superficial self. When as an adult I interrogated them, I discovered similarities in their backgrounds and emotional make-up to my own. And naturally I found it was the same with non-famous women I fancied too. Evidently there was more to attraction than literally met the eye.

Occasionally I'd be complimented by celebrities saying things such as 'I feel you really understand me'. With them, it was like we had a special connection, and that often boiled down to common ground. The more insecure ones I interviewed, the more I realised showbusiness is indeed overrun with souls seeking the attention, appreciation and love they lacked as children. It took one to know one. The tragic thing is no matter how much of that they receive from audiences and fans, it can never replace or match that which should have been supplied by their parents.

When as a youngster desiring fame (and, as a likely consequence, fortune), much of that was about wanting to stick two fingers up to those who put me down then. Now as an adult, there was still no sign of me attaining fame, but I felt it was probably a blessing it hadn't come my way as I'd found it tough enough to deal with difficulties I faced. Many celebrities struggled as a result of their fame, just as I imagined I would have done. For example, some men among them who were popular with women experienced problems settling for one…though that I didn't think I'd mind.

The value of a press interview tended to increase if the celebrity concerned discussed their personal circumstances, and the more of a mess they were or were in the better. A fair number drew the line, saying things like 'It's called a private life for good reason'. However frustrated or disappointed professionally I may have been by that, as someone who found relationships of most kinds complicated, I personally respected them all the more for it, and began to be grateful I hadn't become well-known so my challenging personal situations did remain private.

The way interviewing celebrities tended to go was: ask probing / controversial questions and if you got good answers back you'd probably be in the money, but on reading the resulting article they and/or their representatives might feel they've revealed too much, blame you and maybe not work with you again. Ask nothing controversial and you'd be lucky to get much more than a bland story published, but the celebrity would love you and happily talk to you anytime. However, as celebrities were frequently in demand for interviews and they each had just the one life to talk about, they'd understandably tire of being asked predictable questions and often relish different challenging ones. Some even made up stories to get publicity, and I could usually spot those.

I do think that the vivid imagination I'd had since childhood helped me as a freelance journalist coming up with interview questions and story ideas. That was crucial to my survival, let alone success, as a freelance. In a domain of who dares wins and if you don't ask you don't get, I often asked cheeky questions in interviews, and for the most part got away with it. Maybe my quizzing of celebrities also benefitted from the boundary-disrespectful way I'd been talked to by my Dad and inappropriate conversations I'd had with Mum. I usually found it easier to interview women, but then generally I was more at ease in female company.

I now paid close attention to interviews conducted on television and radio, and I'd wince when lengthy fact-packed questions were asked because the interrogator was clearly trying to make him or herself seem impressive. Of course readers or listeners of my interviews were interested in the people I was talking to, not me. My absence of self-esteem alone ensured I knew my place. I kept my questions concise and to the point for fear of hearing my Dad demand 'Stop showing off!', and in that instance I was glad of it.

Enjoying a drink after a friendly mixed doubles match at my local tennis club one evening, a lady I'd played against - on hearing what I did for a living - said: "It must be very boring hearing people talk about themselves and their lives..." "Far from it" I replied truthfully, "everybody has at least one fascinating life story to tell if you ask the right questions, let them talk and listen carefully enough."

Social conversations had long been sources of anxiety for me. But now when conducting interviews, I controlled those conversations...except with the occasional strong characters who sought to have things go their way. As a journalist I almost adopted a role like an actor did, and I was secure in that role because I usually knew 'my stuff' and could always fall back on that if interviews got challenging. Thus I tended to be calm as an interviewer, regardless of how famous or impressive my interviewee. Yet, as I said, if I talked to some of them in normal non-work circumstances, I could get overwhelmed with nerves like fans might on meeting them.

Fans are curious people. Having been an admirer of various celebrities myself, I knew there's variety in what you want in meeting your idols. Most just want to shake their hand and congratulate them on their success, maybe get autographs or photographs. Some seemed to believe that by gaining proximity to these luminaries they'd share the admiration at their achievements...even though they'd never be able to legitimately claim them. Me, I was among those who wanted to thank them for how they, or their work, had made me feel...particularly in my troubled youth...and in my own way pay them back with positive publicity. Sometimes I hoped a bit of their magic would rub off on me, that I'd become similarly blessed, like how as a kid I wanted a piece of Mark's ability to charm, to make others laugh, to be admired.

24.

AIN'T NO PLEASING THEM

Recording interviews for publication in the popular press was invariably more relaxed than conducting them for broadcast, live or not. It was usually enjoyable to interrogate stars, but I still got nervous at times. Doing a face-to-face exclusive with a major movie actress, nerves put me in a fit of giggles. She was remarkably understanding, explaining that she was all too frequently 'corpsing' during filming, causing costly delays which only made her even more nervous and giggly, so she carried a pin with which to prick herself into being serious.

Another time another famous actress was telling me in detail about her divorce, and I guess the gravity of it brought out the anxious child in me because I smirked and smiled. I just about managed to get a grip on that occasion, but I felt unprofessional...and disrespectful to her as she shared her most personal thoughts.

I cursed my nerves, but was relieved to not now be risking high-profile humiliation by laughing live on telly or radio at a serious moment. I'd had more than enough humiliation in my early life. But humiliation sometimes continued to occur in my adult life too, courtesy of Dad. No matter what I was now achieving professionally or who I met or interviewed, he still didn't treat me as a grown-up or with respect.

As a homeowner in a smart part of the capital with a mortgage and bills and meals, a car, a social life and plenty more things to pay for, I naturally targeted the wealthier domain of the popular press as opposed to going for the higher-brow with lower budgets. Besides, my interests and level of intellect were better suited to the tabloids. I'd been doing alright for a number of years when, with typical tactlessness in front of other people at a function, Dad dismissively referred to me as 'a tabloid reporter', adding "When are you going to do real journalism and write for some proper publications?" Crestfallen, as I'd so often been by his hurtfulness, I explained to him that the so-called broadsheets (The Telegraph, Guardian, Independent, and his beloved Times) he was referring to would then have required me to work much harder than certain tabloids for much less money, which I wasn't prepared to do just to please him. Also to defend my status, I pointed out that, because my work was published, it would survive me and him. "It won't if the World ends" Dad replied.

When I featured Dad's favourite opera singer, he asked me where she lived. It didn't occur to me not to tell my own father, but I shouldn't have because he then wrote her a kind of fan letter in which he explained I'd provided him with her address – something I should never have disclosed to anyone.

I sometimes wondered what I would have achieved in broadcasting had I had paternal support instead of Dad's humiliation and negativity and all else he caused me. Maybe I'd have interviewed celebrities on television instead. For national TV, the interviews would have been arranged and researched for me, and I wouldn't have had to ask risky questions to get the spicy stories the tabloids required. Plus there was a likelihood of becoming rich and famous. My career with the press would never be revered in the same way a TV interviewer's would. It would pale by comparison, go unnoticed by most people. But I had still done well considering initial expectations of me, especially my own.

When I worked in radio, my favourite and most moving moment was when a friend told me that her brother, seriously ill with Malaria while travelling in a very remote part of South America, heard a report of mine broadcast on BBC World Service, and just hearing my familiar voice lifted his spirits and helped him recover. What a sense of privilege that gave me.

One thing that always amazed me as a print journalist was how articles I - who'd long felt insignificant - created in my little office in my little home, were seen as soon as the following day by hundreds of thousands, maybe millions, of people around the country and sometimes the World. Granted, the audience size depended on the publication, rather like performers playing everywhere from their own living-rooms to Wembley Stadium. Yet it gave me a sense of the thrill an author or songwriter must get knowing their books could be read or songs heard in different parts of the globe at any given time. I was chuffed enough to do what I did for a living and the fact that my work was published for other people's consumption.

As my face appearing on television was out of the question, and my voice talking on radio anymore was inadvisable, my best remaining option was getting articles I'd written in national papers and magazines. It was wonderful to know anyone could pop into shops literally all over the UK and many newsagents around the World, and find them there. From when I started getting bylines [your name on articles you've written], it occurred to me to use a pen-name. That was because self-loathing involved even my own name and, as I saw Dad as the source of my self-loathing, I didn't see why I should attach his surname to my accomplishments. I wanted to deny him that. I did end up sticking with my own name though. Though for my first two decades I considered both Luke and Twigg suggestive of weakness, now I realised it was unlikely there'd be any other journalists of the same name, so I'd stand out in that respect, and that's what I wanted.

I wanted those who'd doubted and dismissed me down the years to see my byline in popular publications and be impressed, maybe think "Hey, that's pretty cool!" or "Who'd have thought it?" I'd have settled for either reaction, though I guess my ultimate would be for my bullies to boast "I was at school with him." Unless any of them had become journalists, they weren't to know that getting articles in the national press wasn't *that* difficult. It hadn't proved to be for me in any case. But the very nature of newspapers and magazines meant my pieces in them would be widely read. So even my former persecutors could potentially now see my work, whereas I'd probably be unaware of theirs. I never would hear about any of them achieving anything, though it was perfectly possible they did and I just didn't move in the same circles. I suspect many went into Finance, which was never going to be my bag from the age of nine when Mathematics left me behind. Of course the likelihood was that they wouldn't give a monkey's that I was writing for the national press, and wouldn't have considered it any kind of a victory for me. But in my head it mattered.

The fact is though that pretty much the only people who notice bylines are journalists themselves. I now frequently had articles published in magazines and newspapers both nationally and internationally – including some major exclusives – but very rarely did a non-journalist spot my name. What I was doing had wide audiences, but only extremely rarely did I receive feedback.

After leaving SLI, I was told that one of my English lecturers there had said that I "couldn't string two sentences together". I'd no idea what prompted that, but it made me hope she'd choke on her Corn Flakes one morning when noticing that a story she was reading in her newspaper over breakfast was written by me. Her actual demise was far worse. Turned out she was an alcoholic one day found dead in a cupboard in that English department, an empty bottle of vodka by her side.

I interviewed sports stars Dad admired, and film stars Mum had admired. I think Mum would have been proud, though sadly I'd never hear that from her. As for Dad, well, as he was still alive he could have said that, but he never did. He liked to drop the names of my interviewees to other people, but I could tell that was about kudos for him, and not pride in me which was what I wanted. In contrast, on the rarer occasions when my Goldenboy brother Mark met famous people through his job running a leading London accountancy firm, Dad and Matthew were impressed and demanded details of those encounters. I would enquire about my brothers' careers – not that Matthew ever had much of one - but they never asked about mine, nor bought or looked at any of the newspapers or magazines I had articles in. To my mind there was a particular cruelty about that, though I'd long had time to get used to unsupportive brothers. Mark and

I had far more in common than Matthew, yet they remained a duo and kept me solo. Since seeing a pantomime as a child, they'd reminded me of the Ugly Sisters trying to stop Cinderella stealing their thunder and finding happiness.

I knew I was never going to be good enough for my father and brothers nor able to make them proud. Occasionally I wondered whether they were playing some kind of sick game to undermine me at best. But celebrity encounters, glamorous events, getting articles I'd written – and thereby my name - in major publications did impress some people. To many with regular jobs, it seemed a tad special with its higher profile. My job was often so exciting that I naturally wanted to share stories about it, but the reactions to hearing them tended to be mixed. Either I got the desired effect and questions then ensued, or there was disapproval, resentment even, that I was showing off. A fair number weren't remotely interested, rightly thinking there were plenty more important things in life. I had countless situations which merited the phrase 'Something to tell the grandchildren', but I didn't have children let alone grandchildren. And even if I did ever have any, I doubted they would be interested seeing as my living relatives weren't.

Whether in broadcast or print journalism, I was never going to do so brilliantly as to be regarded as a leader in those fields. That required a backbone and gravitas I didn't possess. Being an editor would have entailed working away from home anyway, so that was never going to be for me. However, I was now already exceeding the expectations I and others had of me as a youth, and that at least was pleasing…to me anyway.

25.

THIS NOBODY'S GOTTA LEARN SOMETIME

My single years were when I really learnt about life. They were like my trial period...full of trials.

I loved living in London, aka The Big Smoke. There was so much going on, so much to do. I couldn't get enough of the excitement, especially after the dragging dullness and misery of my youth. But I rarely stopped to take all this in and appreciate it, I just kept busy. I was hopeless at relaxing anyway – a throwback to Stourback when I never dared let my guard down. And the capital, particularly the West End which I frequented for functions, cinemas, theatres, shopping and socialising, was nearly always lively. I'd get my fix of that, then happily return to the comparative peace and slower pace of Chiswick.

Although I still felt slightly insecure venturing outside the womb of my home territory, London then seemed a vast extension of it – like living in a tiny property with extremely expansive, enticing grounds. I didn't enjoy being beyond its boundaries for long, even for holidays. I'd wonder what I was missing instead. It wasn't as if I could set that to record and play it back on my return; they were events I'd never be able to recapture at a later date.

A perk of my job was free access to films and shows, but I was hard to please on the entertainment front. In concerts, I wanted singers to sound like they did on their recordings – none more so than Bob Dylan and Van Morrison who usually didn't - though that may have missed the point of seeing them perform live. I was bored by all but a couple of plays I ever saw, couldn't stand or understand Shakespeare, and refused to watch horror or violence as real life was tough enough to deal with as it was. Following my early experiences, seeing any person, or indeed any living creature, being bullied, humiliated, tortured, attacked, abused or anything of that nature, whether it was happening in real life or on screen, got to me.

At SLI, there had been a rare occasion when a male student seriously wound me up. I don't recall what he said, but for the only time in my life I wanted to respond with aggression. Yet the punch I tried to deliver to his chubby face inexplicably turned at the last moment into a harmless slap. I guess I just didn't have it in me to hurt anyone physically, and other than at that moment I never tried to. The fact that I was now getting enjoyment and satisfaction professionally, if not yet personally, meant I was anything but an angry man. In fact, for the most part I felt fortunate and fulfilled.

Being based in my own flat suited me in so many ways. I was my own boss and I had my own toilet, for starters. For much of the first few years of living and working alone I felt lonely and so ran up excessive phone bills, but my creativity and celebrity encounters kept me optimistic.

Plenty of people, on discovering I was self-employed working from home, would say something to the effect of 'I don't know how you do it. If I was in that situation, I'd find it hard to get out of bed of a morning and would be tempted to spend all day down the pub.' I'd explain honestly that, as I didn't have the benefit of a salary, I wouldn't get paid when I wasn't working, so slacking was not an option. Anyway, I was very driven to make a success of my life, and I always preferred to get up early and embrace the day rather than lying in. Besides, unlike most British pressmen at that time, I hardly drank any alcohol.

It wasn't long before I developed a routine of rising at 6am, lunching at noon, and having supper at 6pm. Once that was firmly in place, if I ate much later of an evening I struggled to sleep...which meant my next day's routine was threatened.

An added bonus of a regimented work schedule was some much-needed order in my life. In my 20s and much of my 30s, I'd have to admit, I was 'all over the place.' An immature mess, basically. And that was reflected by the untidiness of my flat and car.

Aside from an enjoyable career hopefully with a future, I was blessed with a nice face, a good head of hair, height which I was finally appreciating, a reasonable brain, and what many others perceived as a privileged background and education. That suggested I should be confident, maybe even cocky, but still too often I felt insufficient inside. Some people meeting me for the first time discovered that I was anything but what they expected, and it threw them. For what felt like too long, desirable girlfriends remained for me like the mythological branches of golden apples always moving out of my reach, and I sometimes thought in my despair: 'For f**k's sake, I went to a top public school, I have a university degree, I'm told I'm handsome, I have a great job plenty of people should be fascinated by...yet I can't land a long-term balanced relationship with a physically attractive mentally stable woman to save my life!'

What I wanted was a very physically attractive girlfriend. I wasn't satisfied with plain-looking women; I wanted sexy, alluring, feminine ones ideally with a pretty face and pert body. Their intellect or compatability was of virtually no consequence to me. As long as I found them desirable, I would overlook or wouldn't even notice any negative or unsuitable aspects to them. It was important that I fancied who I was with, of course, and nothing pleased me more than having a woman who other men wanted but now couldn't have while I could. I relished being one-up on other men, and never more so through women. I'd have gained greatest satisfaction from having my father and brothers wishing they were in my relationships. One woman I dated briefly was the spitting image of Mum at a young age, which was disconcerting, and sufficiently embarrassing for me to never introduce her to my family.

Maddeningly, the more physically attractive I regarded a woman I was interested in, the more I was in awe of them. I'd come over all nervous and talk crap, and on mercifully rare occasions my body would get serious shivers. These were not famous women I met through work - I was fine with those as I'd be in professional mode and wouldn't dream of crossing that line – but the ones I met personally. Instead of gabbling and blurting in my nervousness things that were in my head at any given moment. I never thought 'Well, I've had girlfriends before and I didn't have to worry much then, so why now?'

When occasionally beautiful and/or powerful women did show interest in me, I'd think they'd made a mistake, convinced I wasn't worthy. Sometimes I'd scupper the situation before it developed. Having felt personal rejection for as long as I could remember, I was more used to that than to being accepted and loved. So, if an encounter was looking promising, I'd do or say something to spoil it, to put the interested party off me. I couldn't help or stop myself. I assumed again it reverted back to my long-held belief that I had no right to happiness, love…any of the positive things that having a desirable partner would give me.

An expression I wouldn't hear til many years later refers to a person in a relationship with someone better looking as 'punching above their weight'. Well, such was my dismal self-image that I felt I was punching above my weight in most relationships. There were even times I honestly could not understand why any woman would want to be with me. I should have gained some measure of confidence with every relationship I had, but it seemed that the damage from my early years had a stronger influence.

I remember reading that, even in jail, the notorious Kray twins dressed as smartly as they could as that provided a sense of self-respect. 'If convicted murderers can feel self-respect, why can't someone like me who's never committed so much as a minor offence?' I pondered.

Of admiration and mild envy to me was the way many French and Italian men in particular looked effortlessly relaxed, natural and neat in their clothes. Some appeared to only have one nice pullover – and that tended to be draped over shoulders or tied round the waist rather than worn properly – yet they always appeared cool and fresh. Or, in the colder months, they'd wrap a scarf around their necks loosely but stylishly. I had quite a number of different jumpers and scarves but always looked a state.

I didn't think I stood much chance of ever being rich and/or famous myself, partly because I didn't feel I'd earned it…though there were numerous celebrities I encountered who I secretly thought unworthy of it. Even if I couldn't actually be wealthy or well-known, I decided I'd try and look like I could be. I started buying designer clothes because I thought they might finally get me kudos, respect from other guys, and interest from women. But none of that transpired. No-one ever complimented me on what I wore, I suspect due to my never looking or feeling comfortable in anything…as I wasn't comfortable in my own skin. Not even then when I was apparently in the prime of my life. 'Beauty comes from within' as the saying goes, but I couldn't find it within me. Clearly appearing smart was merely papering over my deep-rooted cracks.

Decades of Dad saying 'I wouldn't do that if I were you', indeed everyone and everything that denied me confidence and self-belief, meant I daren't wear anything which would make me stand out. Yes, even when it came to clothes I felt it wiser to not put myself above the parapet for fear of being mocked or knocked down. So I didn't follow English fashion trends such as collars turned up on the cricket field, sleeves rolled back in the late 1980s, and shirts untucked in the 90s and early 00s. Had I done so, and had just one person commented negatively, I'd have instantly abandoned that look in favour of something totally bland. "Don't give them any ammunition" I privately warned myself as if still surrounded by school persecutors.

At least I wasn't one of those people who'd alter their physical appearance in a self-improvement bid – a dangerous road that never ends for some, except in disaster. The needles and surgery, let alone the cost, would have put me off anyway.

But then I couldn't bear seeing my own reflection. I avoided looking in mirrors other than for checking I wasn't unkempt. I tilted the rear-view one in my car away from my face unless use of it became imperative.

For an awful period I had a bad twitch, an external indication of my inner conflict. And worse, when I was driving, I'd suddenly turn the wheel one way or another which would give myself and others a shocking jolt. How I avoided accidents I do not know. I did all this through a lethal combination of self-loathing and desire to sabotage the increasing positivity of my existence.

When I was disappointed, particularly with myself, I'd often eat things I knew weren't good for me, maybe had the ability to harm me, even kill me in excess, due to my family history of heart disease. That was my self-inflicted punishment, I suppose. But then I'd also reach for naughty foods when things were going well for me – maybe another act of sabotage, another example of thinking I shouldn't have happiness and success.

I needed to work alone, doing stories and interviews that had to be kept exclusive. And it didn't pay well enough for me to afford an assistant anyway. I felt fine when working – it was satisfying, entertaining, and a nice distraction – but I occasionally felt anything but when I wasn't.

As I considered myself inadequate, I hoped my job would do the impressing for me. It was giving me thrills that I thought others might be curious to hear about…if little else. Working with celebrities understandably wasn't as potent as actually being one. But I was increasingly aware that most women prioritised personal character and characteristics in a man far more highly than their achievements.

26.

MY LESSONS IN LOVE

An unexpected bonus of interviewing people was that it was teaching me to keep conversations going, partly by asking the right questions and listening carefully to answers. That served me well when I had one-on-one encounters with people, women mainly, like in quiet corners at parties. But, despite successfully conducting countless impromptu interviews with the rich and famous, I was hopeless at small talk. When formal functions involved people standing around with drinks in their hands, I struggled to converse in relaxed fashion. I always feared saying stupid or inappropriate things, and sometimes still did. I regarded most people to be more endearing and together than myself, so anyone accompanying me to dos could cover for me socially and hopefully draw the interest I couldn't. Yet they could be more of a burden than a boon because, when it came to events I attended as a single guy, if a female friend accompanied me there was only so much flirting I could do with others without appearing rude, and if I was joined by a male friend that sometimes meant competition.

Tom, the friend who most frequently joined me at events, was almost as short on confidence as I was. He'd never have admitted that, but I recognised our shared symptoms. Tom was also progressing well within the Media, but his insecurity originated from being adopted as a child, and I guessed we'd come together through a mutual lack of foundation and consequent abundance of ambition. I described that guy as a friend, but he wasn't in the true sense, nor I to him. I noticed little evidence of him liking or respecting me, but I overlooked that due to my preference for a Plus One at parties. It could definitely be said we used each other as crutches to lean on in such situations and, when either of us met women we were attracted to, the other tended to be discarded or made to feel a gooseberry.

I assumed that as Tom had gone to a co-ed comprehensive school, he'd be light years ahead of me in understanding and dealing with the opposite sex. Furthermore, his occasional appearances on television were almost making him a minor celebrity. Yet he rarely got the girl. I noted his tactics: the instant he clapped eyes on a female who took his fancy, he'd shower her with compliments, telling her she was gorgeous, sexy, and so on. He wasn't one for playing it cool and keeping his cards close to his chest; he laid them all on the table, hoping his expressed interest would be reciprocated…and more often than not it wasn't, which baffled and bewildered him. I knew if I tried to offer Tom my thoughts on the matter that it would have annoyed him, and probably made him say 'What do you know?' But he did once tell me he thought complimenting women showed he was kind, made them feel more secure, and strengthened his position with them. Even when that policy failed repeatedly, he still believed in it.

I might have spoken to women the way Tom did if I'd had the balls to. Sometimes when I attained female interest, it would be so flimsy that the slightest unimpressed look or comment from them could destroy it. In new relationships, I'd usually be trying to fathom what did and didn't please the woman concerned.

One situation that both bemused and amused me occurred after I got given a filthy look. "What's up?" I asked. "You should know" she replied. "How can I know unless you tell me?" I pointed out. "You. Should. Know. Especially as you're supposed to be psychic!"

A nurse I saw for a few weeks was applying lipstick before one of our evenings out, and I told her I thought it too bright and gaudy. She turned from the mirror and roared at me "I will wear what I bloody well like – it's not for you to tell me what to put on!" I was taken aback by her reaction, feeling like a child being reprimanded by a teacher yet again. I hadn't meant to be disrespectful to her. Yet there were plenty of times I recognised girlfriends not respecting me, and so wished it wasn't the case. I knew they ought to take my circumstances into consideration rather than me only considering theirs. But sometimes I so wanted them physically, or got hooked on them psychologically, that I found myself dancing to their tune rather than having them dancing to mine.

I'd started out assuming that the way to a woman's heart was to be soft and kind to them. But so far I found the more I was like that, the more they behaved badly towards me. "What makes them feel a need to do that to me? What is it about me that makes them do it? How do I stop it happening in future?" I'd ask myself, just as I had when attempting to figure out my persecution at school. I clearly had a weak side to me that certain people detected, disliked and sought to punish, and I wished I was instead someone who naturally commanded respect. I wanted my exes to say "I used to go out with him" but for a proud reason, and not embarrassed because I'd been lily-livered or a jerk. Above all, I hoped at least some would consider me a cool, calm, self-contained man with an absence of neediness. Then I'd have paid good money to one day be told I was like that.

I couldn't fathom why so many women I desired were clearly more enamoured of men who not only paid little attention to them, but treated them poorly. Most would say they wanted a gentleman, yet an alarming amount showed they wanted anything but. Everything needed to be black and white and logical for me. Instead, relationship rules went against the grain and contained way too many grey areas for my comprehension. And too often when I appeared to have got off to a great start with women, they'd suddenly go cold and distant and play games, so a weird competition would develop whereby neither of us wanted to appear weaker or the loser.

Although I believed I'd already had a few wishes granted in my life, even in lonely times I didn't wish for a girlfriend or lover. I knew that in due course there were bound to be more serious matters I - and presumably countless other people – would seek spiritual help with. So I didn't make what I called Call Outs unless I considered it absolutely necessary. I was also all too aware of the phrase 'Don't push your luck', and I'd been influenced by children's stories in which only three wishes were permitted, so I didn't want to use up all mine in case I really needed them one day. Though I sincerely hoped I get far more than three.

Now that Mum was gone, and knowing that she'd taken a keen interest in spirits and the afterlife as well as my love life, perhaps this would have been a good time to call for her help. But the assistance I'd had in the past had happened in her lifetime, so maybe someone else was looking after me anyway. Though if it was a dead relative or friend, I didn't sense anyone had ever cared enough in this life to want to watch over me from the afterlife…if there is an afterlife.

If I was religious like I'd been raised to be, I'd be putting these requests to God. Since rejecting Catholicism, I'd not known who I was pleading to, but the very fact that I did it suggested I believed that some power (for want of a better term) had the ability to influence my life, maybe even control it. Which made me wonder now: those times when I feel I've messed up, like sabotaged a relationship…was it not my fault after all? Perhaps someone somewhere was acting on my behalf, hopefully in my best interests.

School experiences alone had taught me to keep such beliefs to myself. Go public about such matters and cynics will soon come a mocking like 'Then why not ask for a huge inheritance, or the winning Lottery numbers…?', and so on.

More important to me than becoming financially secure was becoming successful relationship-wise. That almost became an obsession…and I became self-obsessed, worried about what I was saying, doing and thinking and what the women concerned were too. It didn't occur to me that other men – whether from similarly sheltered backgrounds or not – might also struggle with working out the opposite sex. I was naive rather than stupid, and I certainly wanted to learn. So I occasionally sought advice, particularly from the kind of women I wanted to be with and the kind of men I wished I was.

One male friend told me he only ever gave 30% of himself to women in the early stages of a relationship, which was his "treat 'em mean, keep 'em keen" strategy. But that wasn't something I managed to master deliberately. Such was my focus on catering to what these women wanted rather than thinking about what I actually wanted.

Occasionally interviews I did proved handy in learning how the celebrities got to be in the often enviable relationships they were in. When I asked one internationally acclaimed actor for the secret to his long and happy marriage, he replied "It's important to always remember you don't own the other person." At the time I was impressed – after all, I'd made the mistake of thinking I had exclusive rights to Luisa for a start. But his response took on a whole different meaning years later when I heard widely held rumours he was having an affair with a World-famous woman.

I noted that some smart women I met or interviewed said they were attracted to guys 'who have their own thing going on'. It was a fashionable phrase describing people whose focus was on their own busy lives, who weren't suddenly going to drop everything to devote themselves to those they just met. Well, I now loved the work I was doing and the life I was leading in London, which meant I had a lot to be busy with. I didn't believe enough in me personally and often looked at others wishing I was them with their strengths, but by now it wasn't that their lives seemed preferable to experience instead.

It took me far too long to understand that the more I went on the front foot, boasted and showed off, the less likely I was to attract. Women I met didn't want overtness from guys, certainly didn't appear to expect it from guys like me. It was pleasing when those I wasn't trying to win over responded favourably. The lesson from that was obvious, but infuriatingly I didn't act on it. I knew what was required but I just could not change things, or if I did for a while I'd eventually revert to my old ways and in doing so torpedo those situations.

Something I did notice from time to time was that, when I wasn't looking at other people, I could sense them looking at me. Yet if I then glanced at them they'd immediately look away, as if they only wanted their glances unobserved. Lydia Edwards, a well-known English actress I befriended observed me as I entered a restaurant beside her and, knowing mine was a lonely heart, advised me "Keep your head down and eyes lowered. Don't look for love, it'll happen when you least expect it." The very opposite of the Bible quote that had stuck in my head: 'Seek and ye shall find'.

Lydia was far from done. "Unless you're engaged in conversation with them, don't look at people, particularly at women, or it'll look needy and as if their world is more desirable to you than your own. You'll be of far greater fascination to them if you're in your own world. Let them wonder about you and your life, and be intrigued and ideally enticed by it. And just because you find a woman attractive, don't treat her like a celebrity – even if they are a celebrity! - but like any normal person. With your job, you should already be used to doing that.

"Remember how we are warned – sometimes as youngsters by parents – not to 'have our head turned', to not allow other peoples' status, power, wealth and so forth to enchant and influence us? Well, the same applies to other people's looks and personality. So many men are so taken by physically attractive women that they literally turn their heads to look at them, and easily find themselves under their spell. That happens to weak men, certainly men who women consider weak – most red-blooded men, in fact. Strong men don't have their heads turned. And, because they're in a minority, they're of most interest to women. So be a strong guy and don't have your head turned."

It had been many years since I'd last looked at The Bible, yet here was another reminder. In my overactive imagination I was now reminded of Lot's wife who was turned into a pillar of salt after ignoring a warning to not look back when fleeing the city of Sodom during its destruction by God.

I asked Lydia "But if I don't look up, how will I see and engage with who I like?" "You focus on you, not them. Let them do the looking" Lydia replied. "And they can't fail to see you at 6'5"! Besides, to coin an Irish phrase: What's meant for you won't go by you".

That was her way of saying I should trust fate and wait for it. So after all the thoughts and theories I'd had about the keys to being successful with women, I was now being told "Do nothing. You don't need to do anything. In fact, you mustn't do anything. Don't even try to be funny. Just be yourself." For me this was easier said than done as I didn't really know who I was, and I certainly wasn't comfortable with myself. I also wasn't good at waiting for things to happen; I feared they might never happen and I was rarely certain they would. I was a go-getter, which worked at work when I usually needed to be proactive. I liked the idea of letting go, letting life happen to me, rather than being Front Foot Luke and in the driver's seat. My history and resulting insecurity meant I didn't think I really was one for 'letting go', yet when I thought about it relationships had actually materialised when I did do that.

I listened to Lydia because she was the kind of class lass I wanted to attract…not that I thought I stood a chance with her. Her closing words of wisdom here were "Let go and smile. Contentment is the most desirable quality. If you come across content, other people will want a piece of that."

I liked these insights into how the female mind works. I also liked the idea that we never stop learning, and was fond of the expression 'Every day is a school day'. It would have saved me a helluva lot of time and trouble if someone in the know had taught me this sort of stuff in or out of school. But better late than never, and I liked to think taking Lydia's advice led to some interesting situations.

A captivating blonde Swedish waitress at a West End pizza joint took my number, and I was shocked when she called the next day and suggested we meet. After about 20 minutes chatting in a fairly empty pub, she leaned in to me and whispered in her hurdy-gurdy accent "Do you want to make lurve to me now?" Although about all I could convey was a nervous gulp and nod, I certainly did…and we did, after dashing back to my place. But following the fun and frolics, I didn't call her as I was convinced someone as stunning as her wouldn't want to see me again. Several days later she dropped a parcel off at the reception of Class magazine, containing clothes I'd left at her flat and a furious note at my lack of follow-up.

A publicist for a top department store took me out for what I assumed was a networking-style lunch. She then revealed she lived nearby and invited me back to hers for coffee. We'd barely made it through the front door when she grabbed my tie, pinned me against a wall and snogged me. Eventually allowing me to breathe, she told me "You've been asking for that all lunchtime!" It was news to me, but I obviously didn't mind at all. Yet somehow I then managed to annoy her and that ended our encounter.

The exquisite ex of a by then slightly passe pop star once visited me in my flat, and we chatted happily for some time. After she'd gone, I noticed her handbag was left where she had sat on my sofa. So I drove to her house, gave her the bag and went straight home, which seemed the correct course of action. "You idiot!" exclaimed a female friend of mine. "She will have left it there on purpose to ensure you saw her again, but she won't have wanted you to just hand it back and leave it at that!" If my friend was right, I assumed I'd blown any interest there might have been and so took it no further. Anyway I couldn't imagine the super-pretty ex of a pop star then settling for the mess that was me.

While I could have considered those successes, to my mind they were failures because they didn't develop into relationships. I assumed self-assured men would have effortlessly made the most of such situations, but I wasn't so didn't. I just didn't trust women I wanted's interest, certainly not that it would last.

Considering my parents' marriage was such a catastrophe, Matthew's first had failed within 18 months, Mark had wed an incredibly difficult woman, and my debut relationship imploded prematurely, let alone countless other couples parting around me, it's a wonder I believed in love. But I was determined for things to go well personally as well as professionally despite my early difficulties. Maybe it was all those fairytales from childhood in which couples 'lived happily ever after' that kept me believing I would find such a situation eventually. The need for sex remained a major motivation too, it must be said. So no amount of mistakes I made with women, whether in trying to get them to date me or while dating them, was going to stop me persevering. I'd long heard it said, though not directly to me, that if you want something enough, and if you strive hard enough, you get what you want eventually. And eventually I felt I did...finally meet a princess after kissing many frogs.

Yes, I managed to land a serious girlfriend in Jane. This was through a friend who said he knew I would not just be extremely attracted to Jane but get on well with her too. And he was right, as was evident from the moment she and I met.

Unlike the learning curve that was my College romance with Luisa, this was a love equally balanced between both parties. For a start, literally, when I was anxious and nervy in trying to woo her, it didn't bother Jane. Finally, I'd found someone who accepted me for what I was, faults and all.

Jane was delightful, smart and driven, and came from a solid Kentish family. She was mature enough to have easily settled down young - the scenario that both my brothers had, through tradition and/or insecurity, fallen for. But, while I considered myself more insecure at that stage than Matthew and Mark combined, their disastrous decisions to marry the first candidates who came along had made me cautious. I knew I had loads of living and loving to do before I could commit for good...if I was ever going to be able to commit at all.

Jane and I went through the kind of 'honeymoon period' common to most couples – that thrilling spell when they're all you think about when you're apart, and you can't keep your clothes on and hands off one another when you're together. During those early heady days when my body desired hers, I was with her as much as I could be, and when I couldn't be I was wishing I was. Her happiness was then paramount in my mind, whether that entailed ensuring she felt secure or doing and occasionally buying thoughtful things for her.

A unique indication of my then reverence for Jane was that she was the first person I wanted to take to a significant place in my past: Parkstone Prep, and most significantly its ornamental gate. I hadn't had any desire to go back prior to that, due to predominantly bad childhood memories. But, although it wasn't like I was returning a hero, I did feel I was finally doing things career-wise I could discuss with some pride should anyone there ask what I was now up to. And I also considered it an achievement to have a smart, good-looking girlfriend at my side. All that amounted to more than I dared hope for when standing at that gate in my youth. While I didn't tell Jane any of this when we went there, in my head it was as if I was saying to the gate 'I don't know if you remember me, but many years ago I used to stand here, look through you at the road and wonder where it would lead me, and what the future held for me. Well, I've not been gone too long, but I'm not doing badly so far. Better than expected anyway.' And I imagined the old gate giving me a knowing smile and in a slow deep voice replying: 'I remember. Better than expected, yes. Keep going. Keep going!'

An American acquaintance I introduced to Jane described her as 'a keeper'. And indeed all was wonderful between Jane and I for a fairly long time. And then, gradually after a couple of years or so, it wasn't. At least, it wasn't for me - I could only speak for myself. My physical desire for her had waned.

I felt Jane had become increasingly moody and bossy - wearing the trousers, as they say, in our relationship. Perhaps that stemmed from my reduction in interest in her, and all it entailed. Whatever, to me she was no longer the alluring feminine angel I'd fallen in love with. The more she took on what I regarded as the male role, the less I fancied her. I soon stopped fancying her altogether. Worse, I started finding other women more attractive – including, awkwardly, a couple of her friends, and I wanted to now be with them, sexually anyway.

What's more, I discovered the fancy I had for those other women was reciprocated. I'd lacked confidence as a singleton, but in this relationship knowing I was wanted I now had confidence…and ironically that was making me attractive to others. That seemed so unfair to Jane, though it might equally have been the case for her.

I could have stuck with this unsexy situation, because Jane was so important to me in other ways. But I could tell I would henceforward be secretly lusting after other women, and I never wanted to be unfaithful to her, yet those thoughts alone amounted to infidelity in my opinion. Plenty of principled people of previous generations would have 'hung on in there', but I didn't believe that led to happiness, certainly not satisfaction. I was always aware how my sheltered youth in all-male environments meant I was way behind most other men of my age in terms of relationship experience, and I wasn't just keen to catch up, I felt I needed to. I daren't tell Jane that was my problem; she'd have left in a furious flash had she known. And although I now wanted to end this relationship, I wanted to retain our friendship.

I never did explain to Jane my change in feelings for her. I may have claimed that the relationship no longer worked, but I didn't try to make it work. I just managed to make it obvious it was no longer working, so the suggestion that we part wouldn't be surprising.

It was a difficult, unpleasant, situation to be in…mainly because I still loved her. But for me it had become more like a sibling love, and strong messages emanating from my groin wanted sexual love as well…more in fact. If I was honest I'd have said to Jane "I have no desire to cause you pain, it's just that I have no desire." Fortunately I didn't need to, as one night she turned to me and said "You don't love me anymore. I can tell because not only do you not want to **make** love with me anymore, you don't want to spend as much time with me as you used to, and you aren't as attentive and considerate as you used to be." I instantly denied it, but the more I thought about what she'd said the more I knew she was right.

Since my ardour towards Jane had diminished, so had my everything else towards her – devotion, kindness, generosity...the lot. Instead, I was ready to transfer my focus and all else to women who now took my fancy more, which again was unfair to Jane and sad for both of us. That was my first true realisation of the incredible influence sexual desire, and the lack of it, had on aspects of my behaviour, and presumably the behaviour of many men. In this case, the shameful admission that how well I treated girlfriends corresponded with how attractive I found them at the time. I'd never been aware of that before. Any woman I was in love and lust with could expect my equivalent of 5-star treatment for as long as they made me feel that way. Yet when that waned in me, so shamefully would my attentiveness towards them...and to a devastating extent if my interest was taken by another. I realised too that only women I fancied could make me feel jealous. If I didn't fancy them, I wouldn't care who else they were with, interested in or pursued by.

Nor had I experienced anything like Jane's hysterical reaction when I told her it was over between us. The look of despair in her eyes, the Neanderthal scream that emanated from deep within her...it's stayed with me ever since. Even though we'd been together more than two years, the depth to which it upset her shocked me. Never before had anyone really shown that I truly mattered to them. I was so used to feeling like nobody gave a toss about me.

"Why would you throw all this away?" she asked, perfectly fairly because in most departments aside from the bed one latterly we'd got on great. "Do you think maybe you don't deserve love and happiness?" That was extremely astute, but I didn't admit it.

I hated hurting anyone, least of all my first real love. I offered consoling hugs but understandably Jane now pushed me away. I told her I still loved her but understandably she found that weird in the circumstances. I genuinely did love her, but as I say like the little sister I'd never had. I couldn't bear the thought of never seeing her again. As well as mostly enjoying her company, I'd grown so attached to Jane emotionally, and I didn't want to reject the first person who I knew definitely loved me. I didn't want us to part; I wanted us to remain close. Yet I also wanted to sleep around...to have my cake and eat it.

Jane, however, wanted a clean break. And, despite having engineered the end myself, I was bereft. I no longer had Jane as a supportive crutch, aside from anything else. At times I had to remind myself that I'd made the decision so I could see other women conscience-free. Now I simply had to go out in the big wide World and spread my wild oats...if I could get the opportunities. The infuriating thing was, while I was in the security of that relationship, I'd found myself attracting at least the attention of other women with relative ease. Yet, once I was without that security, I couldn't. To an extent my frightened, nervous child mode returned, as if I'd fallen into the open sea without a lifebelt not believing I could swim. In fact, I'd chosen to swim away from the mainland Jane represented and out to explore various appealing islands, and sometimes midway across I'd panic that I wouldn't be able to return. And those were thoughts I had when I was awake...

For literally years afterwards, even when I did have physically fulfilling relationships with other women, I didn't care about any of them as much as Jane.

The split had another unexpected consequence as well. This was the first of my girlfriends who my father and brothers had got to know and love. Not very well admittedly, but enough for them to tell me that they'd miss her. Until then it hadn't occurred to me that anybody beyond the couple concerned could ever be affected by a break-up. Mark even admitted he'd fancied her which bolstered my ego. So Jane retained a place not just in my heart, but in that of my family.

Confusing Jane by telling her I still loved her but no longer wanted to be with her did her head in. During one angry outburst she declared: "After putting all that time and effort into this relationship for it to come to nothing, I wish I'd never gone out with you from the start. What a waste of those years!" I told her I thought that a great pity because in all honesty I felt only gratitude towards her and the relationship we'd had. That exchange took me back to my old Mind Games for a moment... Whenever I lost a set at tennis that I'd put loads of effort into, I'd think 'If I'd known I was going to lose it, I shouldn't have bothered; I should instead have given my opponent that set and conserved my energy for the next set', though of course that wouldn't have been in the spirit of the game. Now this relationship hadn't ended in marriage but instead died without hope of salvation after all that time, I was inclined to think it was a helpful life experience - a learning curve. I would certainly come to that more satisfactory conclusion from the education I was about to undertake which would prove the best and most important of my existence. And that came about because Jane said the three words I then most needed to hear...

"You need therapy!"

That is only half the story, so it is… TO BE CONTINUED

horrid.child@outlook.com

www.ingramcontent.com/pod-product-compliance
Lightning Source LLC
Chambersburg PA
CBHW052017070526
44584CB00016B/1788